Beautiful Christmas Cards

Alexandra Adami

Beautiful Christmas Cards

Foreword by Lady Helen Taylor

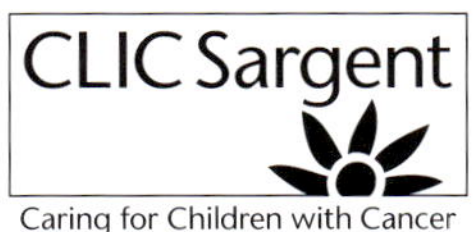

teNeues

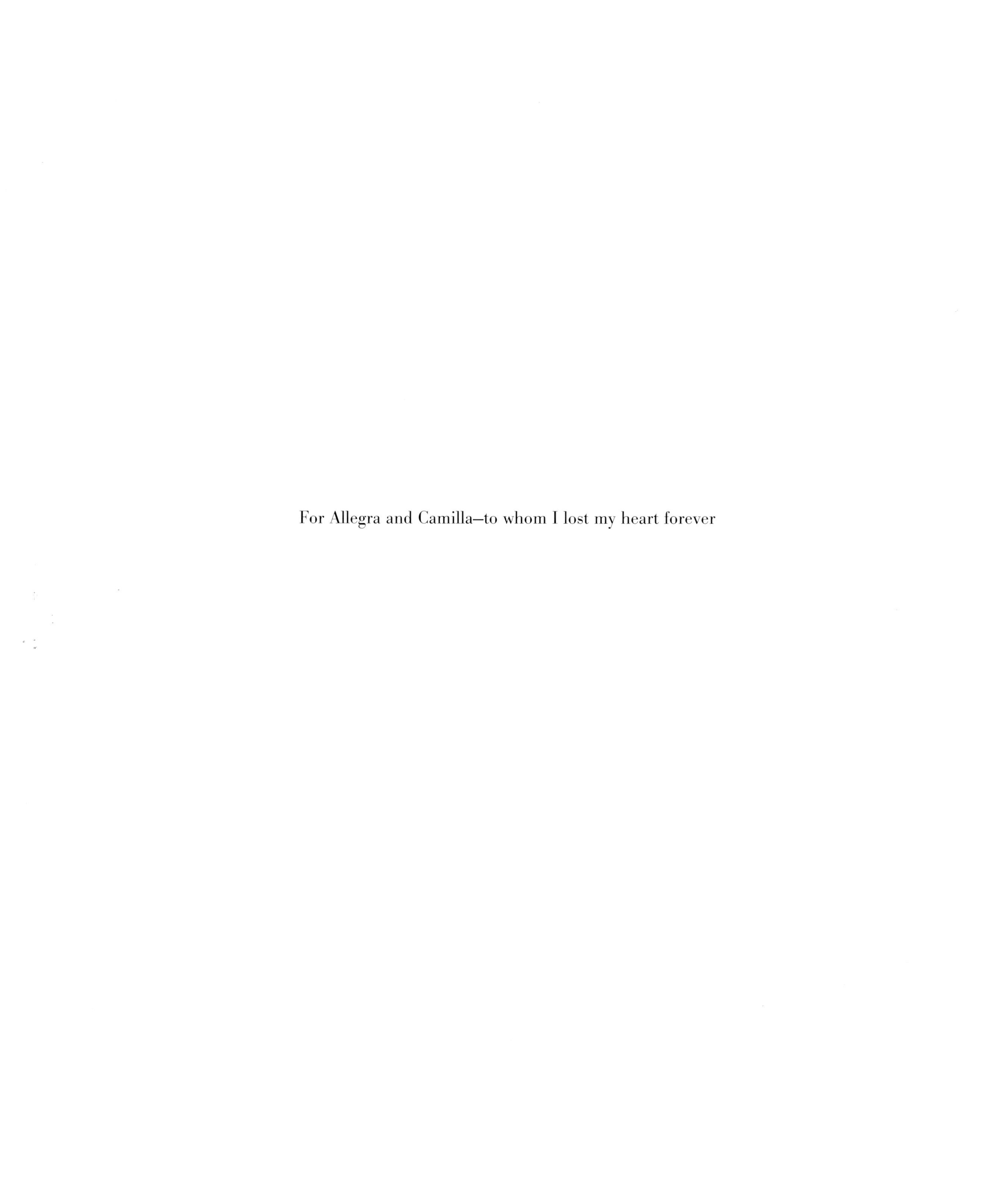

For Allegra and Camilla—to whom I lost my heart forever

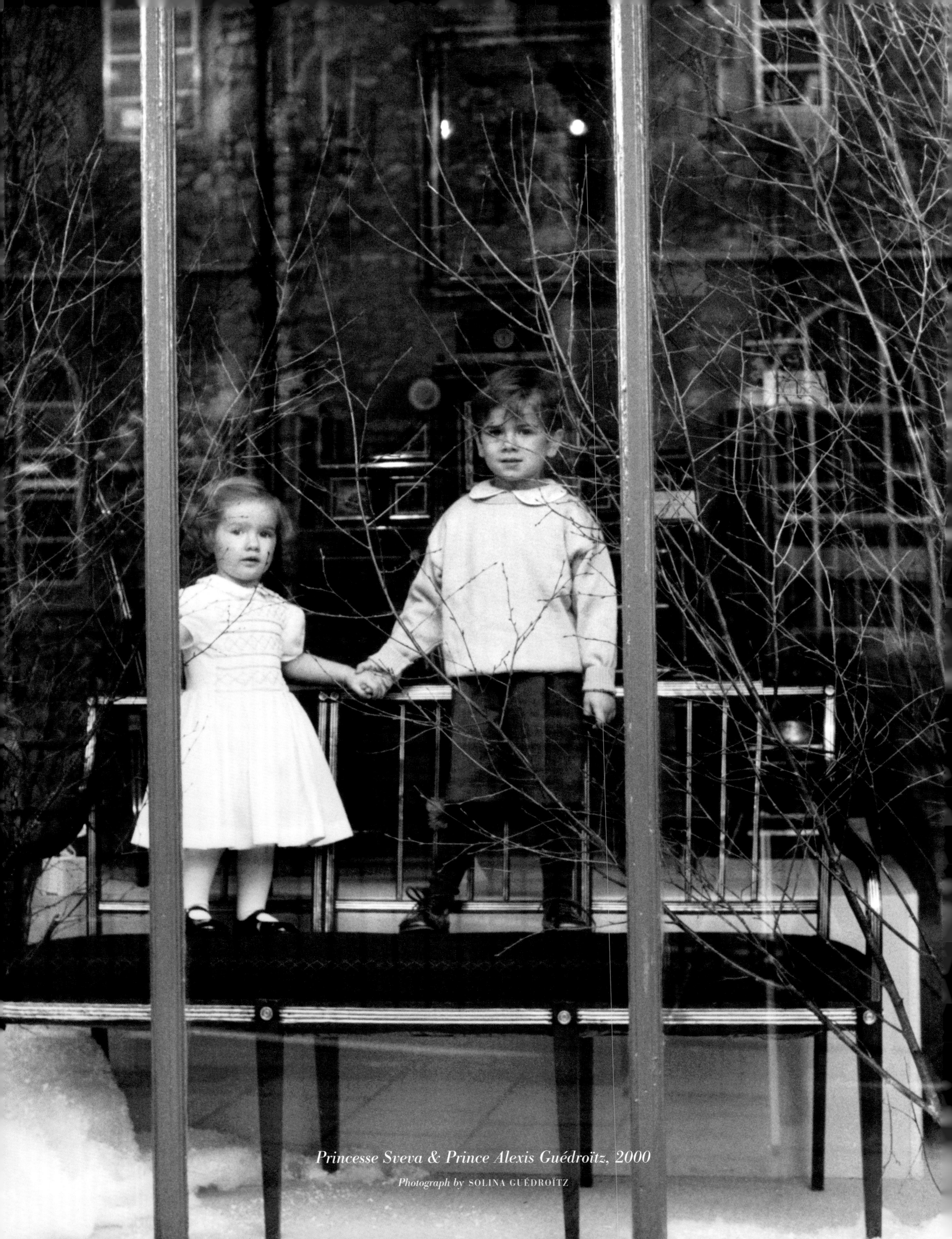

Princesse Sveva & Prince Alexis Guédroïtz, 2000

Photograph by SOLINA GUÉDROÏTZ

It was my great grandmother Queen Mary who established one of the most wonderful collection of Christmas cards from the first examples in Victorian times up to the 1950s. Eighteen beautiful albums give a profound insight into the history of this fascinating social and art form.

The first recorded example of a Christmas card was commissioned by the founder of the Victoria and Albert Museum, Sir Henry Cole in 1846. Early on, Christmas cards were quite frequently used as happy means of ending disagreements, repairing broken friendships and strengthening neighbourly ties in all walks of life. By the beginning of the 20th century this admirable custom had become the social convention that we know today.

Whatever the motivation, Christmas cards until this day undoubtedly represent the most beautiful, the most creative, the most festive form of congratulations.

Already produced to the highest standards, religious subjects represented the main themes in the early days. The famous lithographer and banknote printer Thomas de la Rue was one of the pioneers of early Christmas cards. Thanks to his inventiveness and creativity in printing techniques he produced his masterpieces in delightfully bright colours which were welcomed by a colour-starved Victorian public.

The second famous name inseparable from the Christmas card is Raphael Tuck, who for his laudible efforts was granted a royal warrant in 1893. With him the strictly religious theme disappeared and gave way to more worldly, modern motifs. His two biggest clients at this time were Mrs Grover Cleveland, the wife of the President of the United States, and HRH Queen Victoria.

Her Majesty reportedly ordered one thousand cards of a very elaborate children's design to be sent out to relatives and friends all over Europe. This card represented the culmination of the Christmas card at the time. Standing up proudly, it occupied a space of 12 in high by 10 in wide. Tuck noted that the whole was presented in a most lavish manner, which left the beholder in wonder as to how the Christmas card might ever be improved upon... little did he know!

It is nevertheless true that during this period many cards with their romantic children's motifs and their masterful execution would even today represent brilliant examples of a Christmas card.

Today, just as hundred years ago, there are original, lavish, creative, elaborate or just beautiful Christmas cards. Many hours, days, weeks of creative time is spent by mothers, photographers and professionals in order to maintain this beautiful custom. With all this effort one should try not to forget the original purpose of sending Christmas cards. I am delighted to contribute to this magnificent book not only in support of a lovely idea but above all because a part of the sales proceeds will benefit our great charity CLIC Sargent.

Lady Helen Taylor

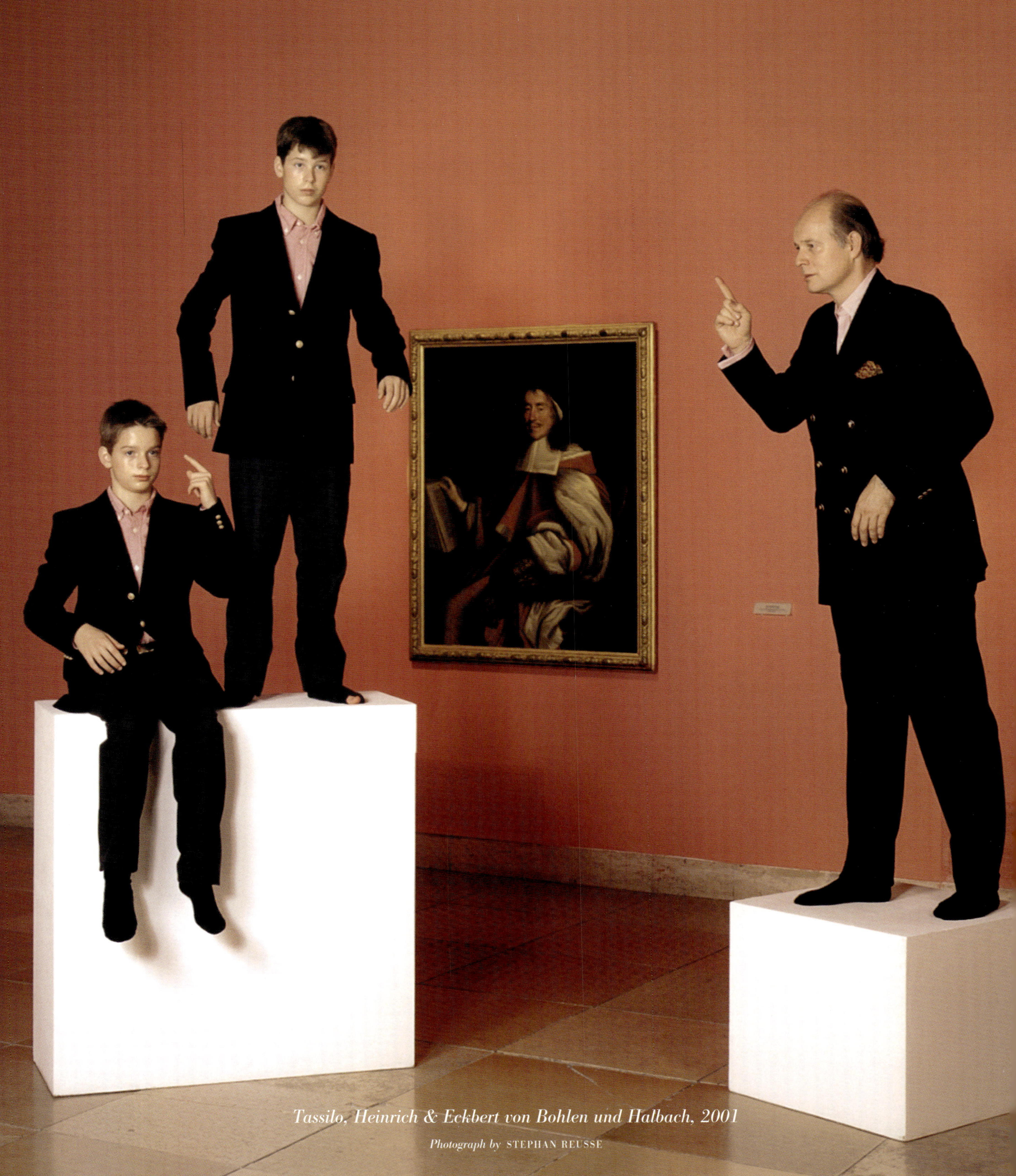

Tassilo, Heinrich & Eckbert von Bohlen und Halbach, 2001

Photograph by STEPHAN REUSSE

Es war meine Urgroßmutter, Queen Mary, die eine der wunderbarsten Weihnachtskarten-Sammlungen ins Leben rief, deren früheste Exemplare aus der viktorianischen Zeit stammen und die bis hin zu Karten aus den 1950er Jahren reicht. Achtzehn wunderschöne Alben vermitteln einen tiefen Einblick in die Geschichte dieser faszinierenden Form der Kunst und des gesellschaftlichen Miteinanders.

Das erste belegte Exemplar einer Weihnachtskarte wurde im Jahre 1846 von Sir Henry Cole, dem Gründer des *Victoria and Albert Museum*, in Auftrag gegeben. In den frühen Jahren dienten Weihnachtskarten in allen Gesellschaftsschichten häufig dazu, auf nette Art und Weise Zwistigkeiten beizulegen, zerbrochene Freundschaften zu erneuern und die nachbarschaftlichen Bande zu stärken. Zu Beginn des 20. Jahrhunderts war aus dieser schönen Sitte schließlich der soziale Brauch geworden, den wir heute kennen.

Doch ganz gleich, welchen Zweck sie einst erfüllten, Weihnachtskarten sind zweifellos auch heute noch die schönste, kreativste und festlichste Form, jemandem Glück zu wünschen.

Anfangs waren religiöse Themen die Hauptmotive und auch damals schon wurde bei der Herstellung von Weihnachtskarten auf höchste Standards Wert gelegt. Der berühmte Lithograph und Drucker von Banknoten Thomas de la Rue war einer der Pioniere der frühen Weihnachtskarten. Mit seinen einfallsreichen und kreativen Drucktechniken verlieh er seinen Meisterwerken herrlich leuchtende Farben, die bei der nach Farbe hungernden viktorianischen Bevölkerung auf große Begeisterung stießen.

Ein zweiter, ebenso untrennbar mit der Weihnachtskarte verbundener Name, ist Raphael Tuck. Ihm wurden für seine verdienstvolle Arbeit im Jahre 1893 ein *Royal Warrant* und damit die Rechte eines Hoflieferanten verliehen. Unter seinem Einfluss verschwanden die streng religiösen Themen und wichen weltlicheren, moderneren Motiven. Seine zwei größten Kunden waren damals Mrs. Grover Cleveland, die Gattin des amerikanischen Präsidenten, sowie Ihre Königliche Hoheit Queen Victoria.

Aufzeichnungen zufolge gab Ihre Majestät eintausend Karten eines äußerst kunstvollen Kindermotivs in Auftrag, die an Verwandte und Freunde in ganz Europa verschickt werden sollten. Diese Karte war zur damaligen Zeit der künstlerische Höhepunkt der Weihnachtskartengestaltung. Aufgestellt besaß sie die stolze Höhe von 30,5 cm bei einer Breite von 25,5 cm. Tuck berichtet von einer derart üppigen Aufmachung, dass der Betrachter sich fragen musste, wie die Weihnachtskarte je noch verbessert werden könnte ... hätte er nur in die Zukunft schauen können!

Dennoch muss man sagen, dass viele dieser wahrhaft meisterlich gefertigten Karten aus jener Zeit mit ihren romantischen Kindermotiven selbst nach heutigen Maßstäben hervorragende Beispiele einer Weihnachtskarte darstellen würden.

Genauso wie vor hundert Jahren, gibt es auch heutzutage originelle, üppige, kreative, kunstvolle oder einfach nur schöne Weihnachtskarten. Mütter, Fotografen und Fachleute aus vielerlei Branchen wenden unzählige kreative Stunden, Tage und Wochen auf, um diesen schönen Brauch zu erhalten. Bei so viel Aufwand sollte man dennoch nicht vergessen, welchen Zweck Weihnachtskarten ursprünglich erfüllten.

Es freut mich sehr, einen Beitrag zu diesem herrlichen Buch leisten zu können, nicht nur, indem ich so eine schöne Idee unterstützen darf, sondern vor allem, weil ein Teil des Erlöses unserer Wohltätigkeitsorganisation für krebskranke Kinder, *CLIC Sargent*, zugute kommt.

Lady Helen Taylor

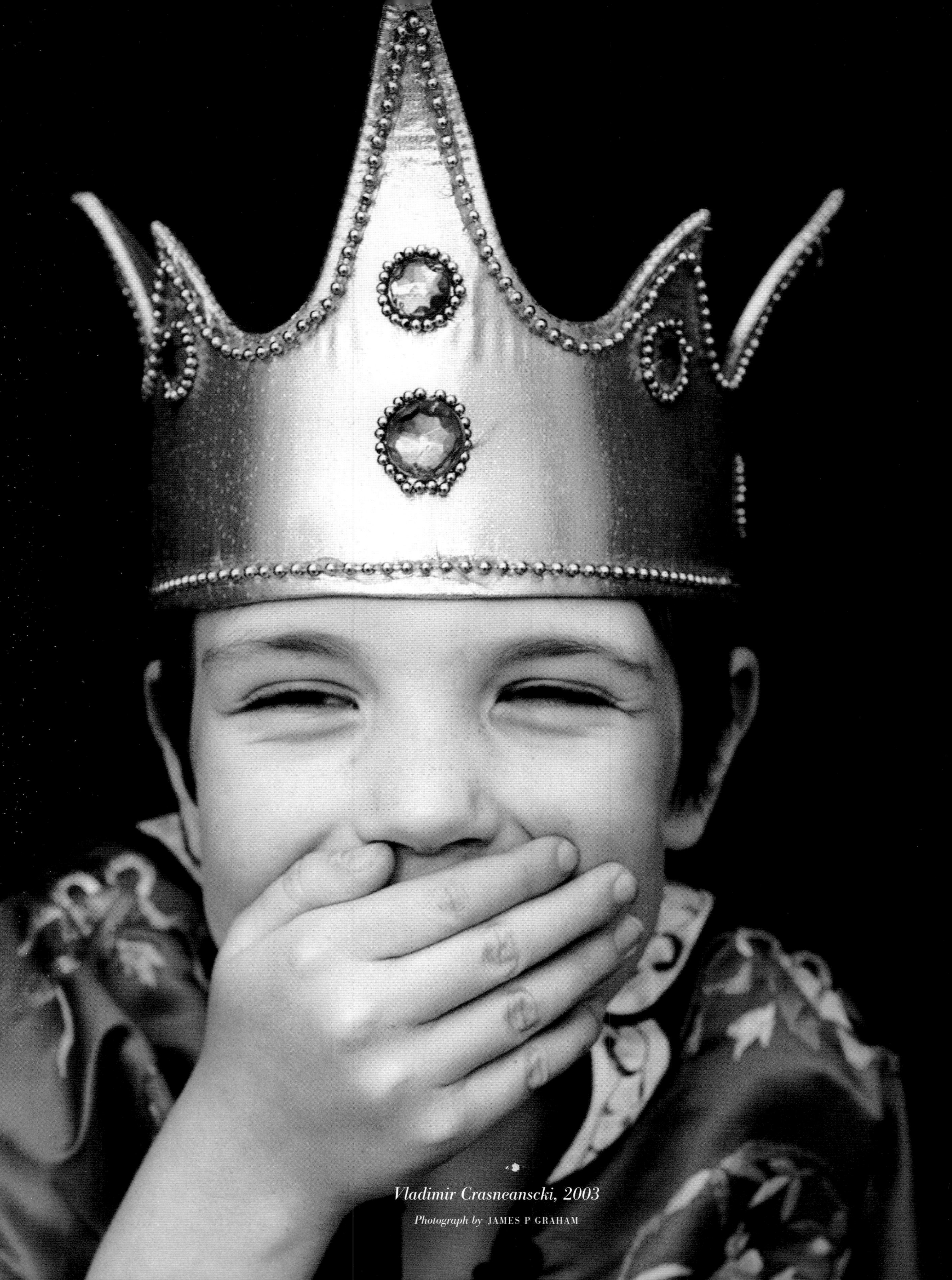

Vladimir Crasneanscki, 2003

Photograph by JAMES P GRAHAM

C'est mon arrière-grand-mère, la Reine Mary, qui donna naissance à l'une des plus belles collections de cartes de Noël dont les premiers exemplaires datent de l'époque victorienne et les derniers des années 1950. Dix-huit albums superbes nous plongent dans l'histoire de cette forme fascinante d'art et d'entente sociale.

Le premier exemplaire de carte de Noël dont nous avons connaissance fut commandé en 1846 par le fondateur du *Victoria and Albert Museum*, Sir Henry Cole. A leurs débuts, les cartes de Noël servaient souvent, dans toutes les couches de la société, à régler des dissensions, à renouveler des amitiés brisées et à renforcer les liens avec le voisinage de manière sympathique. Au début du 20ème siècle, il ne reste de cette belle habitude que la coutume sociale que nous connaissons aujourd'hui.

Mais quel que soit le but qu'elles remplissaient autrefois, les cartes de Noël restent sans aucun doute aujourd'hui encore la forme la plus belle, la plus créative et la plus solennelle de faire part à quelqu'un de nos souhaits de bonheur.

Au début, ce sont les thèmes religieux qui constituaient les motifs principaux et à cette époque aussi, la production de cartes de Noël était également soumise à des standards très élevés. Thomas de la Rue, célèbre lithographe et imprimeur de billets de banque, fut l'un des pionniers des cartes de Noël. Grâce à ses techniques d'impression ingénieuses et créatives, il donna à ses chefs-d'œuvre de superbes couleurs lumineuses qui rencontrèrent un grand succès auprès de la population victorienne avide de couleur.

Un deuxième nom également indissociable de la carte de Noël est Raphael Tuck. Il obtint en 1893 un *Royal Warrant* pour son travail digne d'éloges, ce qui lui donna les droits d'un fournisseur royal. Sous son influence, les thèmes strictement religieux s'effacèrent et laissèrent la place à des motifs plus profanes et plus modernes. Ses deux clients les plus importants de l'époque étaient Mrs. Grover Cleveland, la femme du président américain, ainsi que Sa Majesté Royale la Reine Victoria.

S'appuyant sur des esquisses, Sa Majesté commanda un millier de cartes qui étaient destinées à être envoyées dans toute l'Europe, à la famille et aux amis, et dont le motif réalisé très artistiquement représentait un enfant. Cette carte marqua à l'époque l'apogée artistique de la conception des cartes de Noël. Placée à la verticale, elle avait une hauteur de 30,5 cm pour une largeur de 25,5 cm. Tuck parle d'une présentation tellement élaborée que l'observateur devait se demander comment il serait possible de perfectionner davantage les cartes de Noël... Si seulement il avait pu lire l'avenir!

Il faut dire cependant que de nombreuses cartes de cette époque, réalisées de manière véritablement remarquable avec leurs motifs romantiques représentant des enfants, constitueraient, même selon les critères actuels, d'excellents exemples de cartes de Noël.

De même que cent ans auparavant, il existe de nos jours également des cartes de Noël originales, exubérantes, créatives, de véritables œuvres d'art ou tout simplement de belles réalisations. Les mamans, les photographes et les spécialistes de diverses branches consacrent d'innombrables heures, journées et semaines à la création des cartes pour conserver cette belle coutume. Etant donné la somme de temps investi, on ne devrait toutefois pas oublier l'objectif qui était autrefois recherché.

Je suis très heureuse de pouvoir apporter ma contribution à ce livre fantastique, non seulement pour soutenir une si belle idée, mais surtout parce qu'une partie de la recette revient à *CLIC Sargent*, notre organisation de bienfaisance pour les enfants malades du cancer.

Lady Helen Taylor

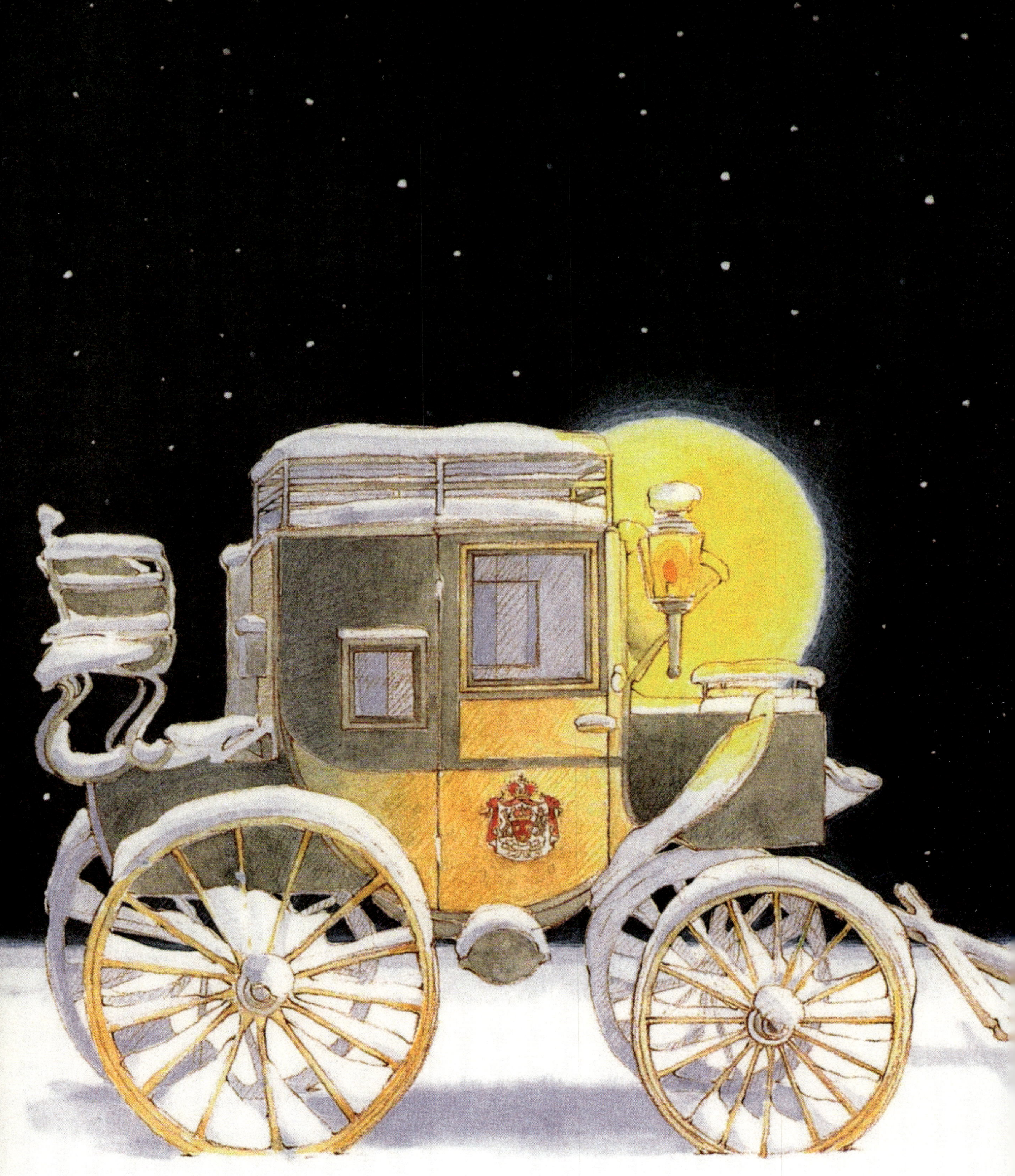

d'Arenberg Coach, 2003

Illustration by LUDMILA D'OULTREMONT

Mi bisabuela, la reina Mary, reunió una de las más maravillosas colecciones de tarjetas navideñas donde podemos encontrar desde los primeros ejemplares de la época victoriana hasta las tarjetas de la década de 1950. Dieciocho preciosos álbumes nos permiten conocer de cerca la historia de esta fascinante forma de la comunicación social y del arte.

El primer ejemplar documentado de una tarjeta navideña fue un encargo de *sir* Henry Cole, el fundador del *Victoria and Albert Museum*, y data de 1846. En sus inicios, la tarjeta estaba presente en todas las capas sociales y solía emplearse para resolver disputas de forma amistosa, para salvar amistades rotas y para estrechar los lazos entre vecinos. A comienzos del siglo XX, esta bonita costumbre se redujo al uso social que hoy conocemos.

Pero no importa qué función desempeñara en el pasado, la tarjeta es también hoy, sin duda, la forma más bonita, creativa y festiva de transmitir nuestros mejores deseos a alguien.

En los inicios, los temas principales eran los religiosos y ya entonces se valoraba de forma especial la calidad en la producción. El famoso litógrafo e impresor de billetes de banco Thomas de la Rue, fue uno de los pioneros en la impresión de las primeras tarjetas navideñas. A través de sus ocurrentes y creativas técnicas, dotó a sus obras maestras de luminosos colores despertando el entusiasmo de sus contemporáneos victorianos, ávidos de color.

Raphael Tuck es el segundo nombre ligado a la tarjeta de navidad. En el año 1893 se le concedió un *Royal Warrant* y, con ello, los derechos de proveedor real. Él puso fin a la estricta temática religiosa e introdujo motivos más mundanos y modernos. En aquella época, sus dos clientes más importantes eran *mrs.* Grover Cleveland, la esposa del presidente estadounidense, y Su Majestad la reina Victoria.

Según se ha documentado, Su Majestad ordenó la impresión de mil tarjetas con un exquisito motivo infantil para enviárselas a sus familiares y amigos de toda Europa. Este ejemplar se convirtió en la mayor expresión artística del momento dentro de su género. Colocada de forma erguida tenía una altura de 30,5 cm y una longitud de 25,5 cm. Según Tuck, la tarjeta era tan espectacular que parecía imposible crear otra que la superara. ¡Si hubiera podido ver en el futuro!

No obstante, también es cierto que muchas de las tarjetas artesanales de esa época, con sus románticos motivos infantiles, siguen siendo hoy magníficos ejemplos de tarjetas navideñas si las comparamos con las creaciones actuales.

Hoy en día, al igual que hace cien años, podemos encontrar tarjetas navideñas originales, ostentosas, creativas, artísticas o, simplemente, bonitas. Madres, fotógrafos o profesionales de diferentes sectores dedican horas, días y semanas llenas de creatividad para conservar esta bonita costumbre. Pero a pesar de este enorme esfuerzo, no deberíamos olvidar la finalidad que la tarjeta tenía en sus orígenes.

Para mí es un placer poder participar en la elaboración de este libro porque no sólo me ofrece la oportunidad de apoyar una bonita idea sino porque, además, se destinarán parte de los beneficios a nuestra organización benéfica a favor de los niños enfermos de cáncer *CLIC Sargent*.

Lady Helen Taylor

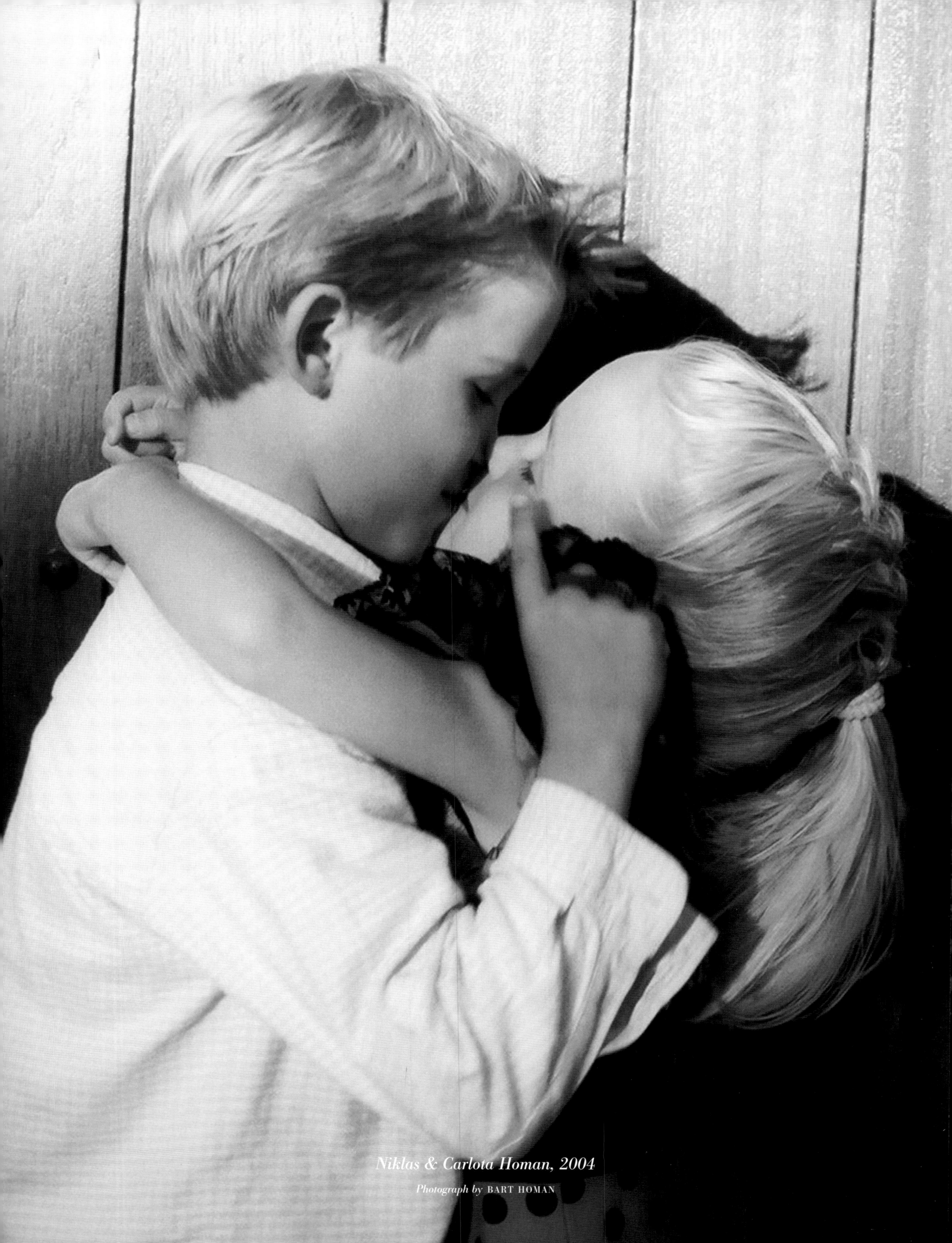

Niklas & Carlota Homan, 2004

Photograph by BART HOMAN

Fu la mia bisnonna, la regina Mary, a dar vita ad una delle più splendide raccolte di biglietti d'auguri di Natale, dai primi esemplari risalenti all'epoca vittoriana fino ai biglietti degli anni '50. Diciotto splendidi album che permettono di immergersi nella storia di questa affascinante forma di arte e di convivenza sociale.

Il primo esemplare documentato di biglietto d'auguri di Natale fu commissionato nel 1846 da Sir Henry Cole, il fondatore del *Victoria and Albert Museum*. Nei primi anni i biglietti d'auguri di Natale venivano spesso usati in qualsiasi strato sociale come un modo gentile per appianare discordie, ricucire amicizie rotte e rafforzare i legami di vicinato. All'inizio del XX secolo questa bella consuetudine si trasformò poi nell'usanza sociale a noi oggi conosciuta.

Eppure, a prescindere dallo scopo che un tempo essi avevano, i biglietti d'auguri di Natale sono indubbiamente ancora oggi la forma più bella, creativa e gioiosa di porgere gli auguri.

I motivi principali inizialmente raffigurati erano di natura religiosa, e anche a quei tempi la produzione di biglietti d'auguri di Natale doveva rigorosamente rispondere a standard elevati. Il famoso litografo e stampatore di banconote Thomas de la Rue fu uno dei pionieri dei primi biglietti d'auguri di Natale. Con i suoi procedimenti di stampa ingegnosi e creativi, egli conferì ai suoi capolavori colori di una vivacità e luminosità magnifiche, che incontrarono l'entusiasmo di una popolazione vittoriana assetata di colori.

Un altro nome, anch'esso strettamente legato al biglietto d'auguri di Natale, è Raphael Tuck, che per il suo encomiabile lavoro fu insignito nel 1893 di un *Royal Warrant* come fornitore di servizi della casa reale. Sotto l'influsso di Tuck le tematiche rigorosamente religiose scomparvero, lasciando spazio a motivi più profani e moderni. A quel tempo i suoi due maggiori clienti erano Mrs. Grover Cleveland, la consorte del presidente americano, e Sua Maestà la regina Vittoria.

Come riportano alcuni appunti, Sua Maestà ordinò mille biglietti d'auguri con un motivo di bambini estremamente artistico da inviare a parenti e amici in tutta Europa. Questo biglietto rappresentò il biglietto d'auguri di Natale più artistico del suo tempo. Se messo in posizione eretta, il biglietto misurava la bellezza di 30,5 cm di altezza e 25,5 cm di larghezza. Tuck racconta di un biglietto dall'aspetto talmente ricercato che chiunque lo contemplasse doveva chiedersi come fosse mai possibile migliorarlo ulteriormente... se solo avesse potuto prevedere il futuro!

Bisogna riconoscere tuttavia che molti dei biglietti d'auguri di quel periodo, prodotti con vera maestria e con i loro romantici motivi di bambini, potrebbero soddisfare persino i criteri di giudizio odierni e offrire ancora oggi esempi eccellenti di biglietti d'auguri di Natale.

Proprio come cento anni fa, anche oggi si trovano biglietti d'auguri di Natale originali, ricercati, creativi, artistici o semplicemente belli. Mamme, fotografi e specialisti dei settori più svariati dedicano con creatività innumerevoli ore, giorni e settimane per mantenere viva questa piacevole usanza. Dopo tanto lavoro non si dovrebbe però dimenticare lo scopo originario dei biglietti d'auguri di Natale.

Sono davvero lieta di poter offrire il mio contributo a questo splendido libro, non solo perché mi è stata data la possibilità di appoggiare un'idea così bella, bensì, soprattutto, perché una parte del ricavato sarà devoluta alla *CLIC Sargent*, la nostra organizzazione di beneficenza per bambini malati di cancro.

Lady Helen Taylor

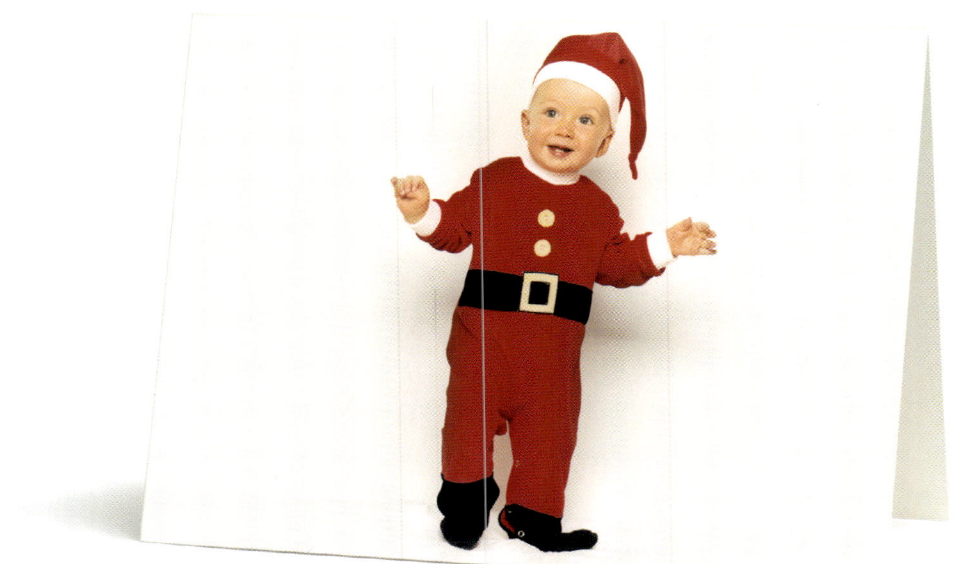

Maximilian Dell, 2003

Photograph by ELIANE FATTAL

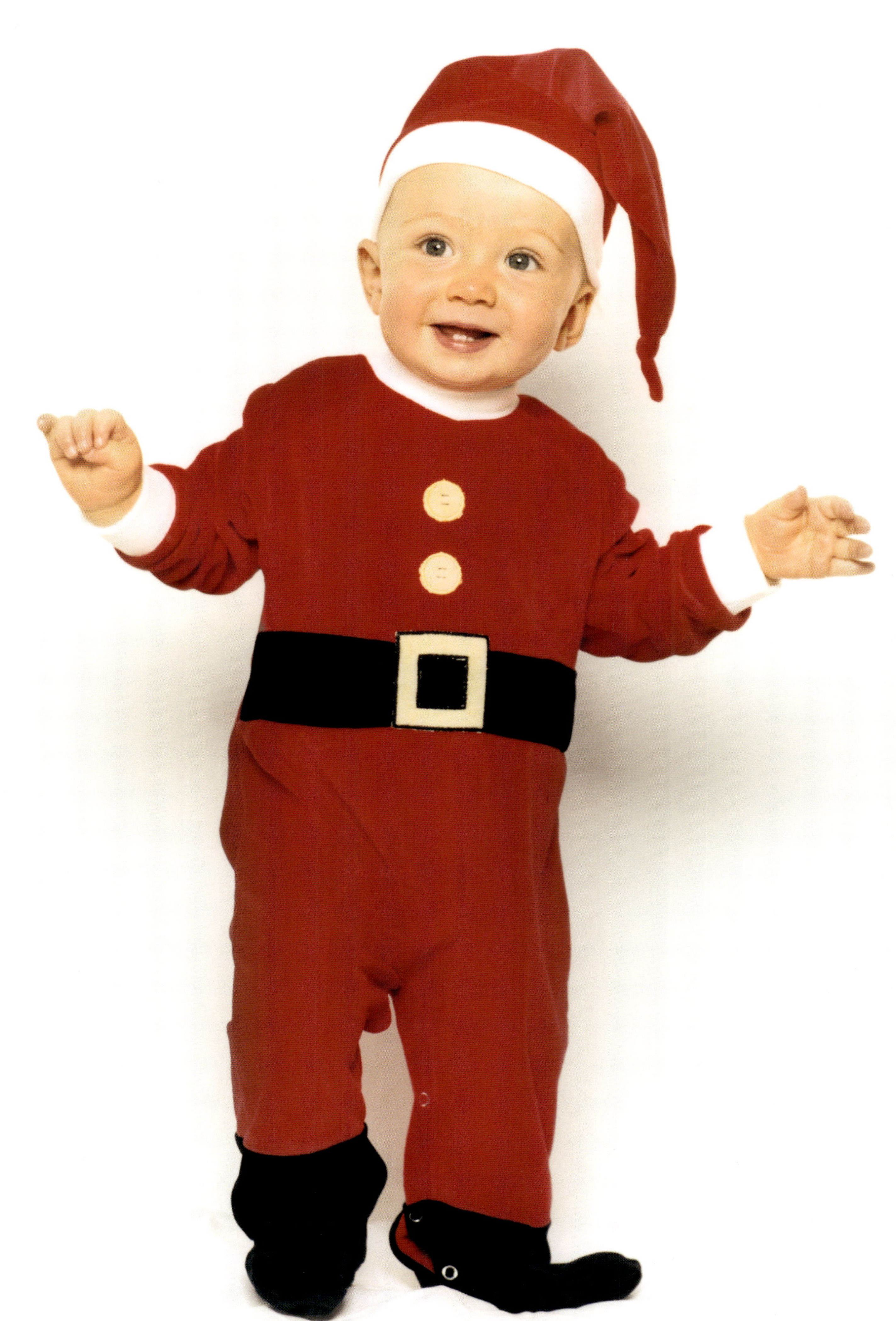

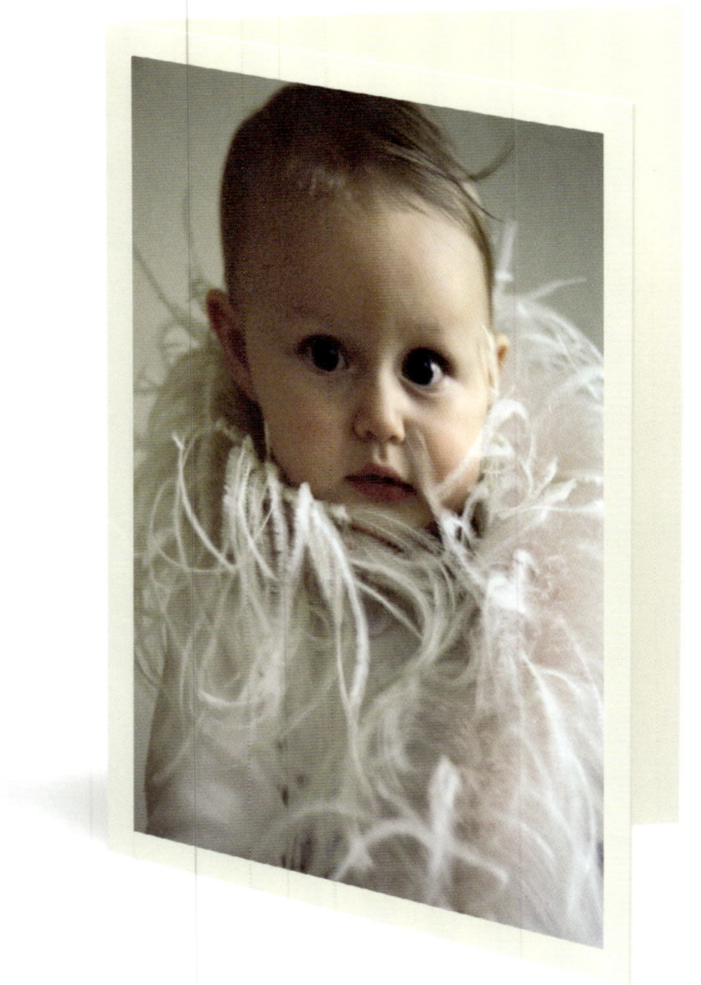

Romy Dub, 2003

Photograph by GERTRUDE DUB

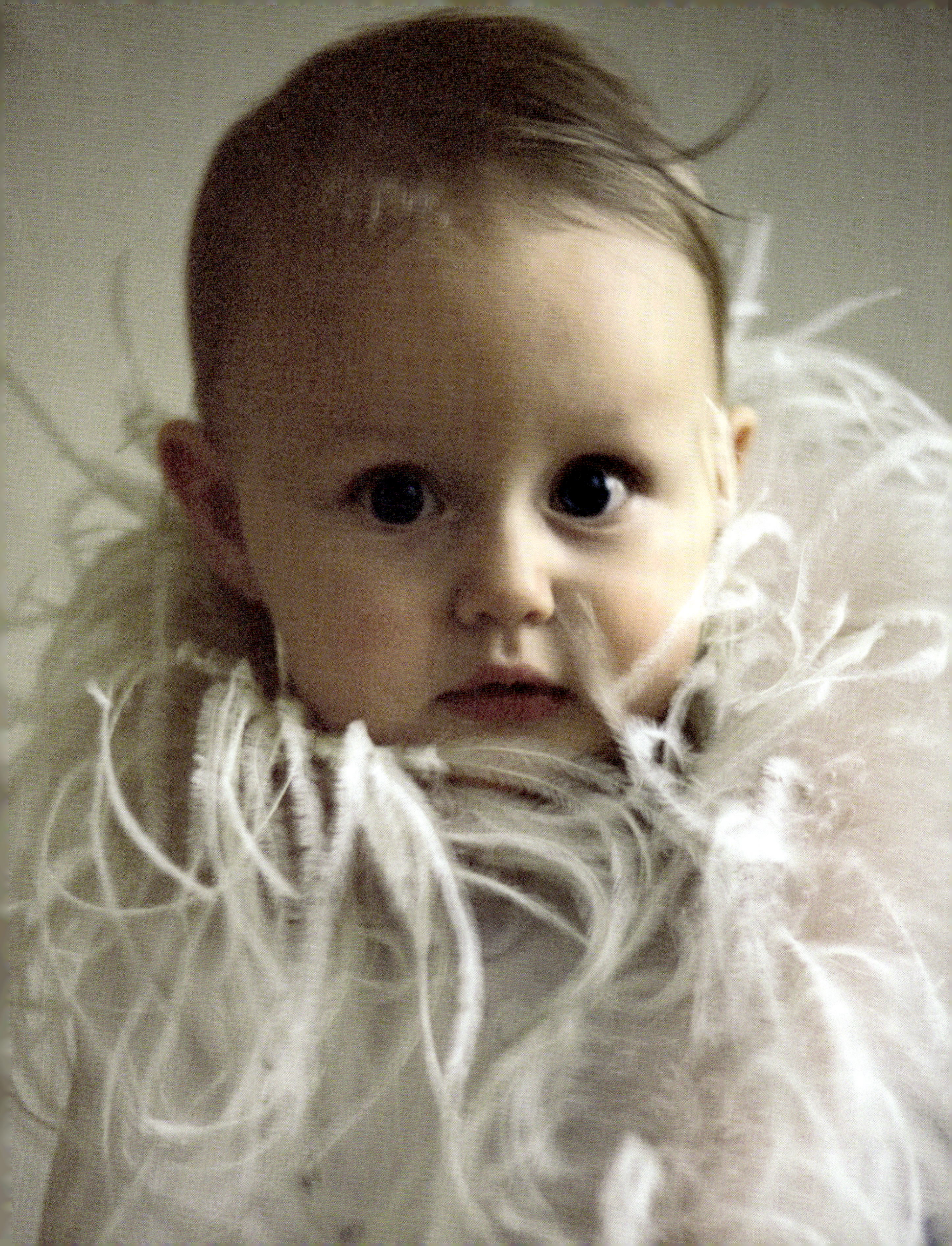

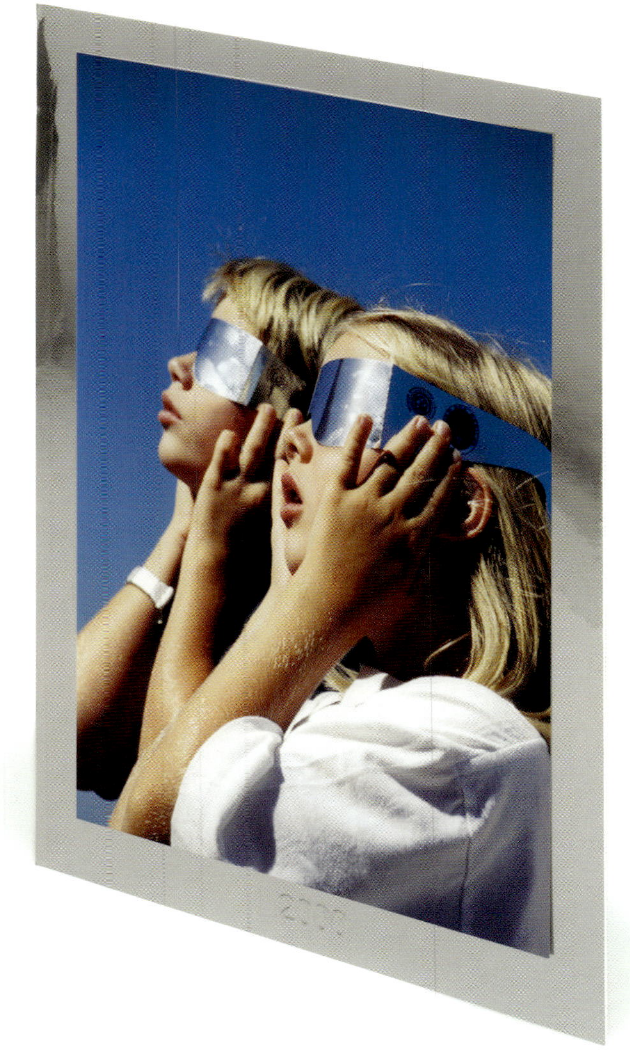

Conte Filippo & Contessa Olimpia
Emo Capodilista, 2000

Photograph by CONTESSA MADELEINE EMO CAPODILISTA

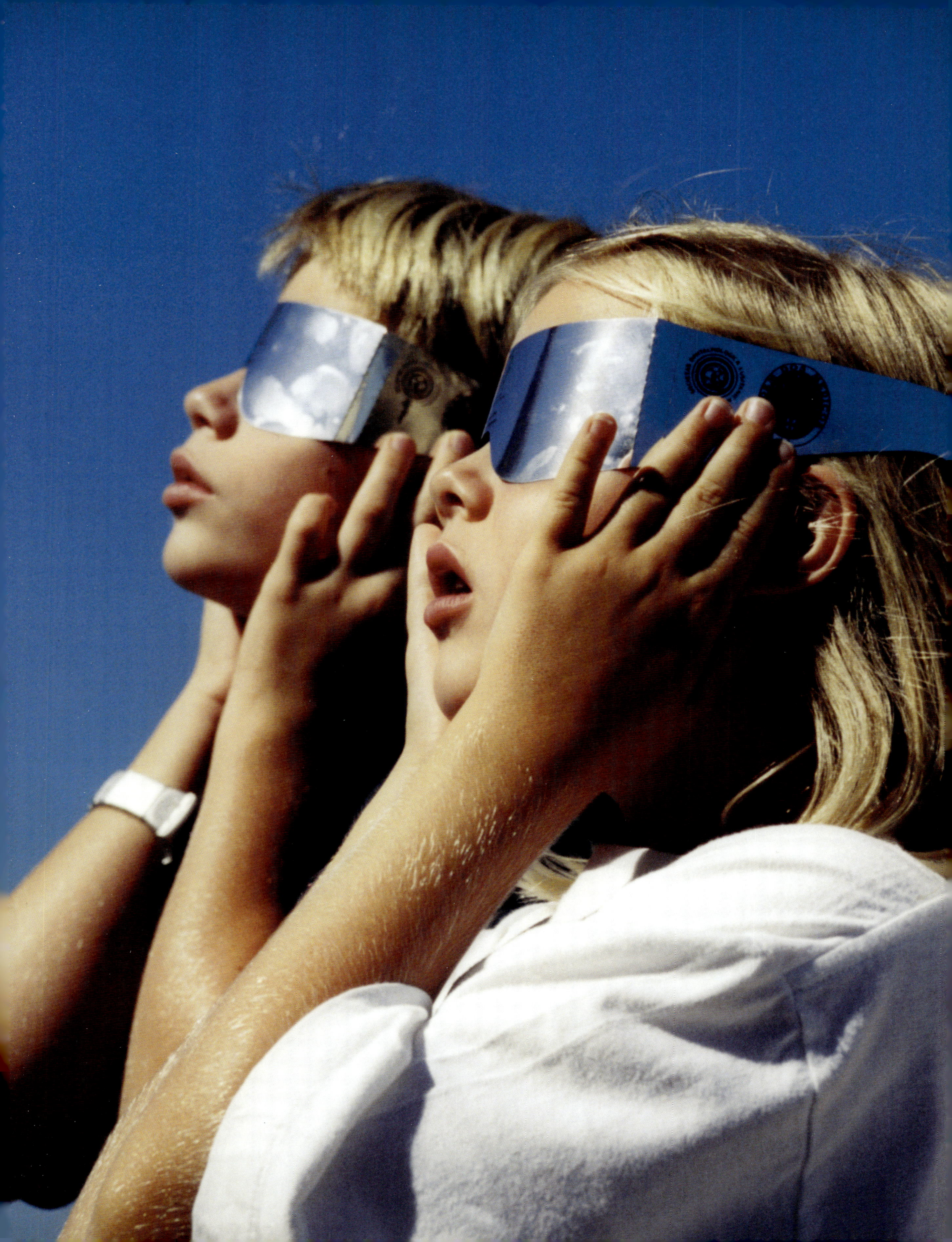

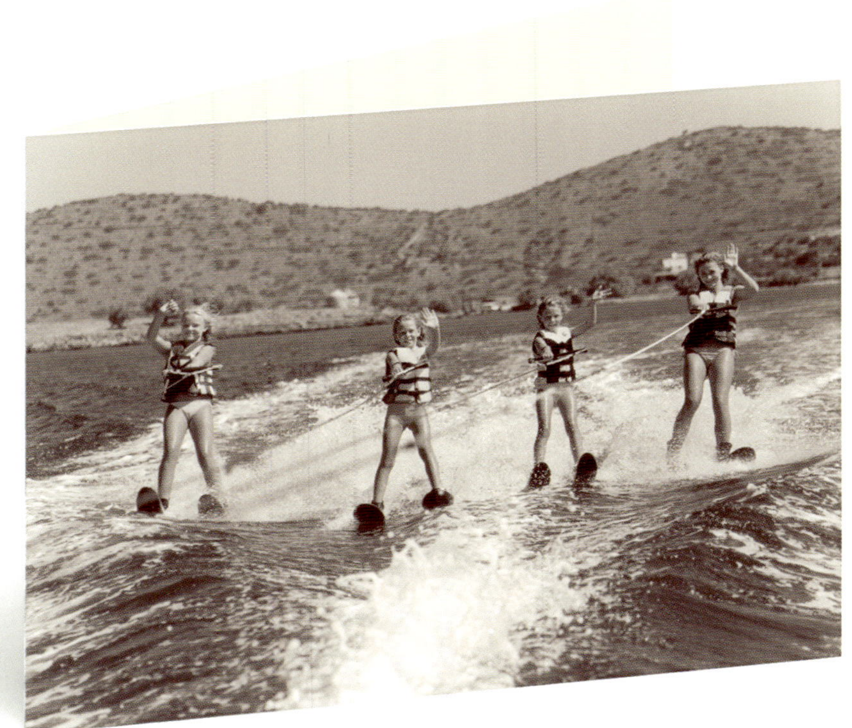

Sophie, Alice, Zoe & Emma Zacharia, 2004

Photograph by MAHFOUZ ZACHARIA

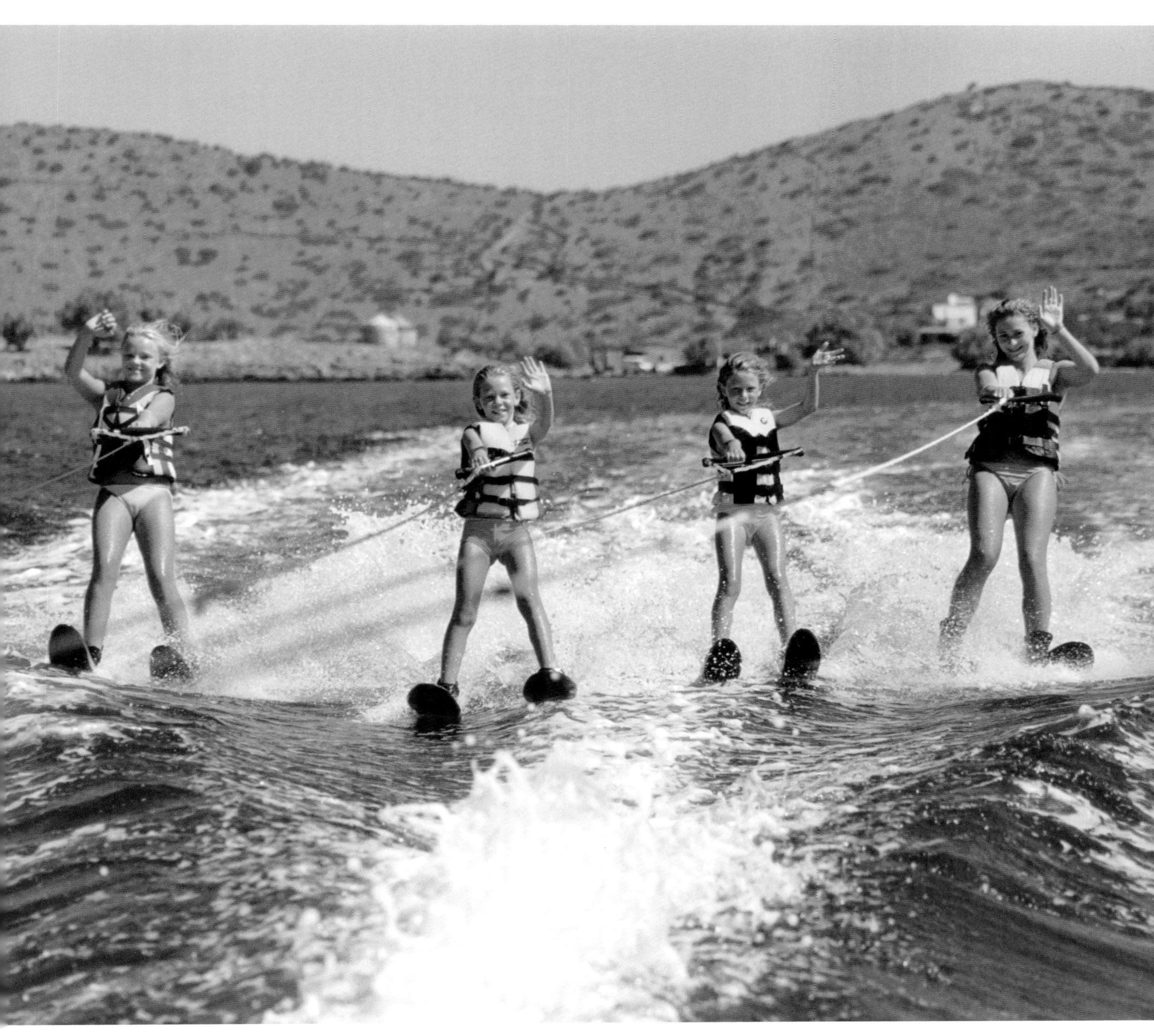

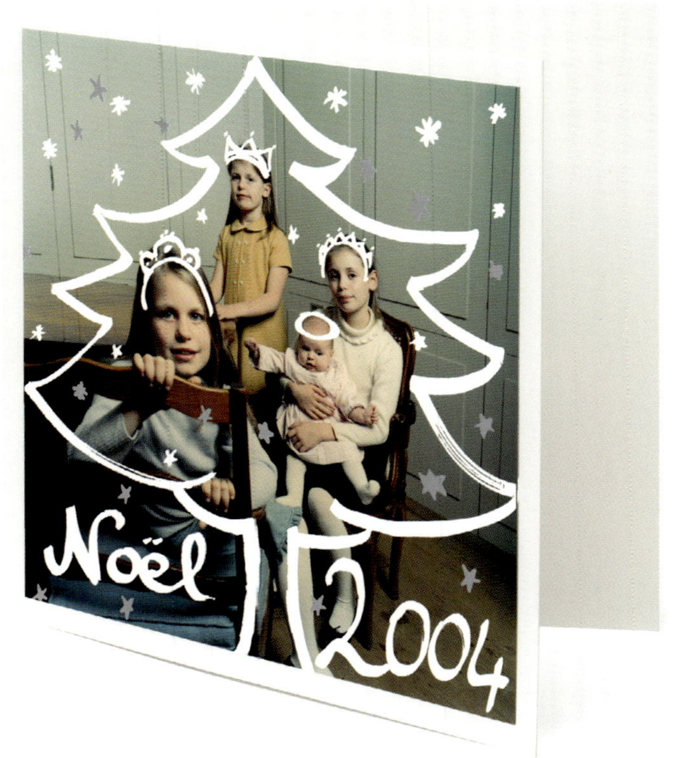

Edwina, Céleste, Evelyn & Gisèle Booth-Clibborn, 2004

Photograph by RICARDO ALCAIDE

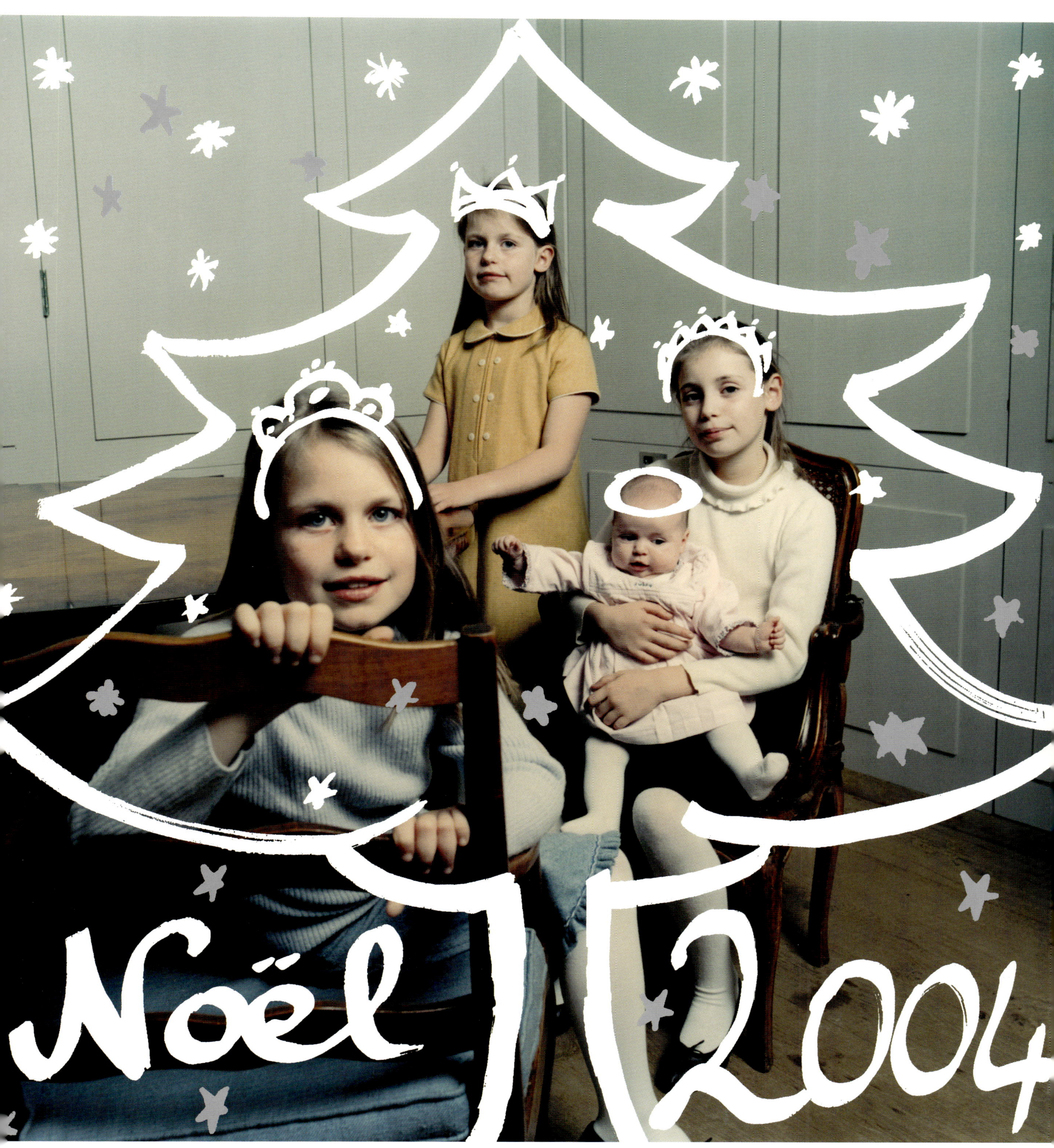
Noël 2004

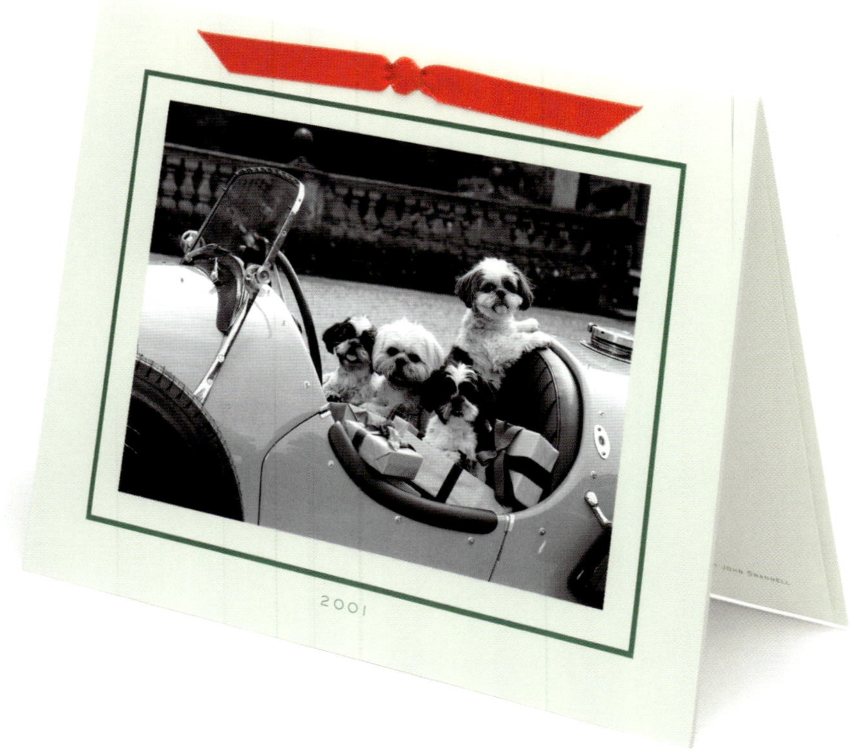

"Minnie", "Fudge", "Jasper" & "Pansy" Bamford, 2001

Photograph by JOHN SWANNELL

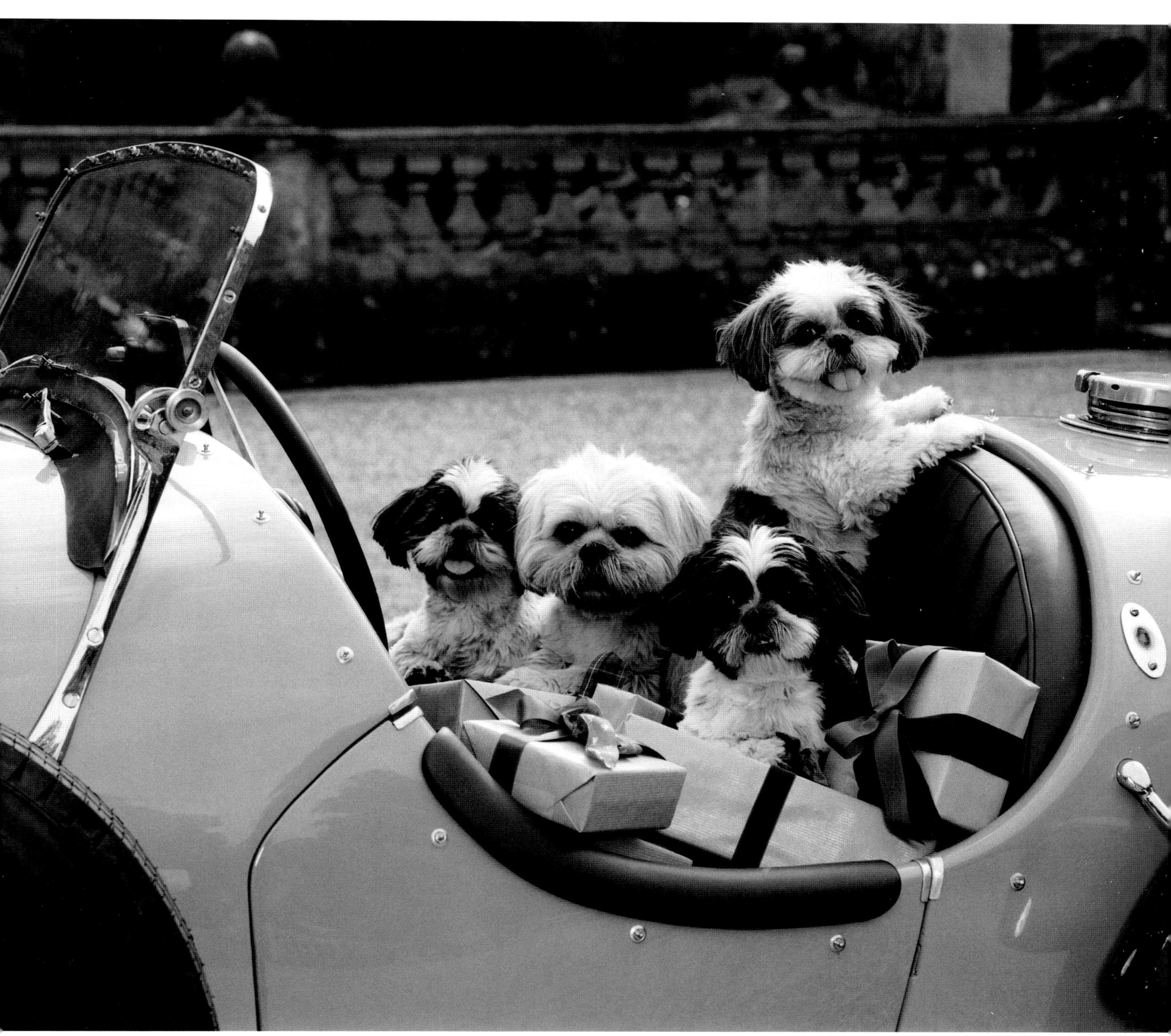

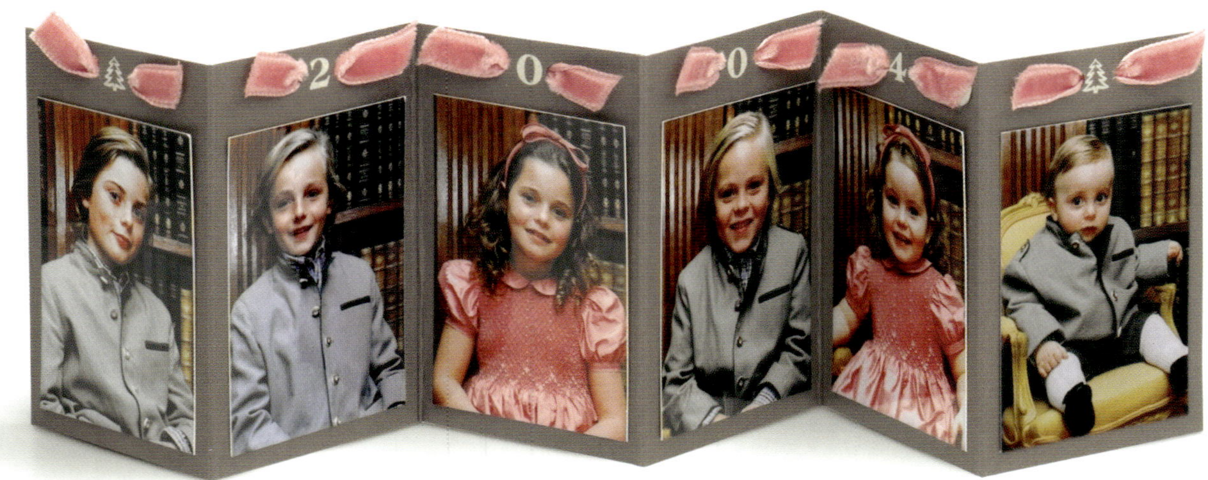

Melchior, Amadeo, Noepy, Rembrandt,
Olympia & Marc-Anthony Dreesmann-Beerkens, 2003/2004

Photographs by FREDERIC FAURE

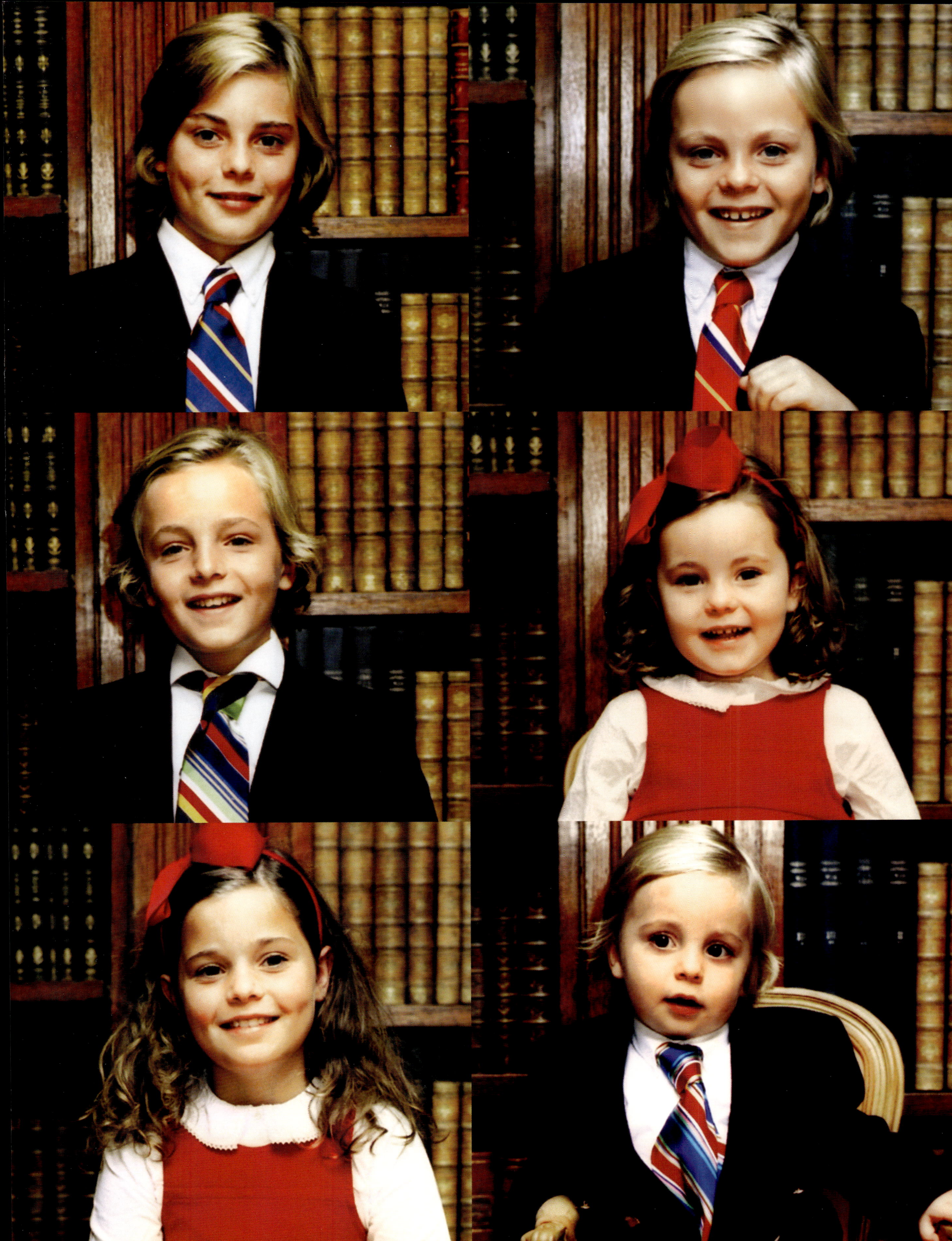

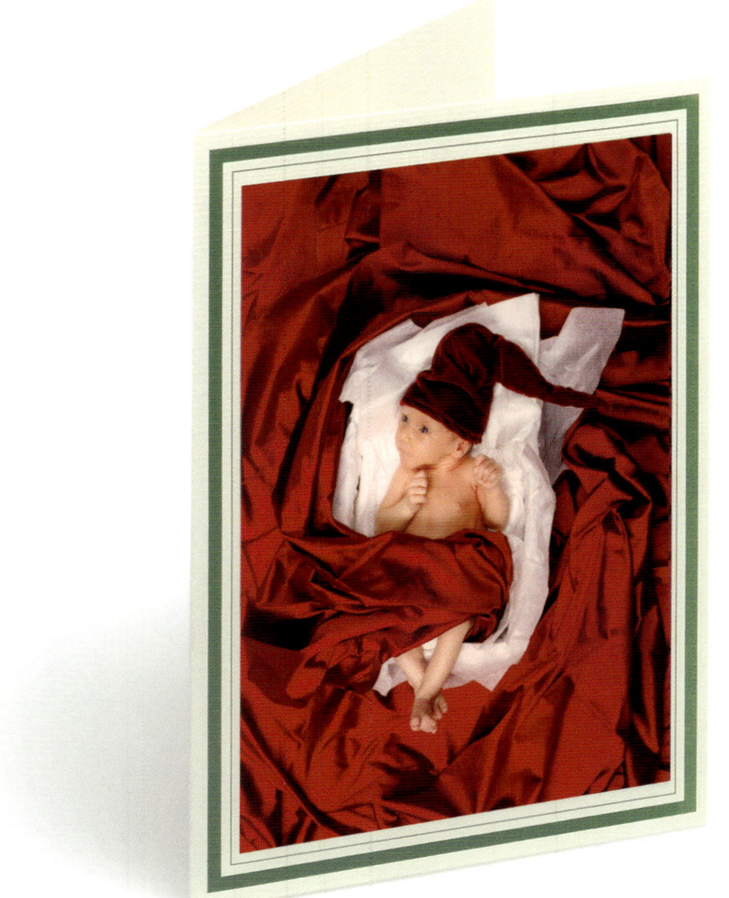

Comte Raoul de Liedekerke, 1995

Photograph by FERDINAND DE LESSEPS

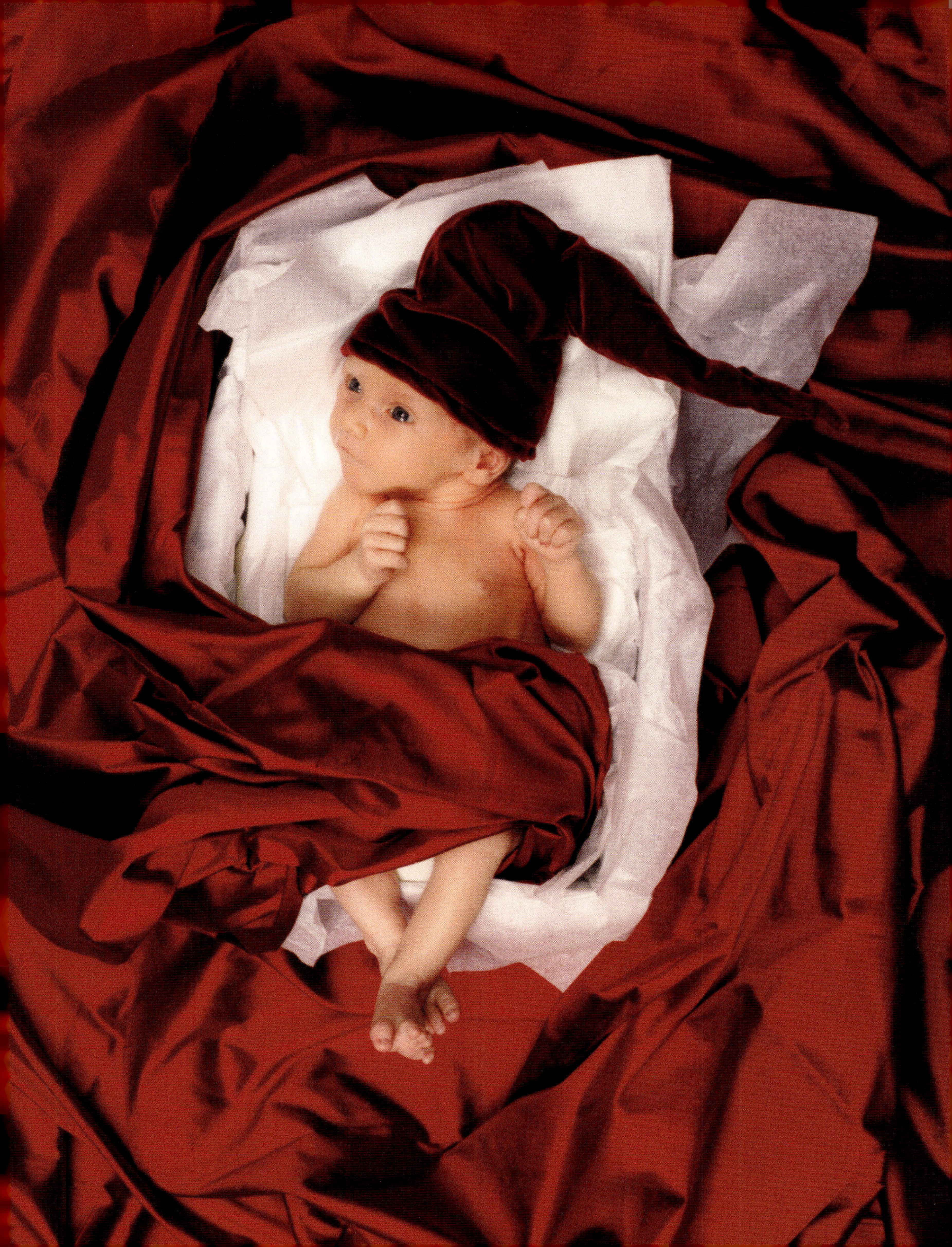

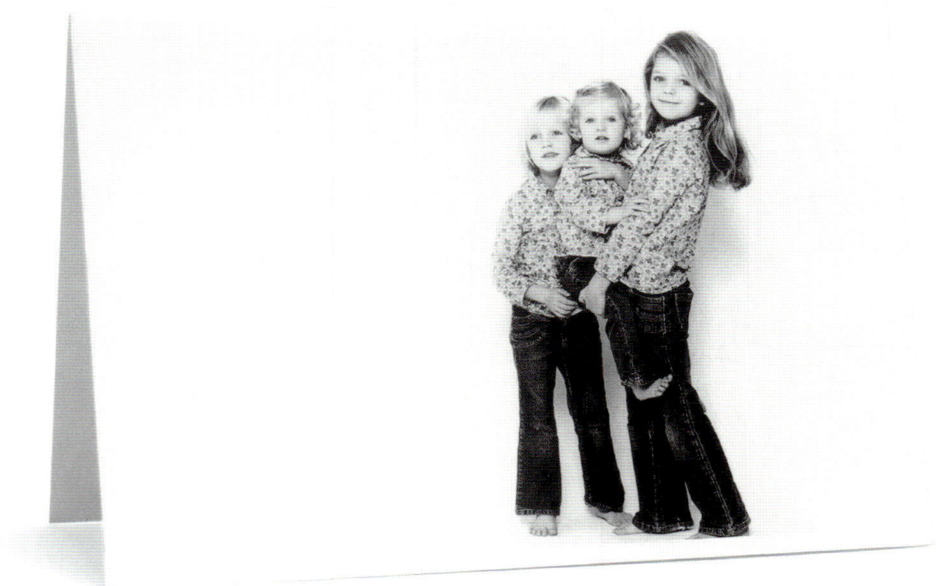

Gräfin Isabel, Gräfin Olivia & Gräfin Mafalda von Stauffenberg, 2004

Photograph by ELIANE FATTAL

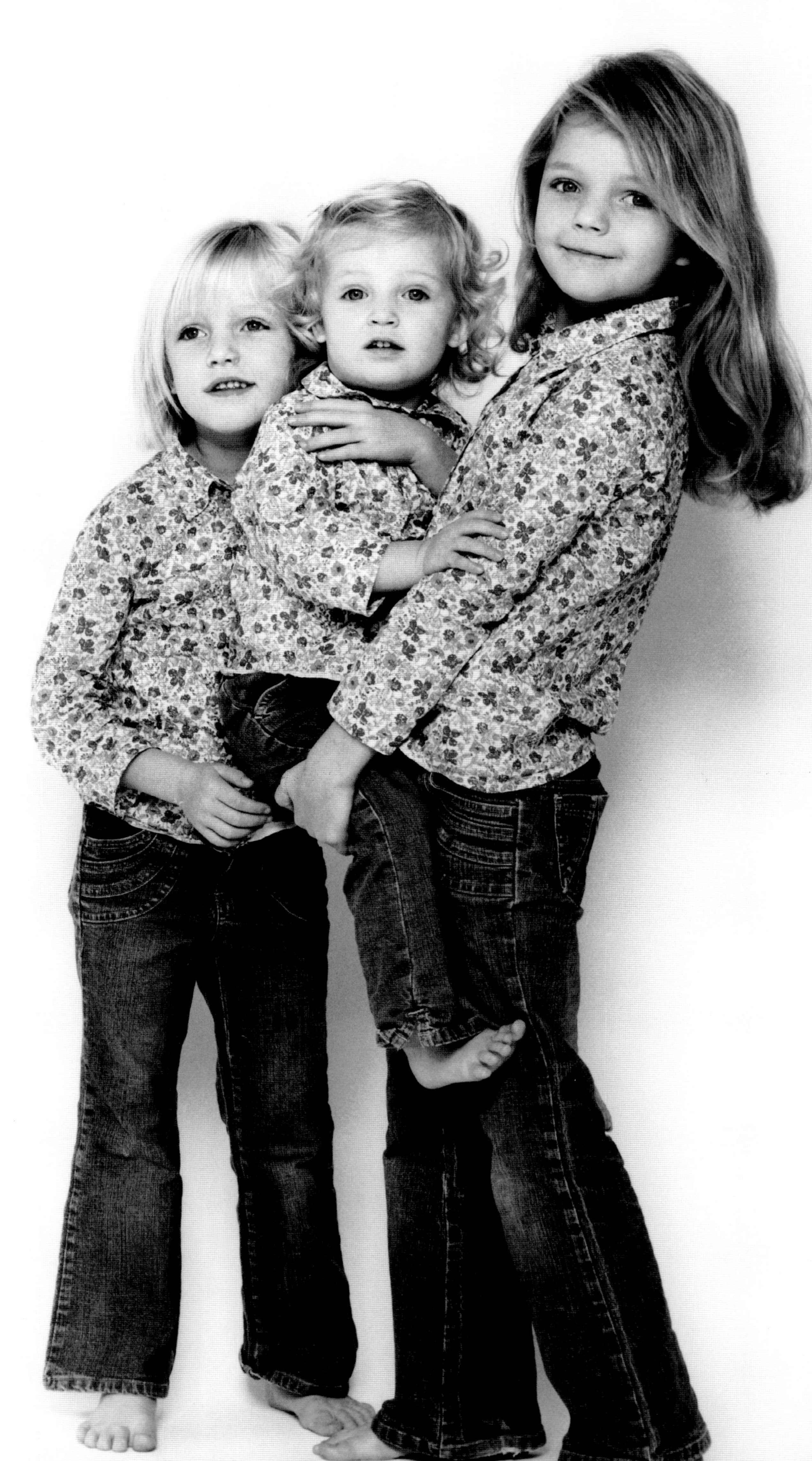

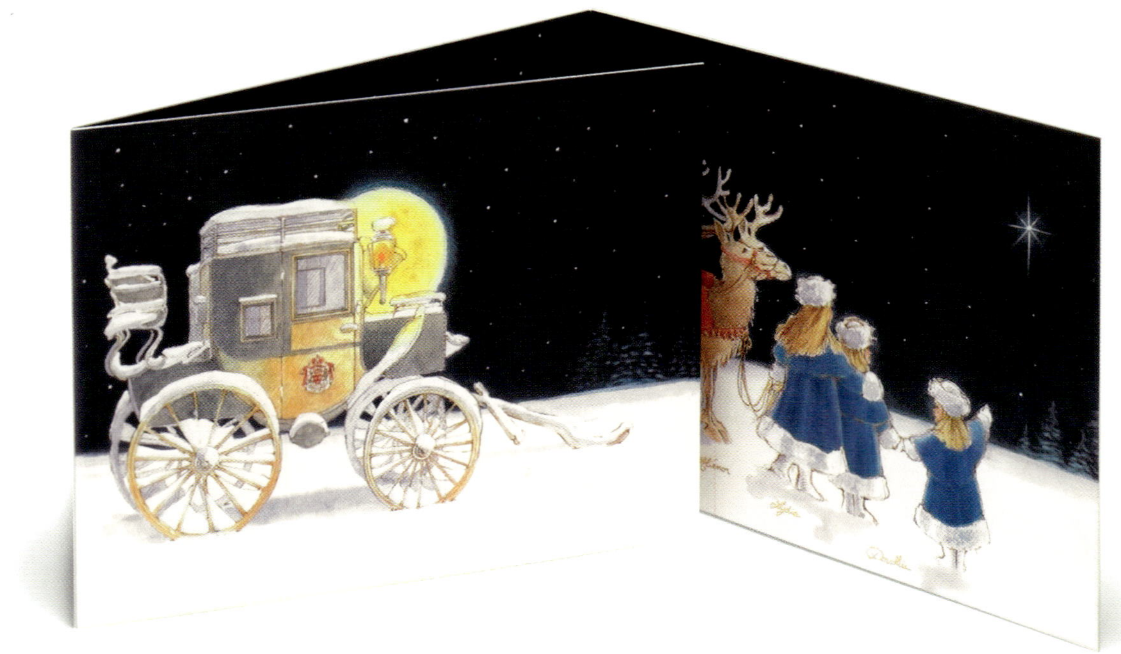

Princesse Aliénor, Princesse Lydia & Princesse Dorothée d'Arenberg, 2003

Illustrations by LUDMILA D'OULTREMONT

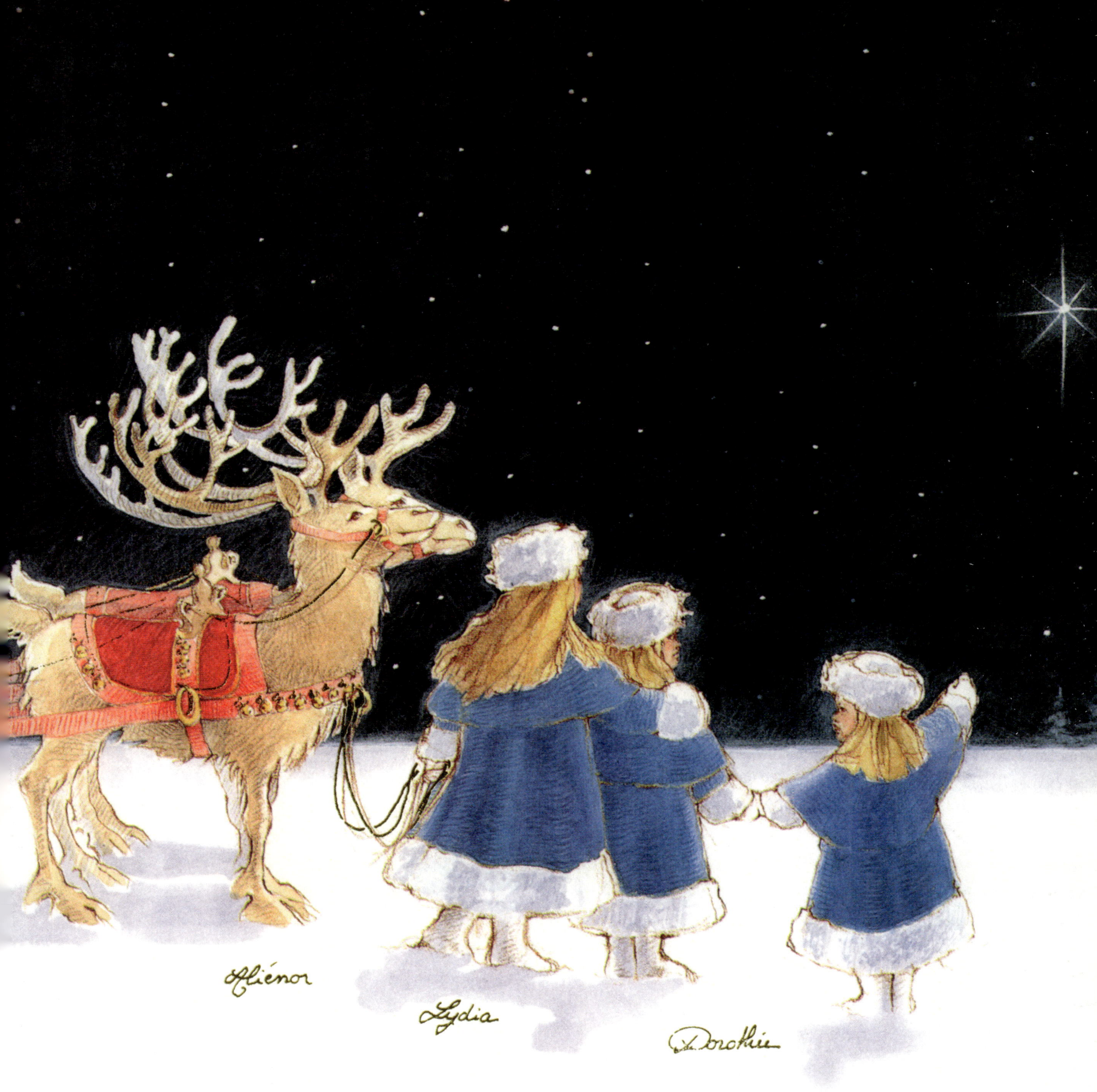
Aliénor
Lydia
Dorothée

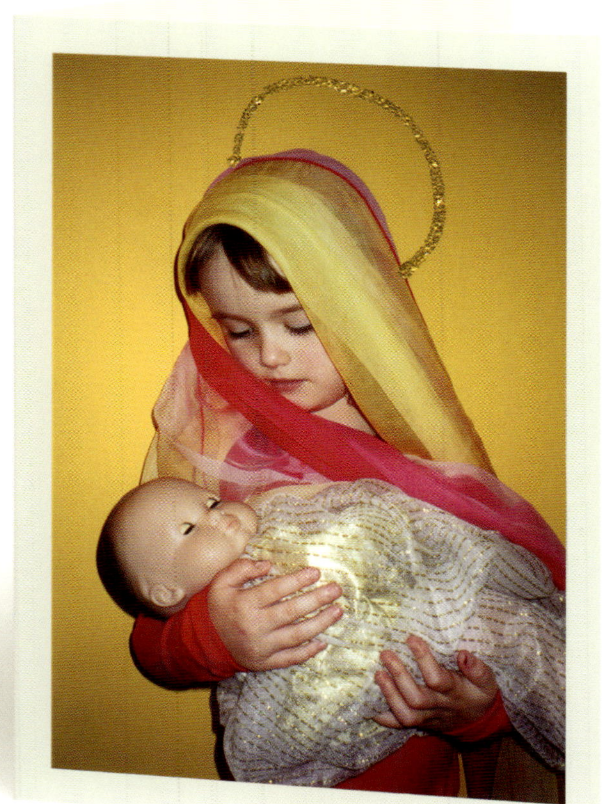

Tara Heather, 2001

Photograph by KIMBERLY DU ROSS

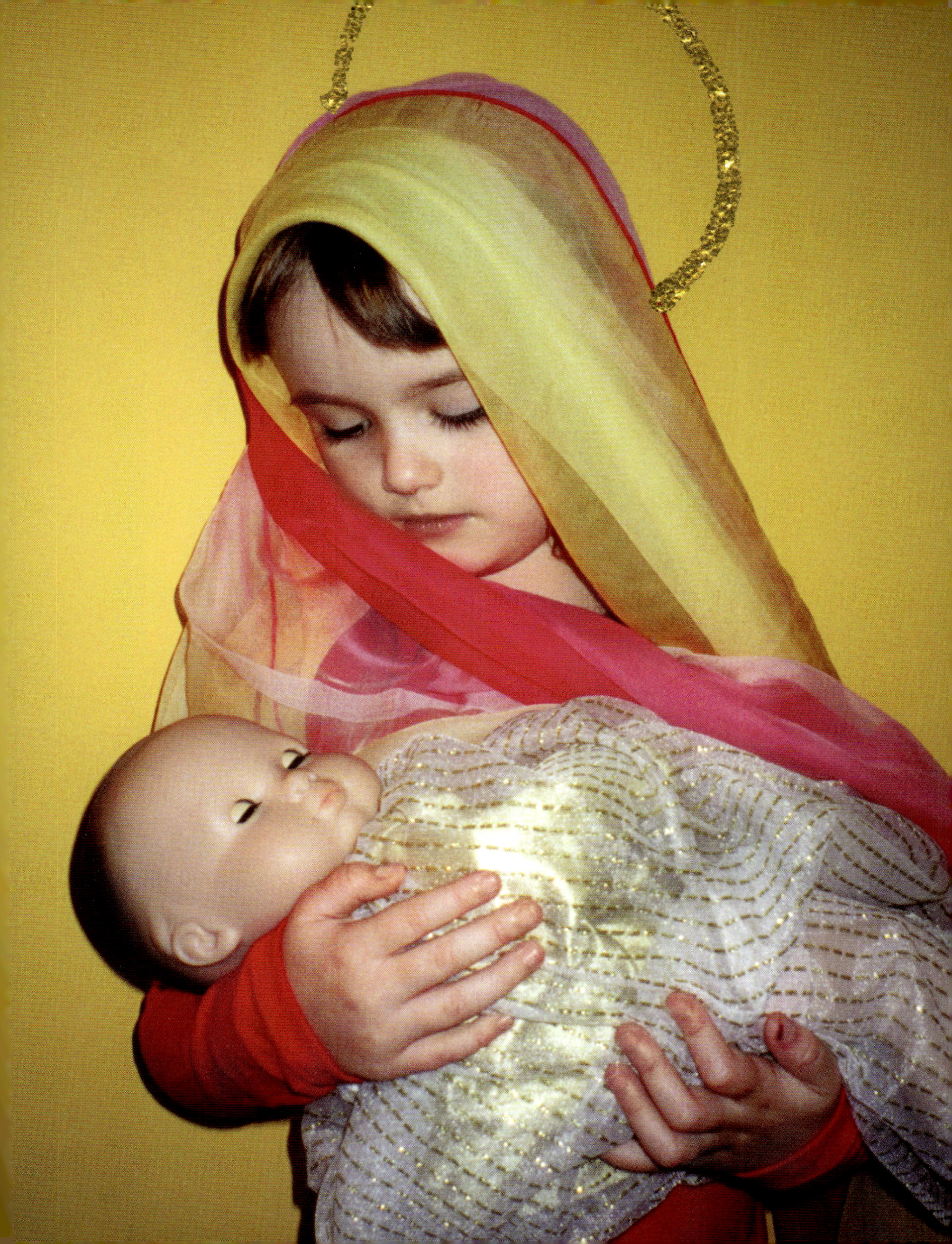

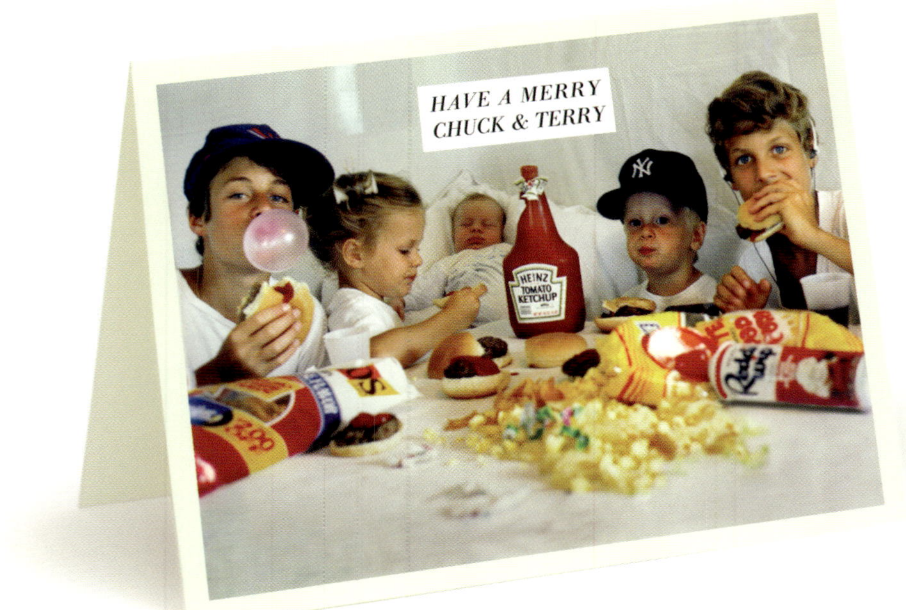

Luis Figueroa y Sayn-Wittgenstein, Gräfin Helena, Graf Clemens, Graf Alexander Kageneck & Juan Figueroa y Sayn-Wittgenstein, 1988

Photograph by GRÄFIN THERESA KAGENECK

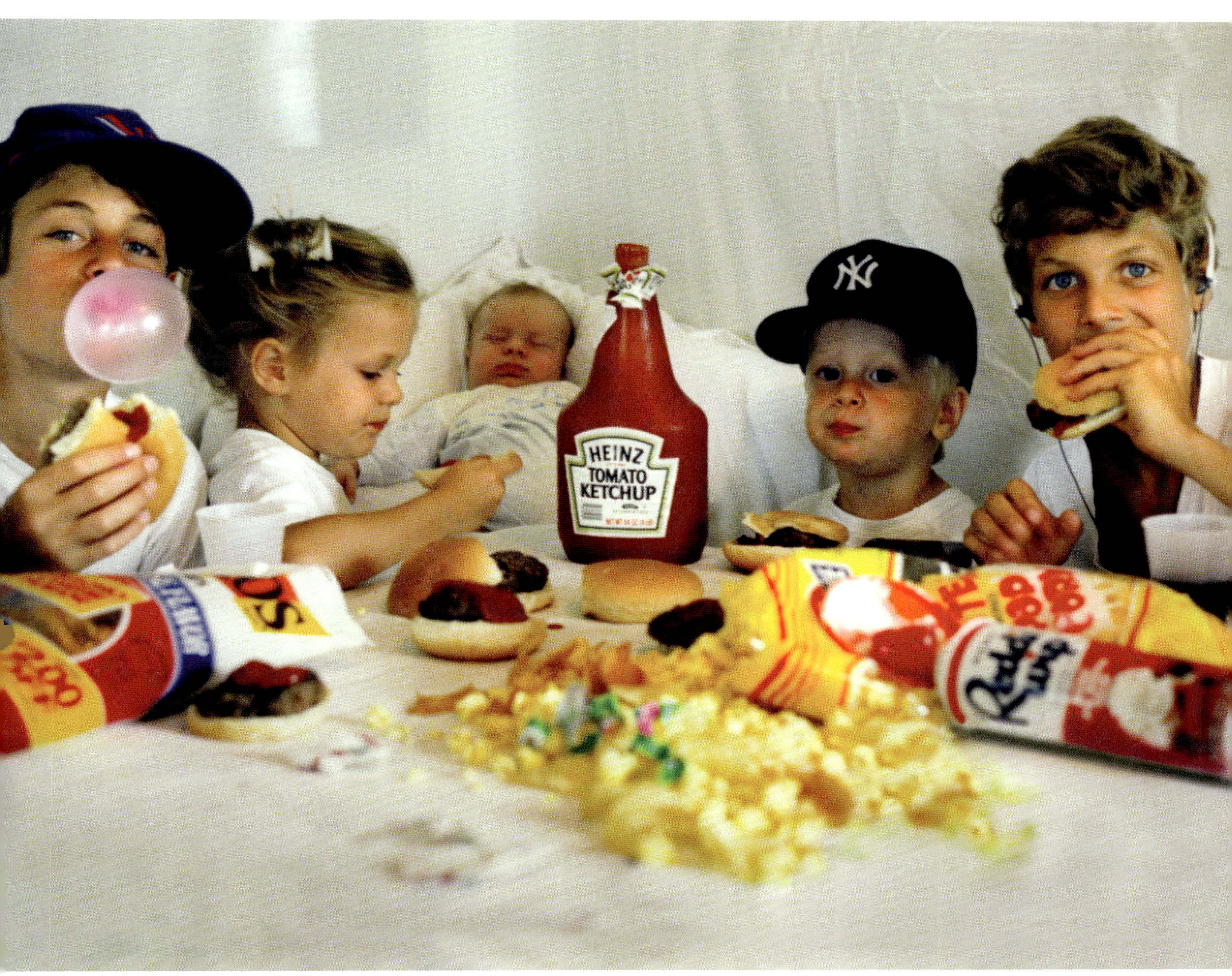
HEINZ
TOMATO
KETCHUP

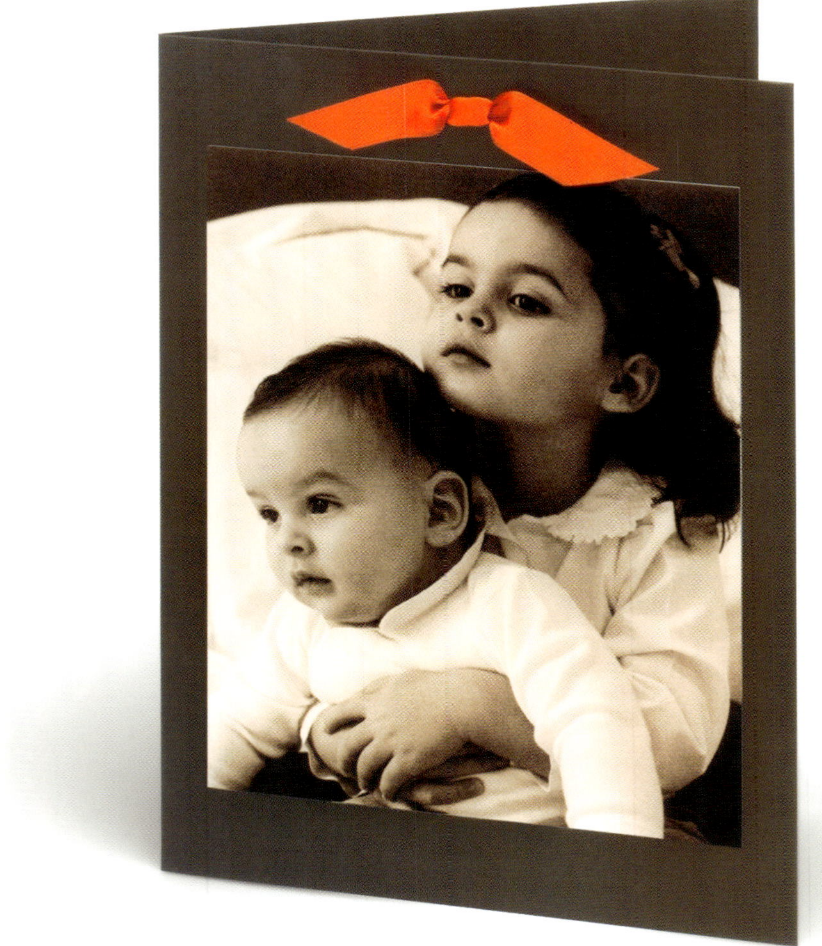

Alex & Ariana Eisler, 2004

Photograph by MARYAM EISLER

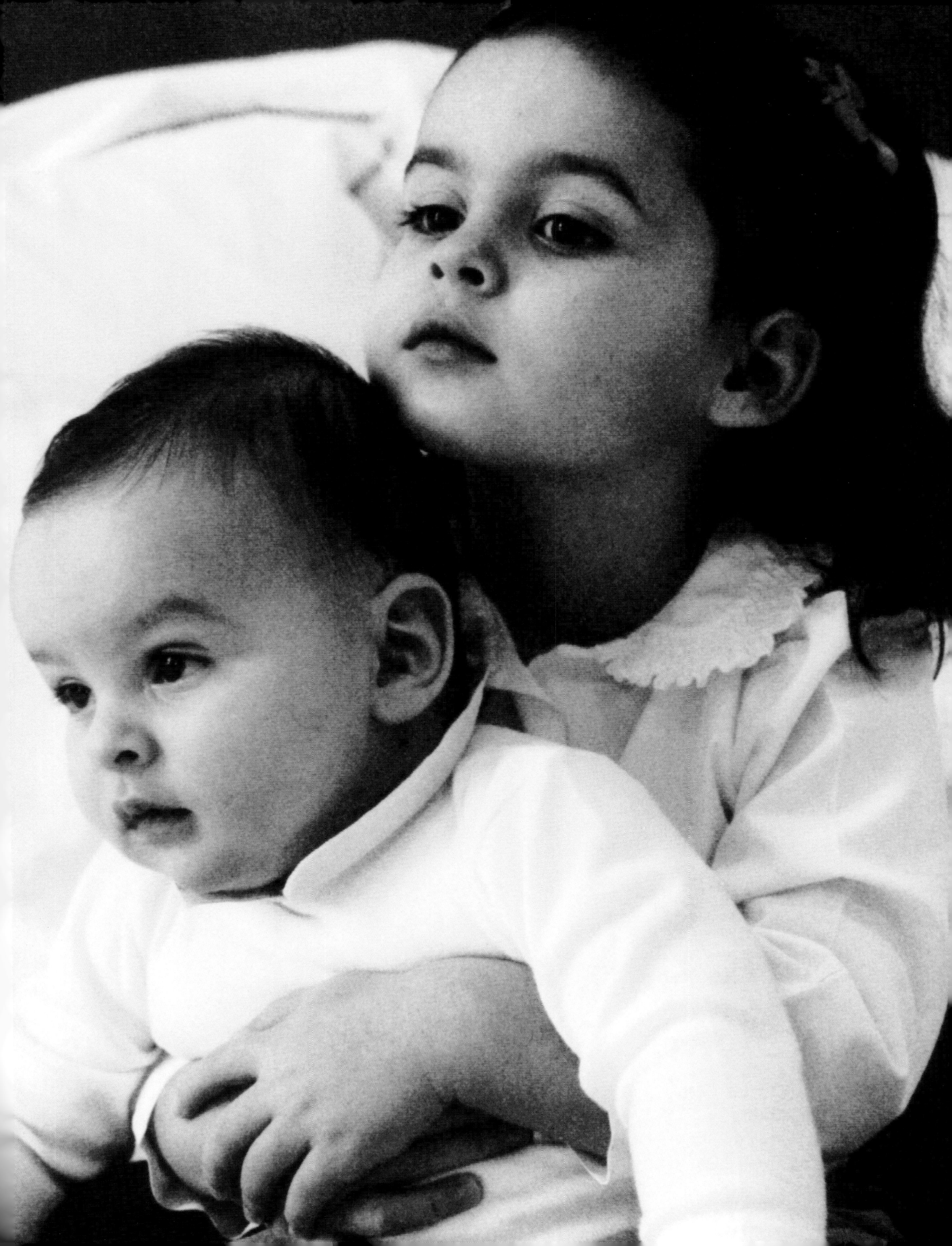

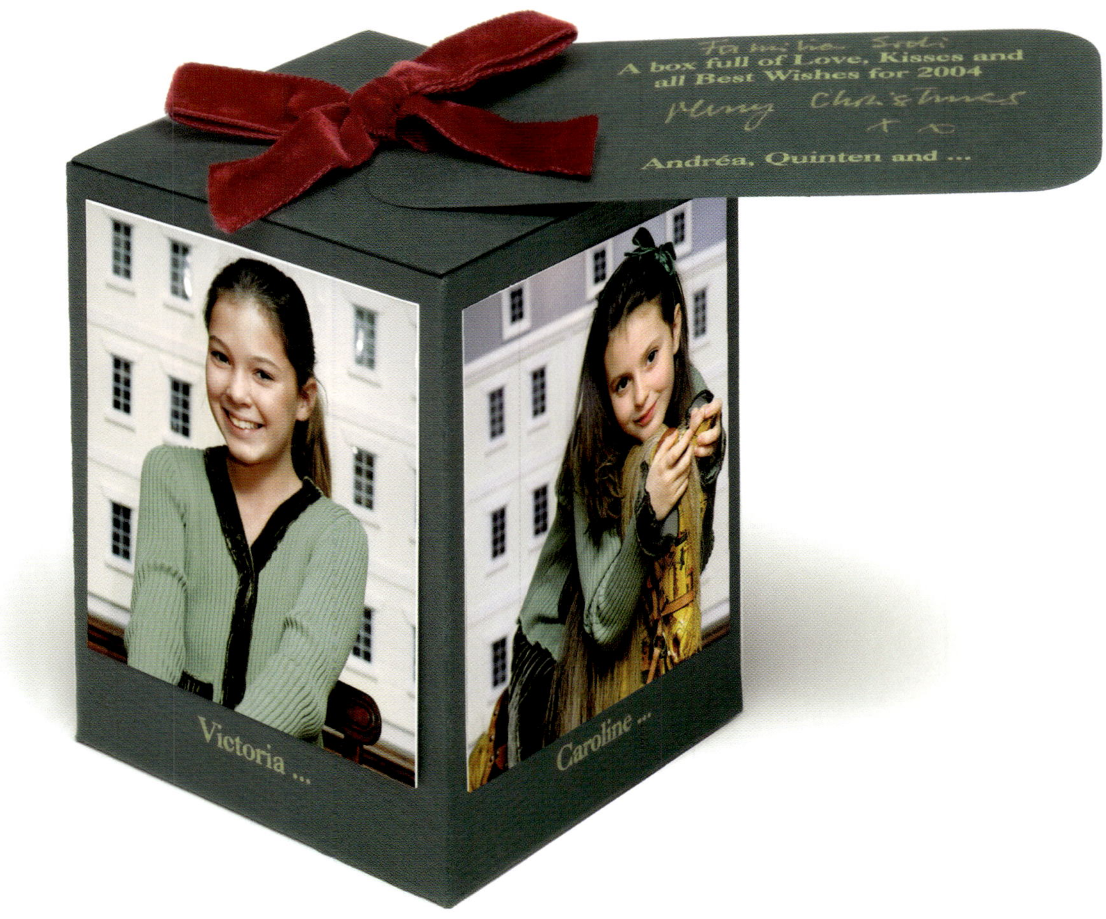

Caroline, Quinten, Felipe & Victoria
Dreesmann-de Botton, 2003

Photographs by FREDERIC FAURE

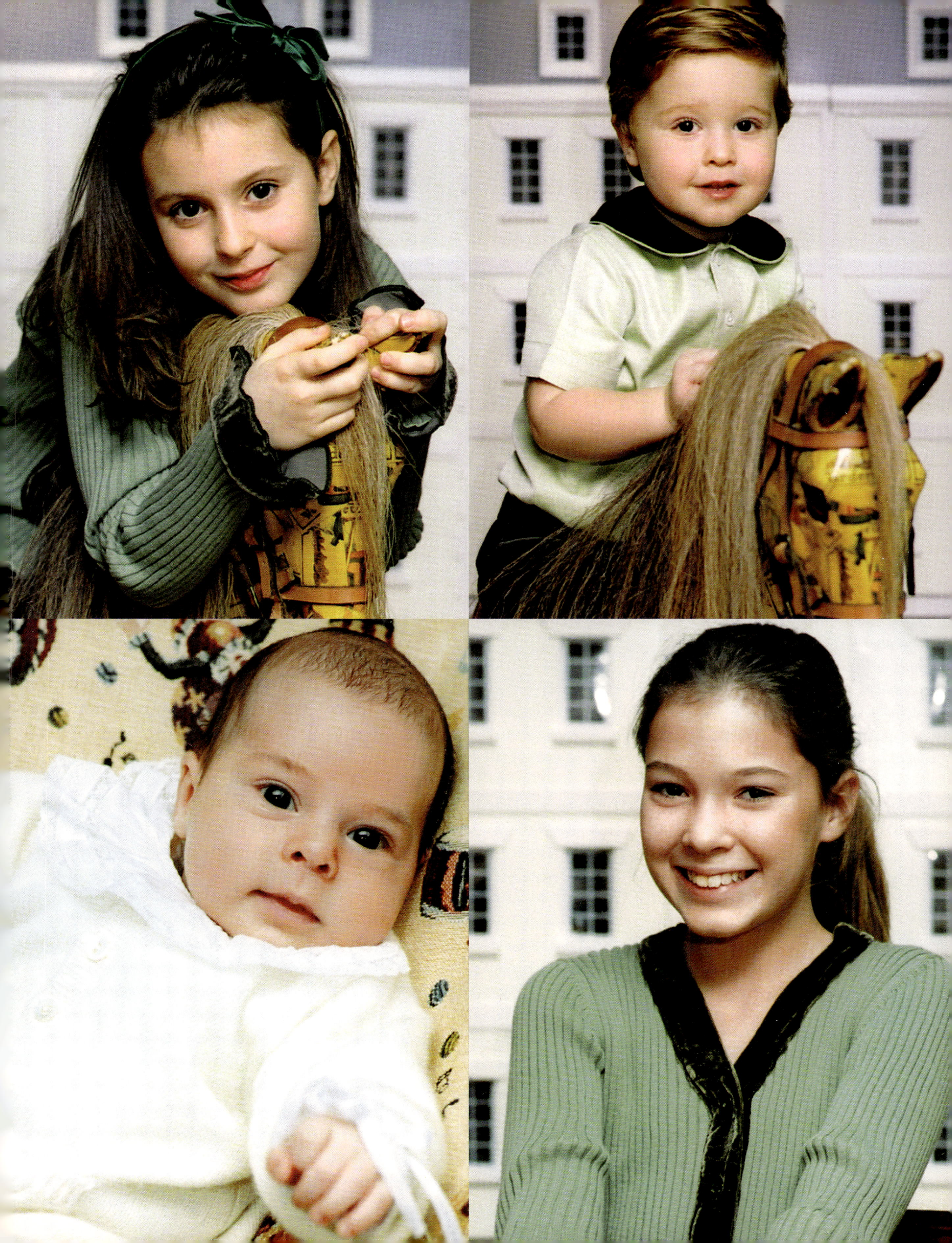

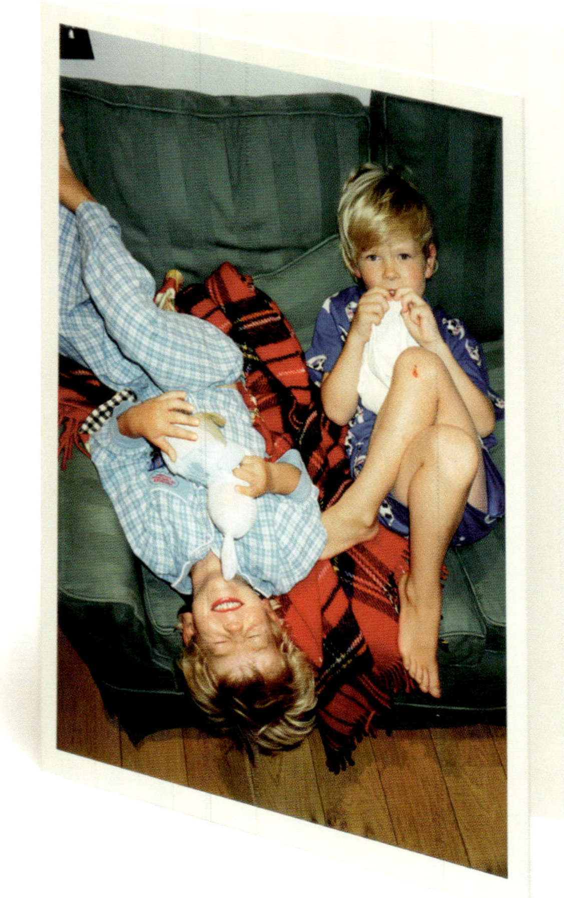

Cassius & Columbus Taylor, 2000

Photograph by MARIO TESTINO

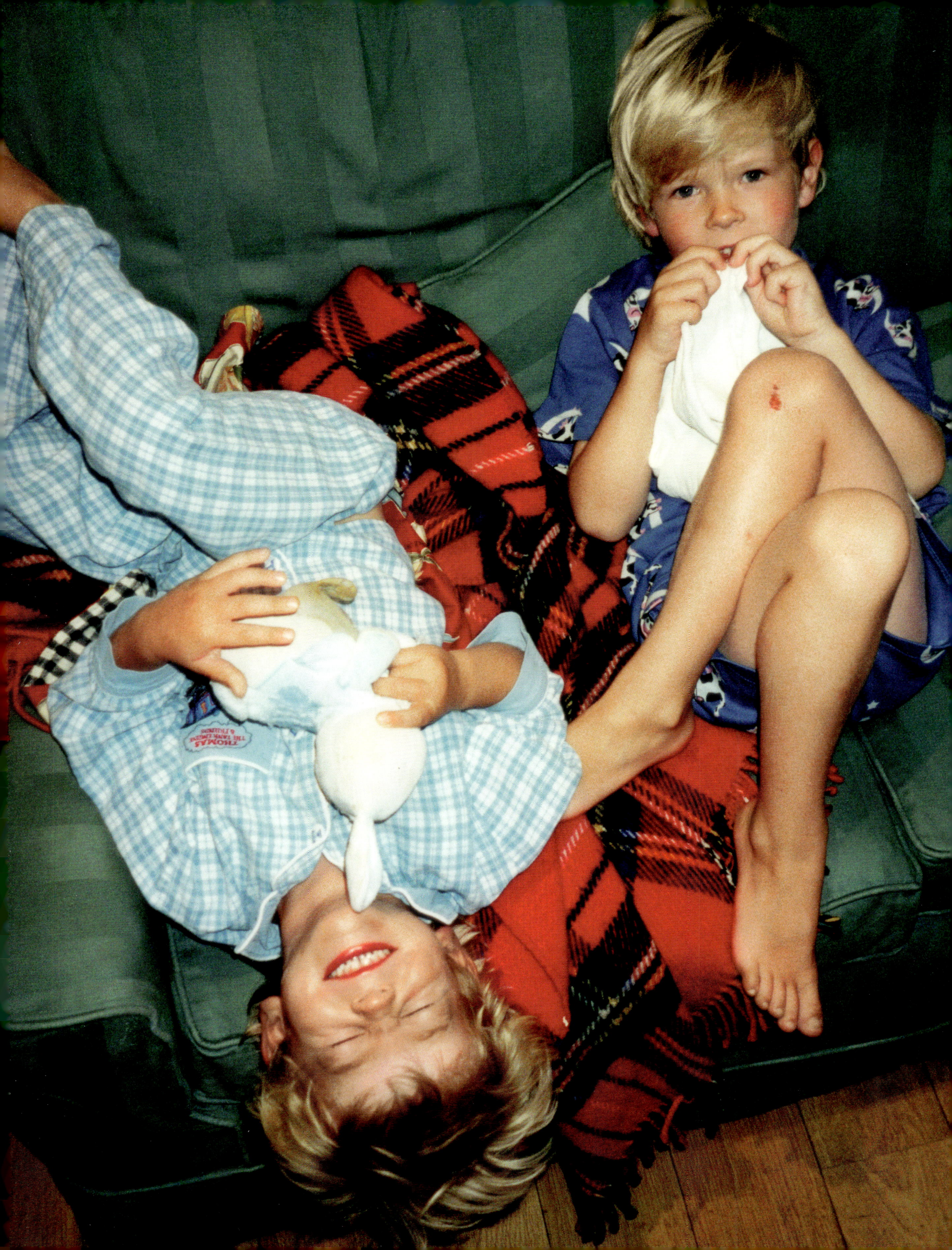

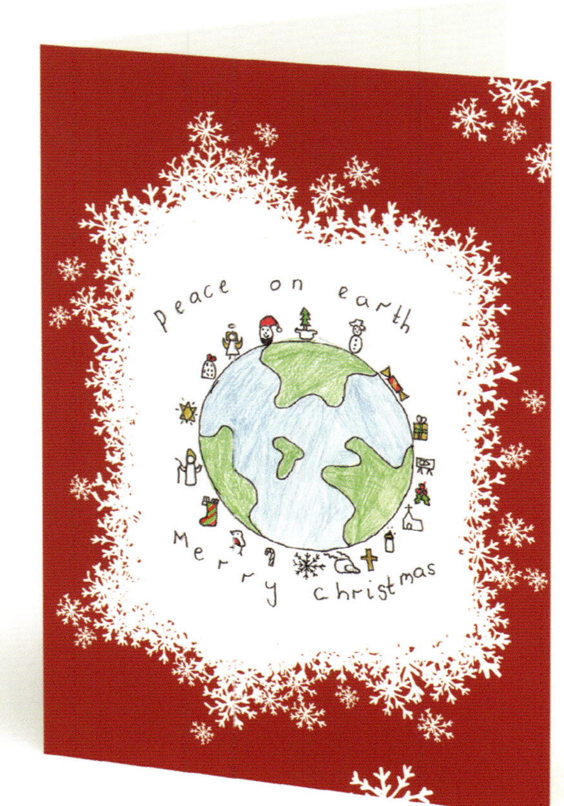

"Peace on Earth – Merry Christmas", 2004

Illustration by FRANCES WOOLSTON

GapArt Christmas Card Competition 2004
(in aid of Sargent Cancer Care for Children, now CLIC Sargent)

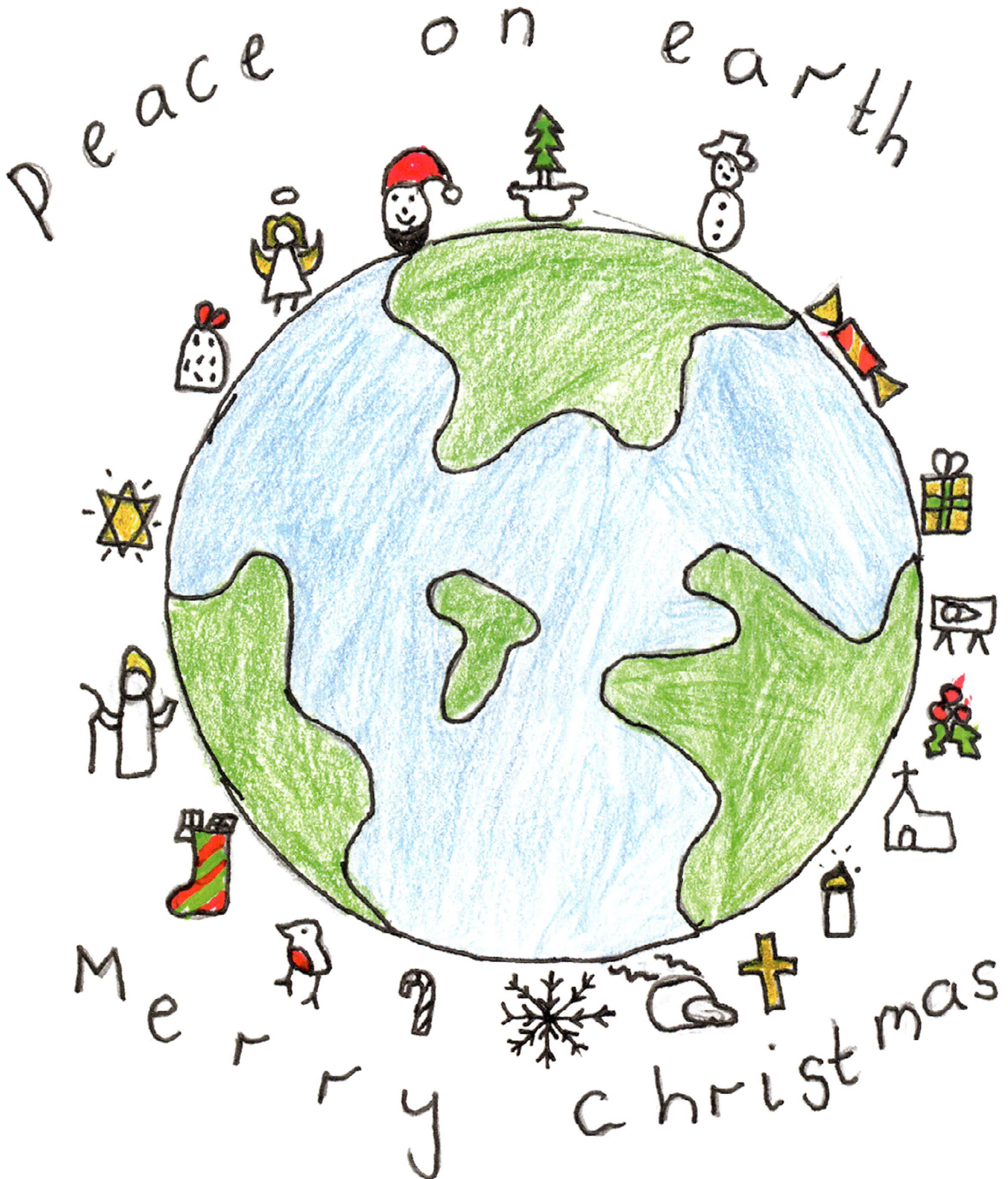

peace on earth
Merry christmas

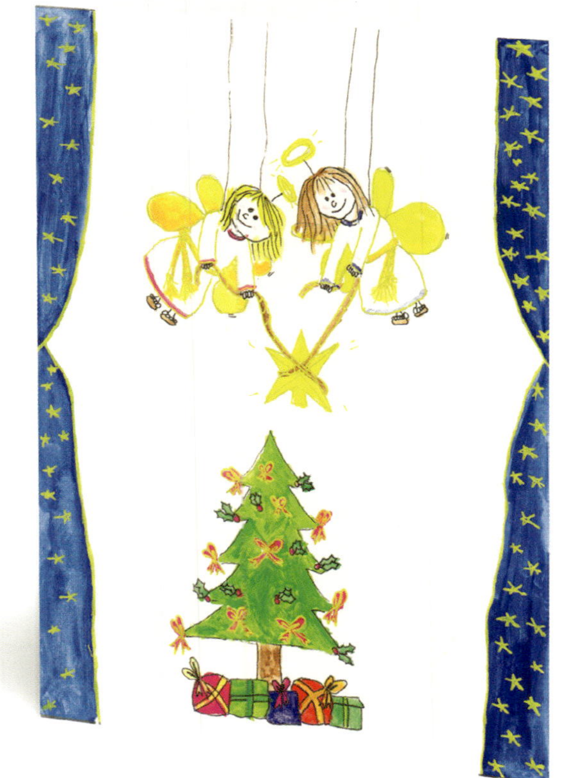

"Angels Decorating Christmas Tree", 2004

Illustration by MICHAELA RAE

GapArt Christmas Card Competition 2004
(in aid of Sargent Cancer Care for Children, now CLIC Sargent)

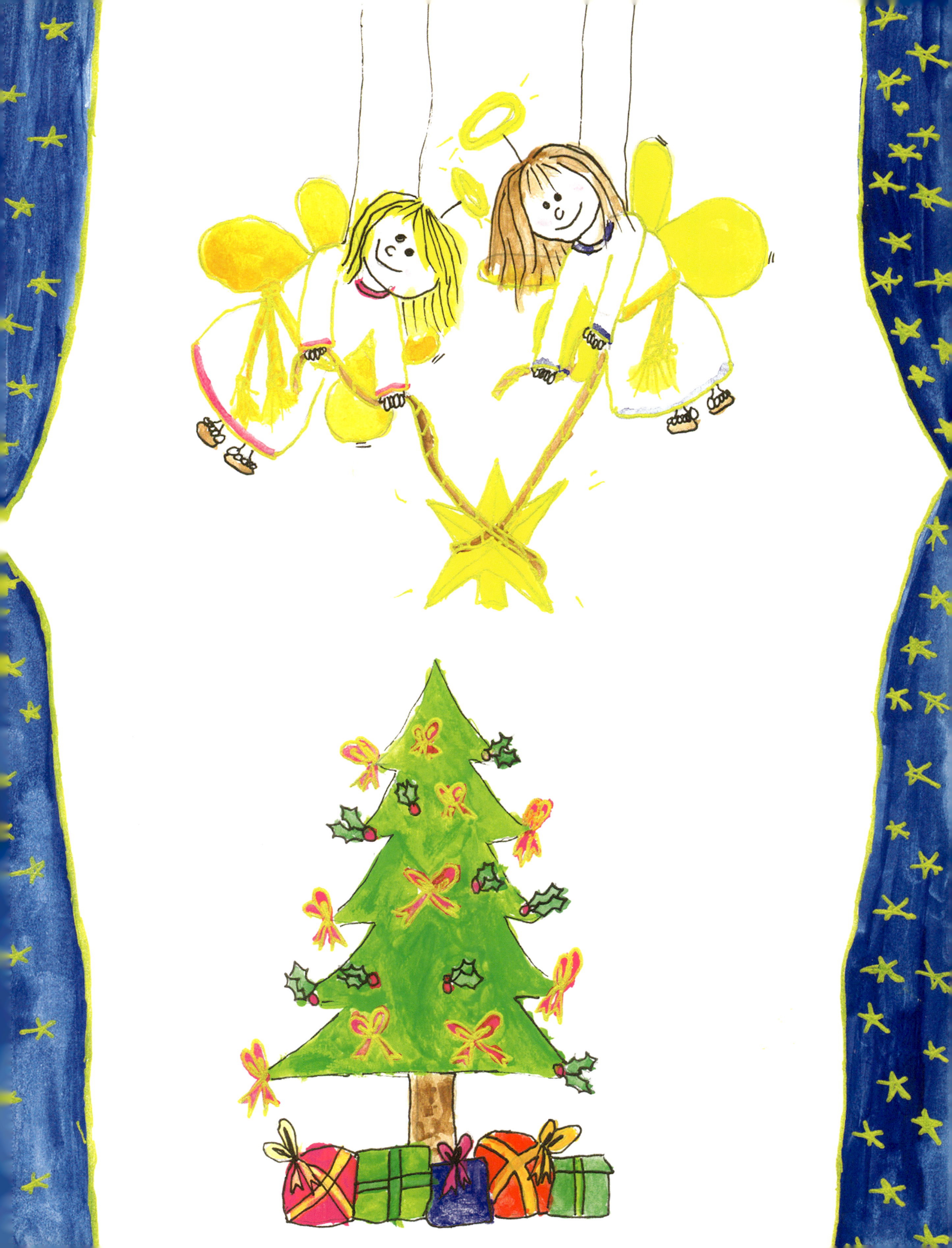

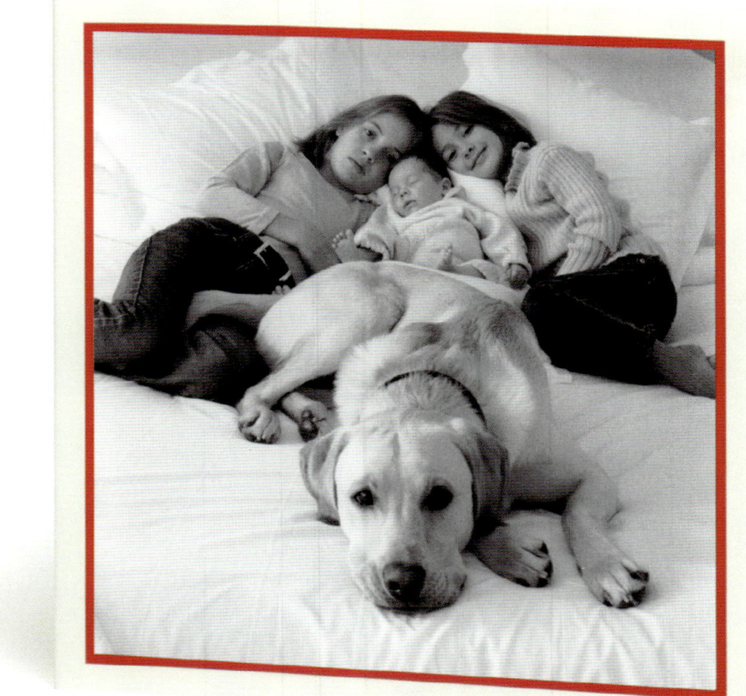

Anouschka, Jasper & Celina d'Abo, 2003

Photograph by TATJANA D'ABO

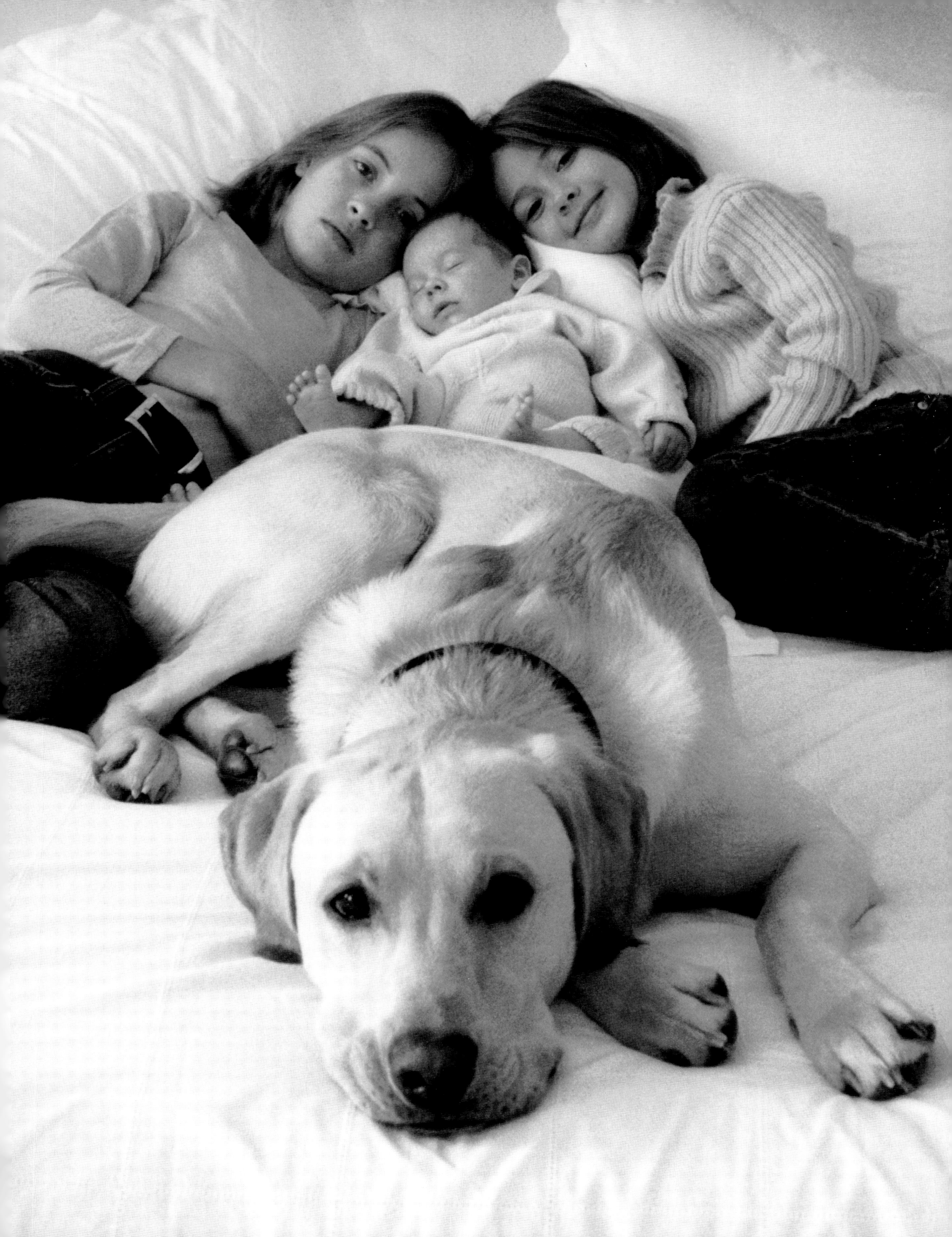

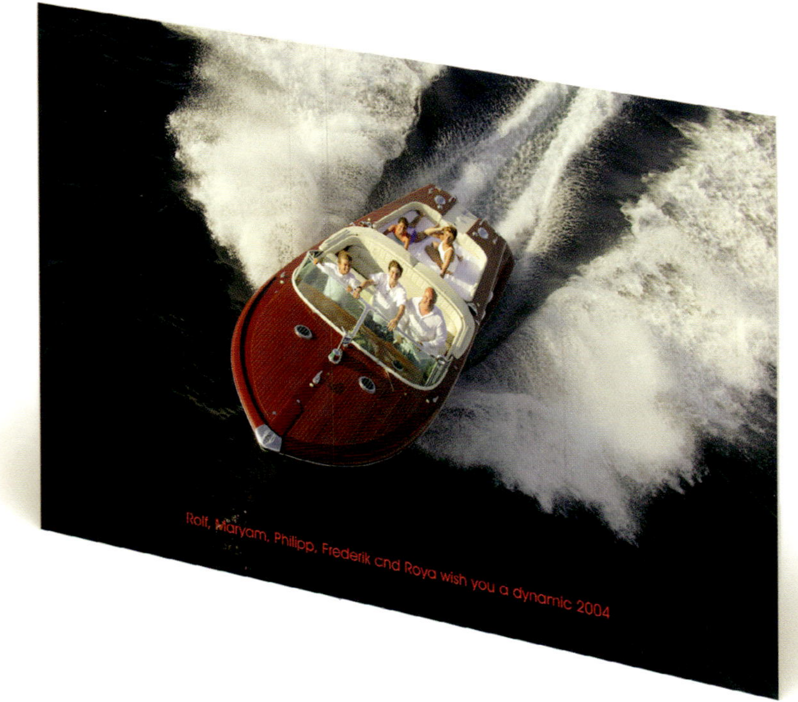

Rolf, Maryam, Philipp, Frederik & Roya Sachs, 2004

Photograph by FLY PICTURES

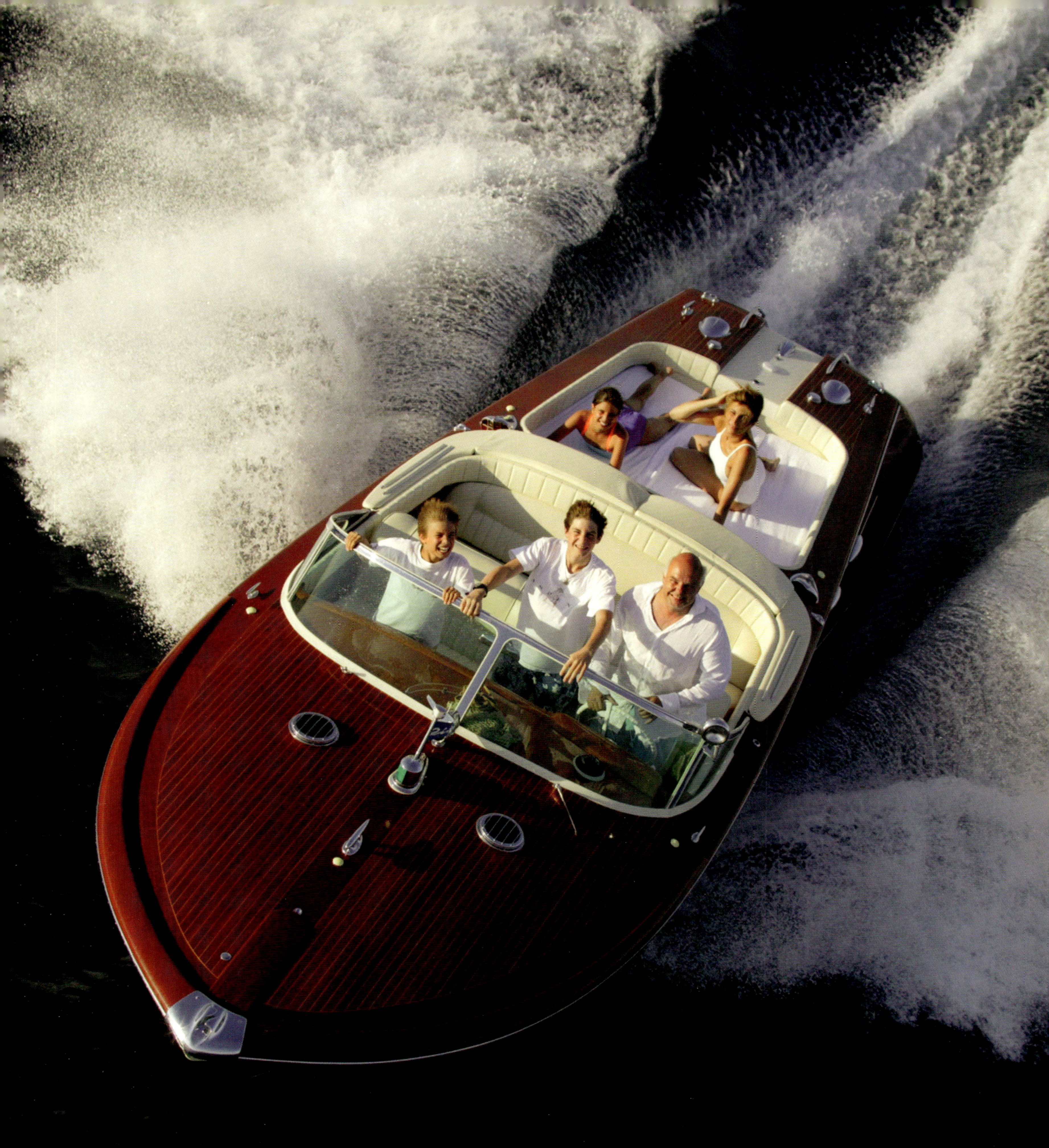

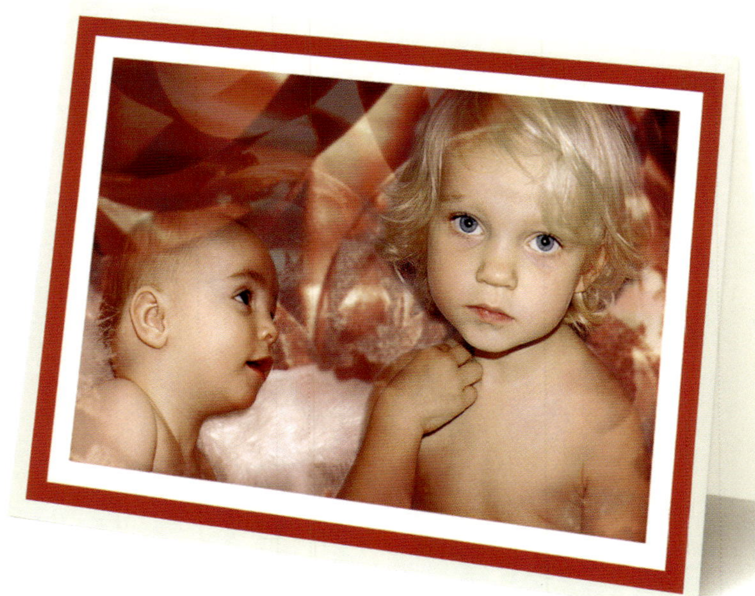

Camilla & Allegra Adami, 2004

Photograph by ALEXANDRA ADAMI

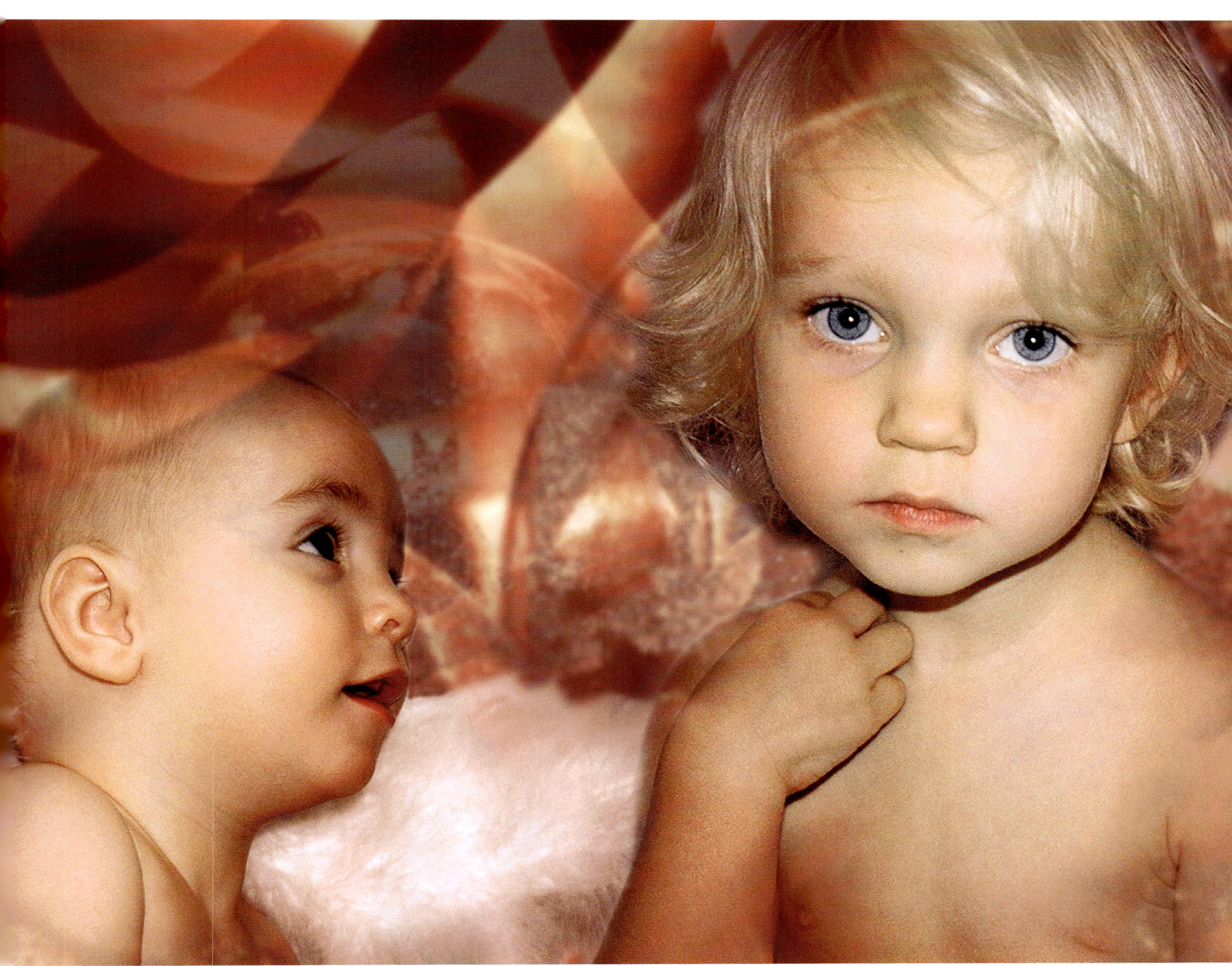

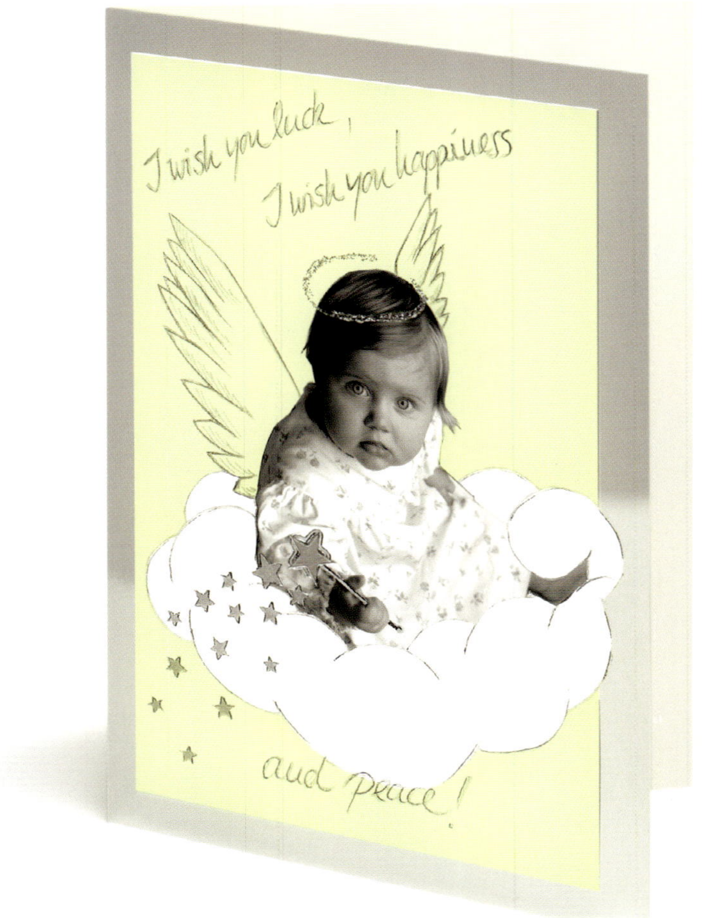

Amalia Schliemann, 2000

Photograph by JOANA SCHLIEMANN

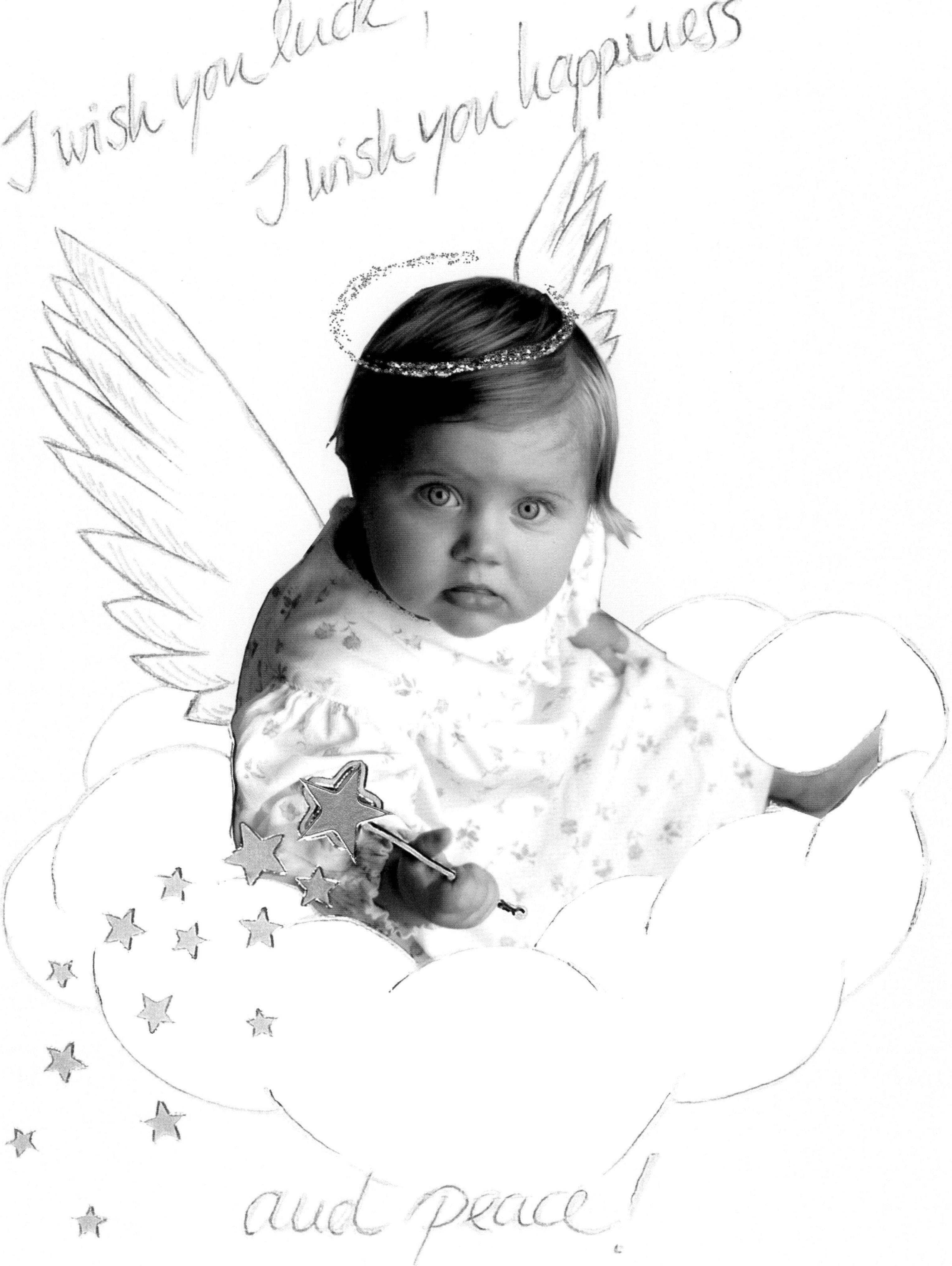

I wish you luck,
I wish you happiness

and peace!

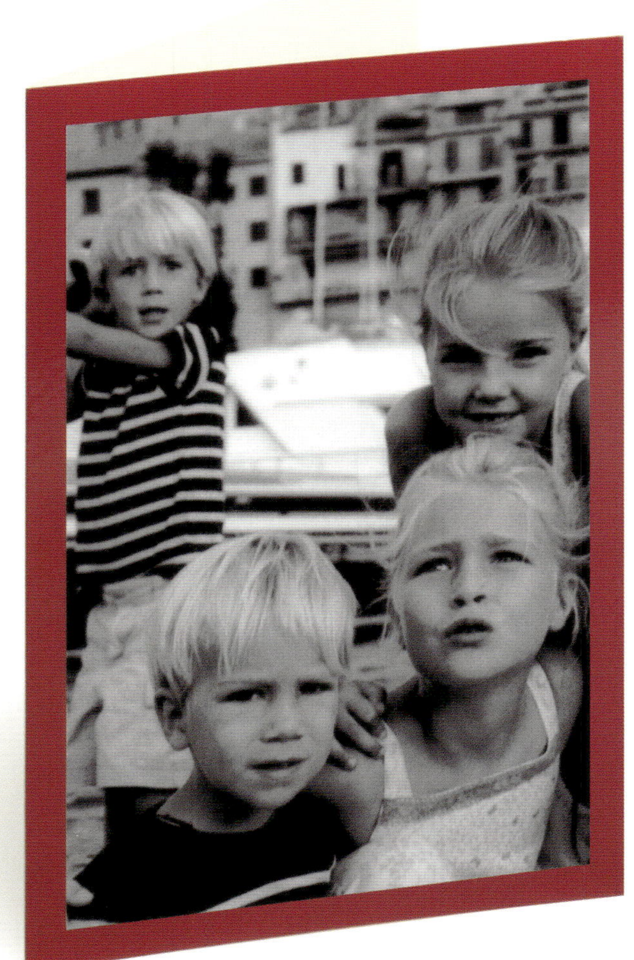

Maximilian, Brando, Nadia & Isabella Sodi, 2003

Photograph by ARIANE SODI

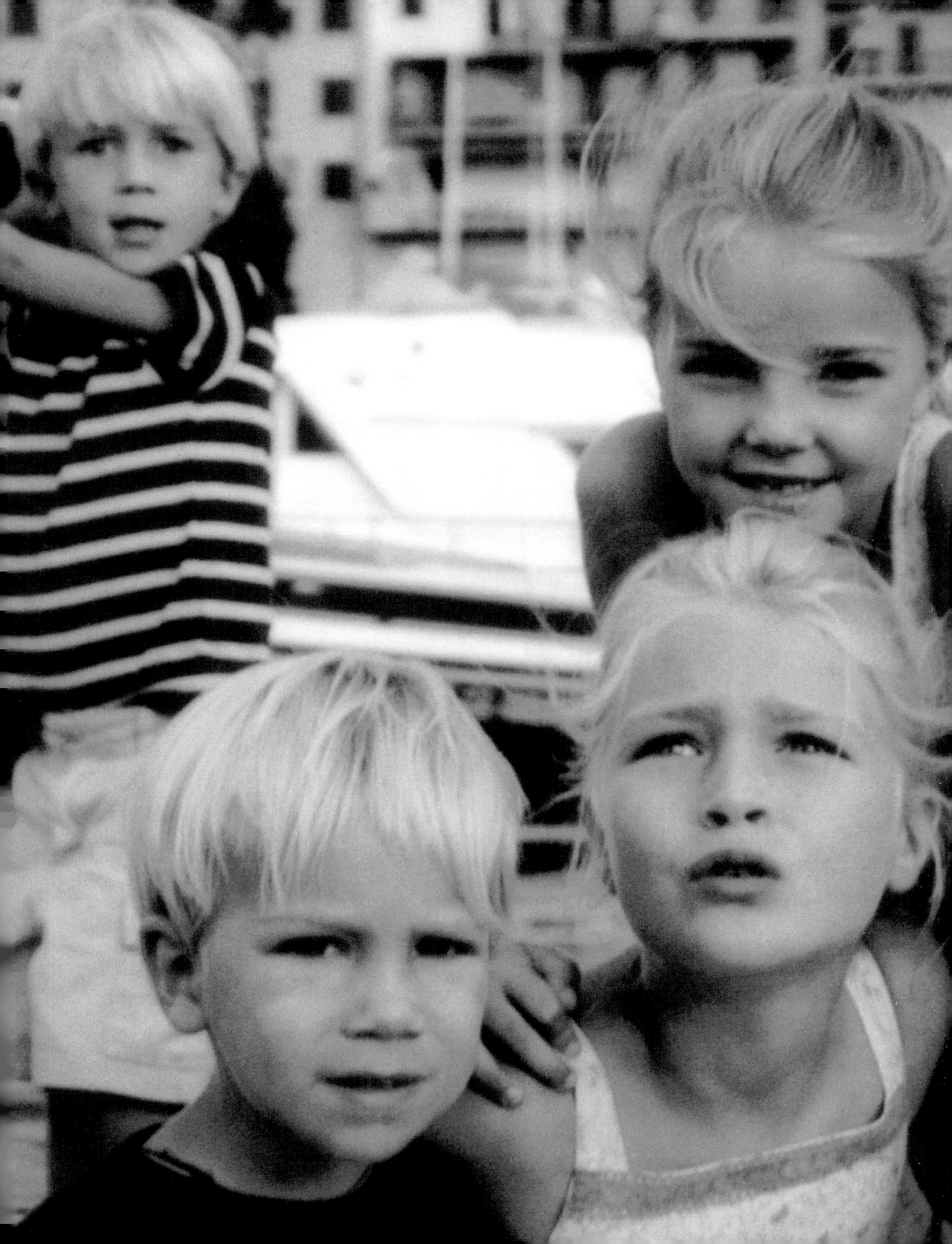

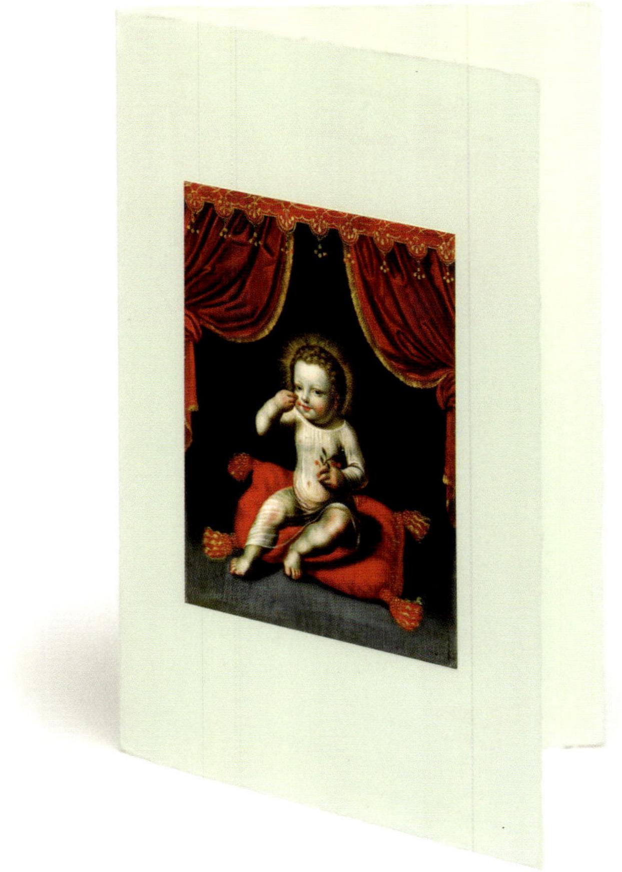

"Das Jesuskind, Kirschen essend", 2002

Painting by JOOS VAN CLEVE (AFTER), SAMMLUNG DER FÜRSTEN ZU SALM

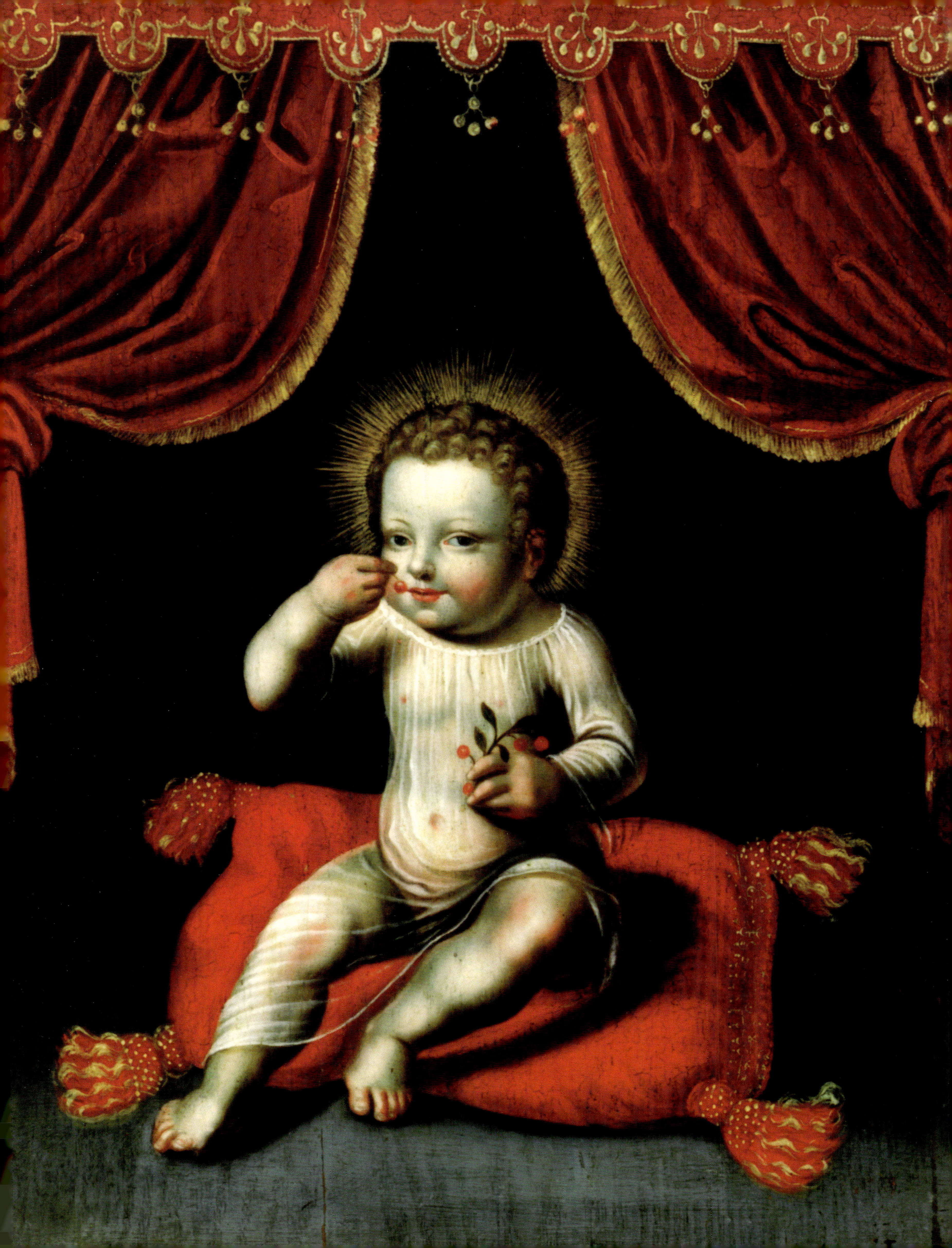

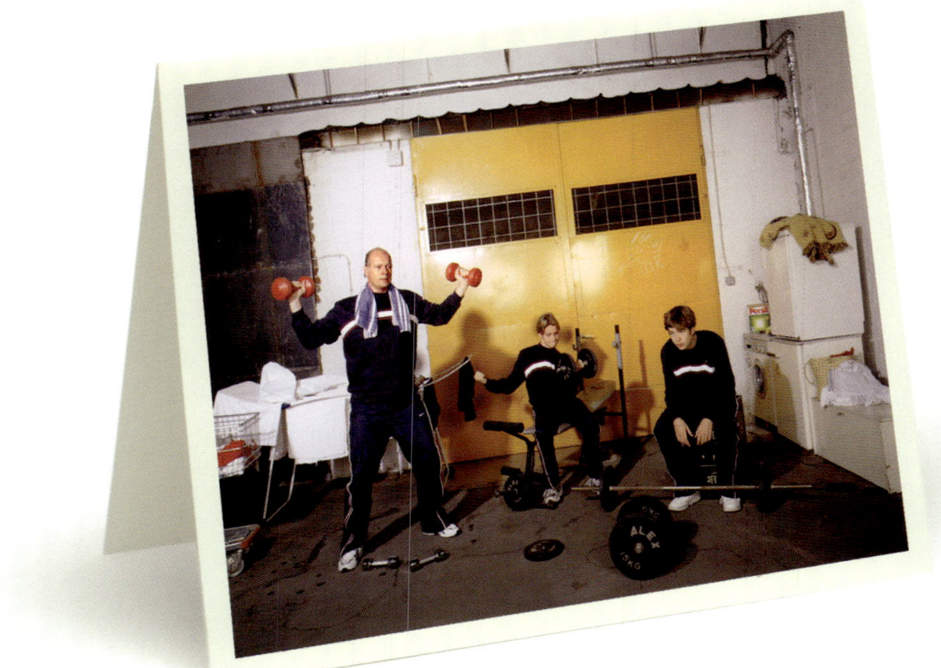

Eckbert, Tassilo & Heinrich
von Bohlen und Halbach, 2003

Photograph by STEPHAN REUSSE

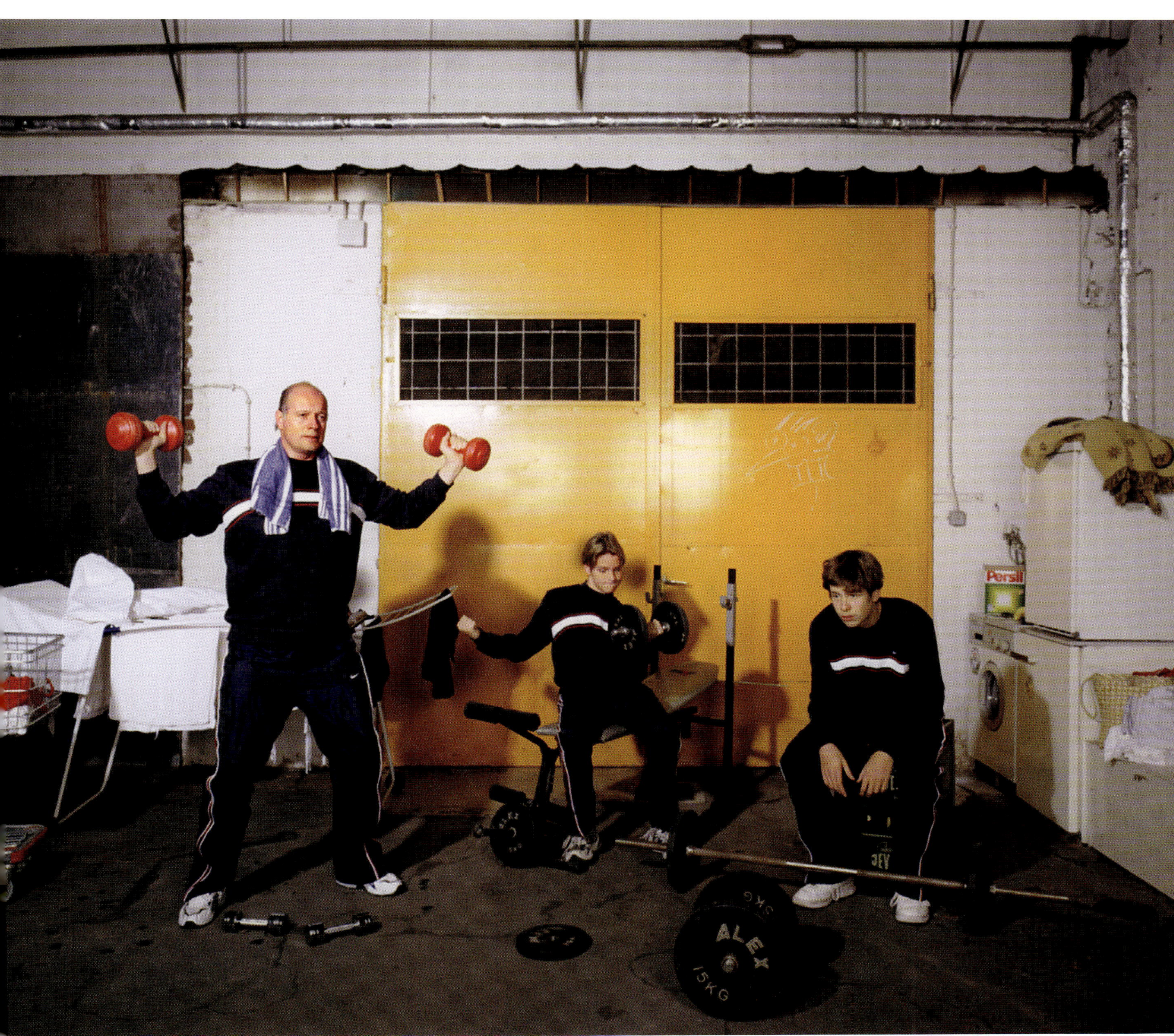
Persil
ALEX
15KG

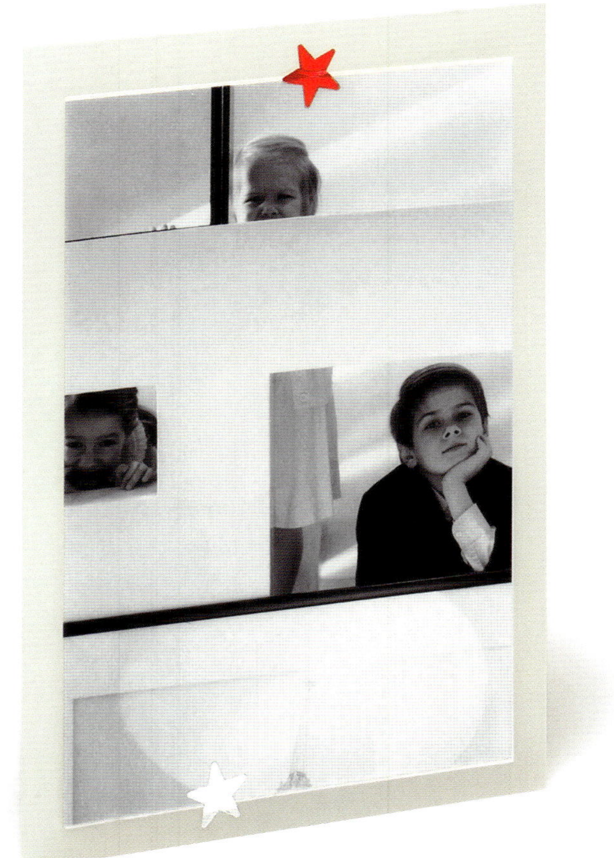

Princesse Sveva, Princesse Assia & Prince Alexis Guédroïtz, 2003

Photograph by SOLINA GUÉDROÏTZ

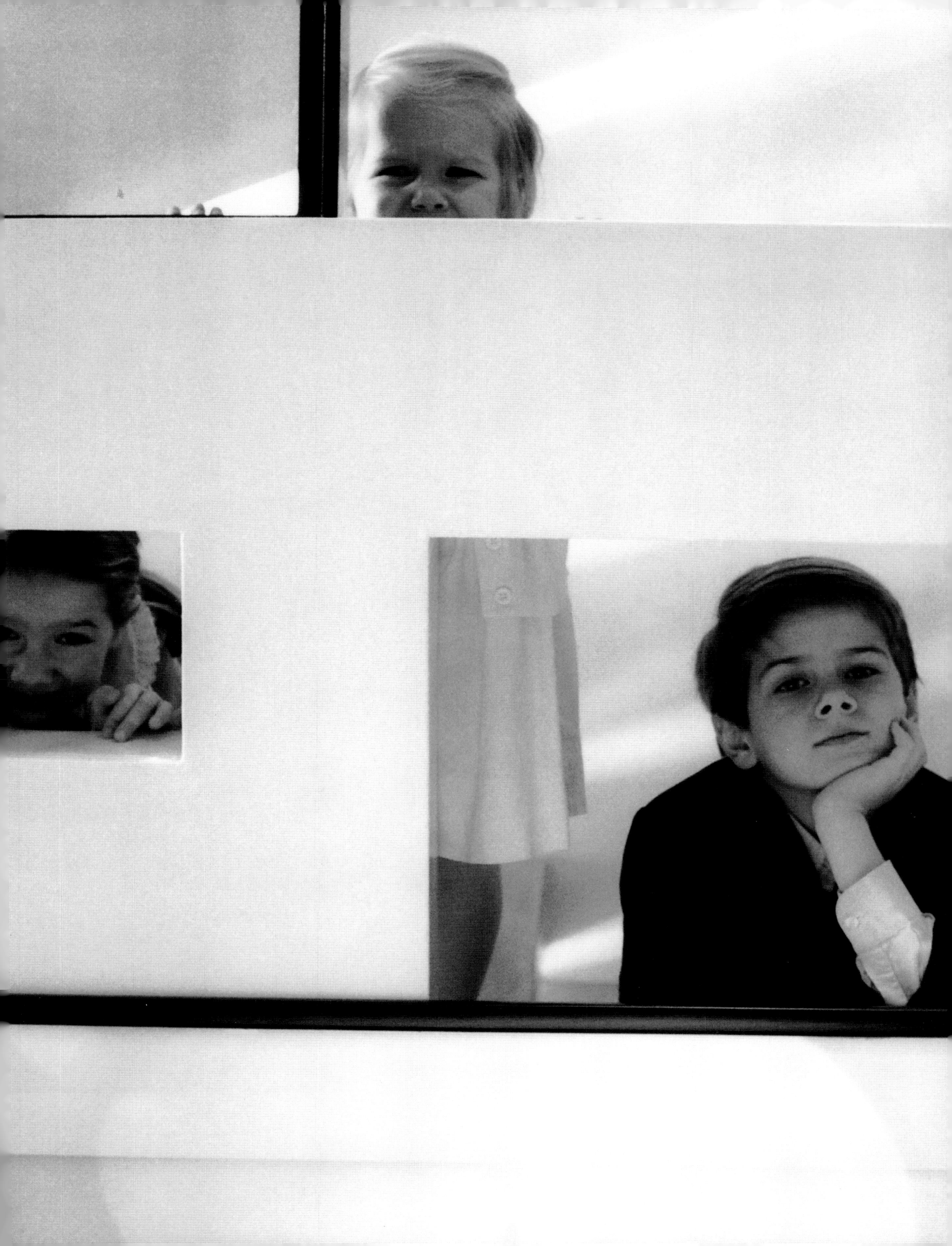

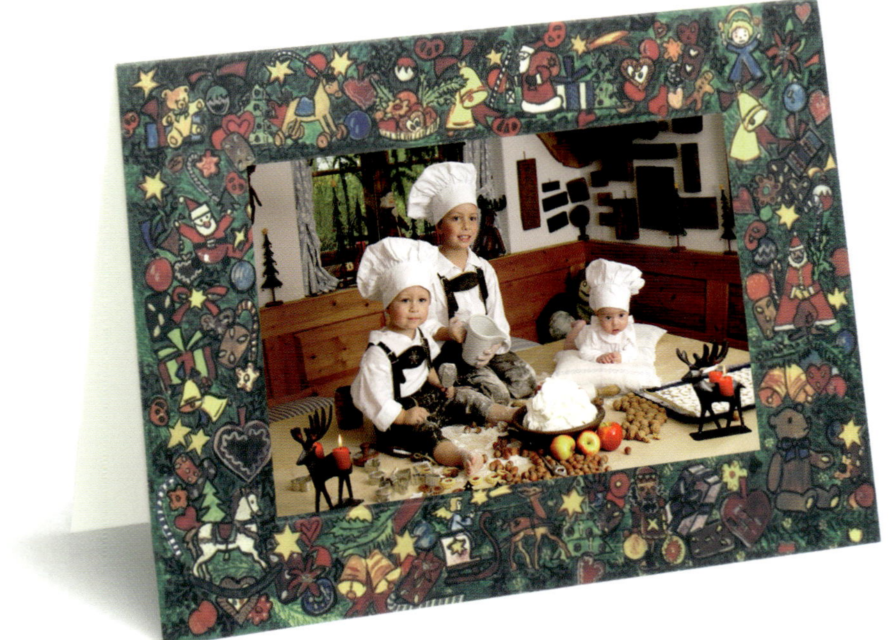

Ferdinand, Leopold & Marie Reuther, 2004

Photograph by MEINEN FOTOGRAFIE MÜNCHEN

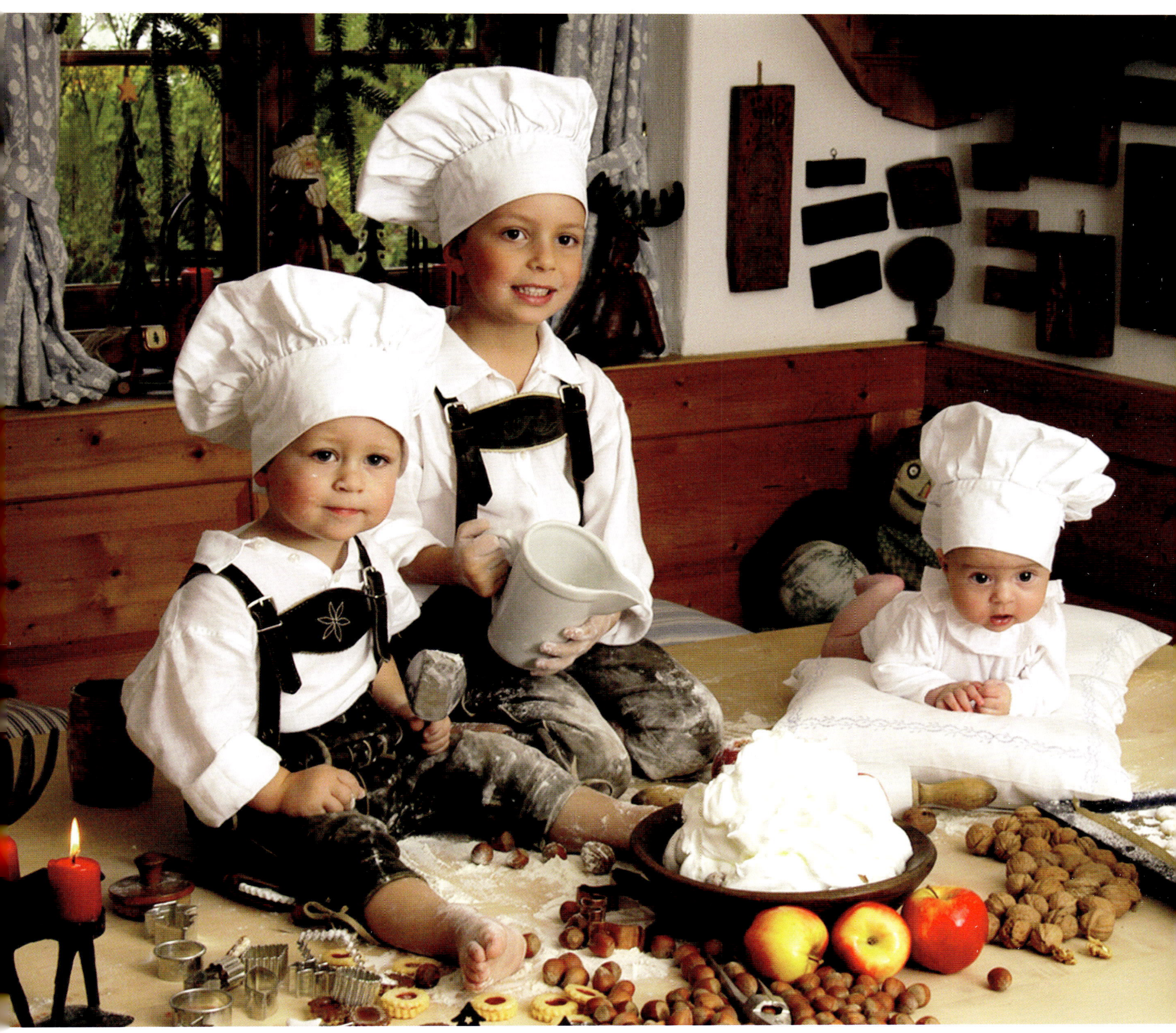

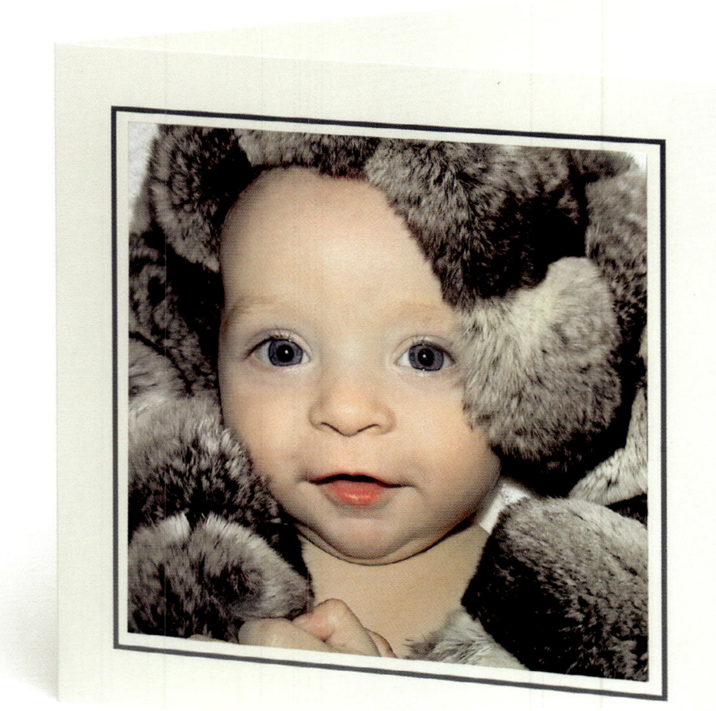

Rigby Swarovski-Adams, 2004

Photograph by NADJA SWAROVSKI

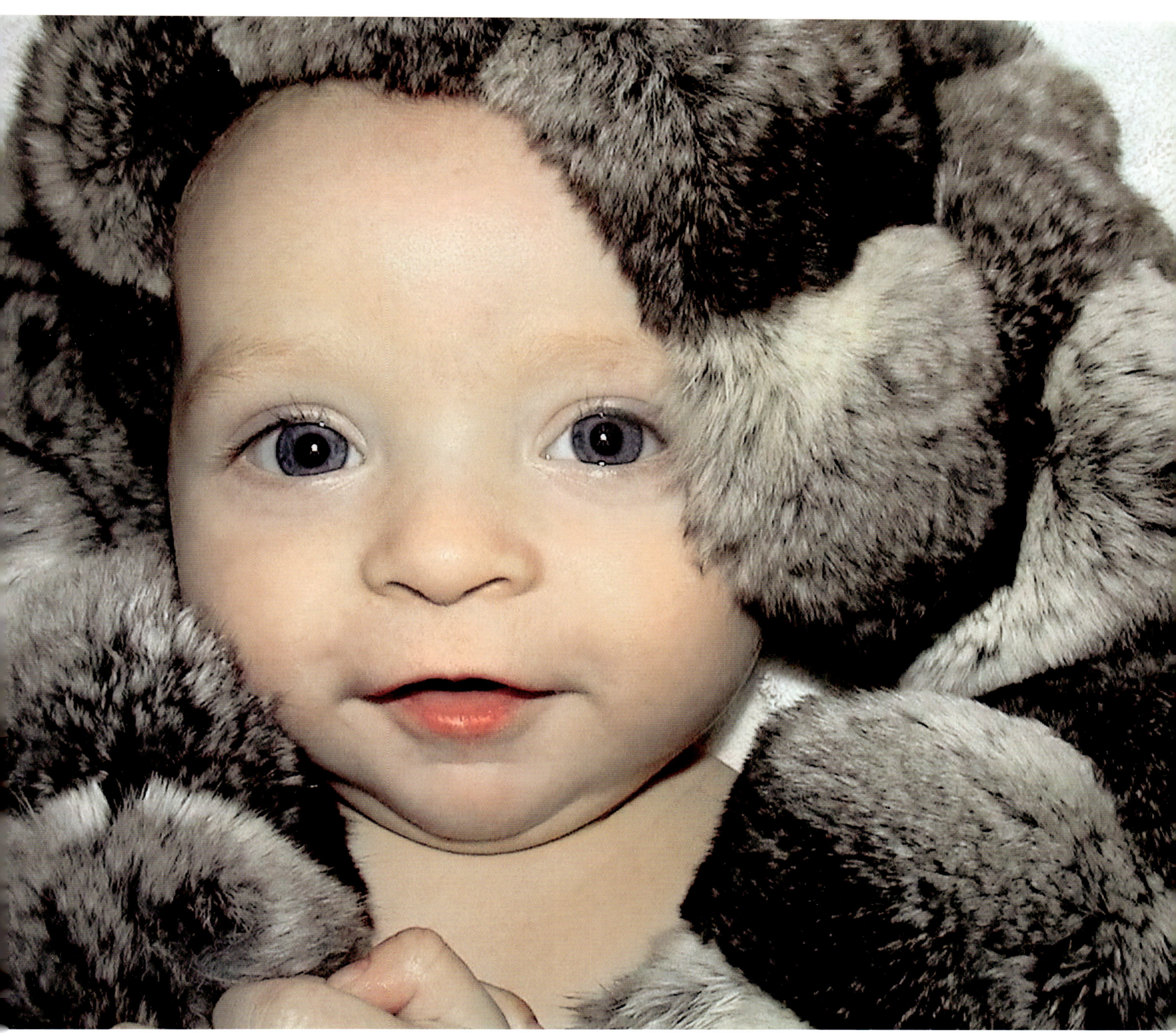

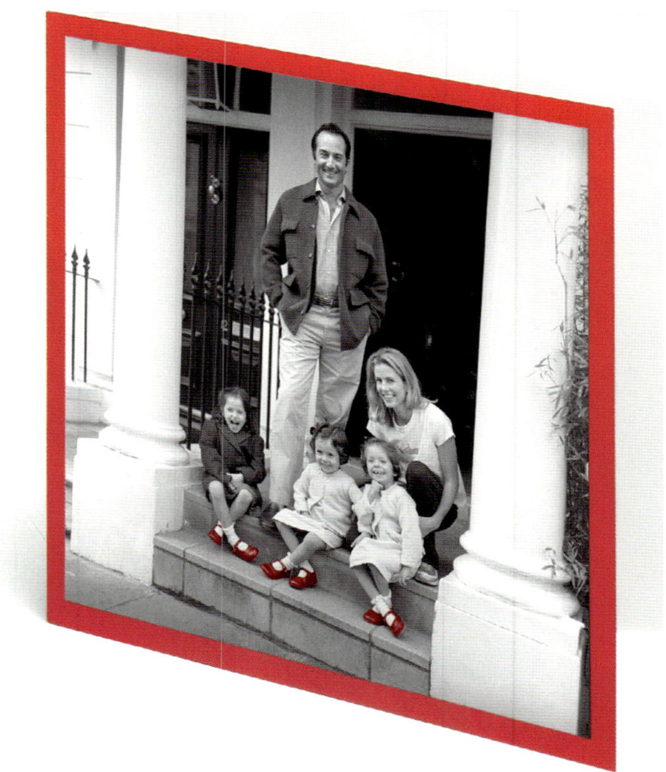

Emilio, Brooke, Inés, Isabel & Marina De Ocampo, 2002

Photograph by JONATHAN BECKER

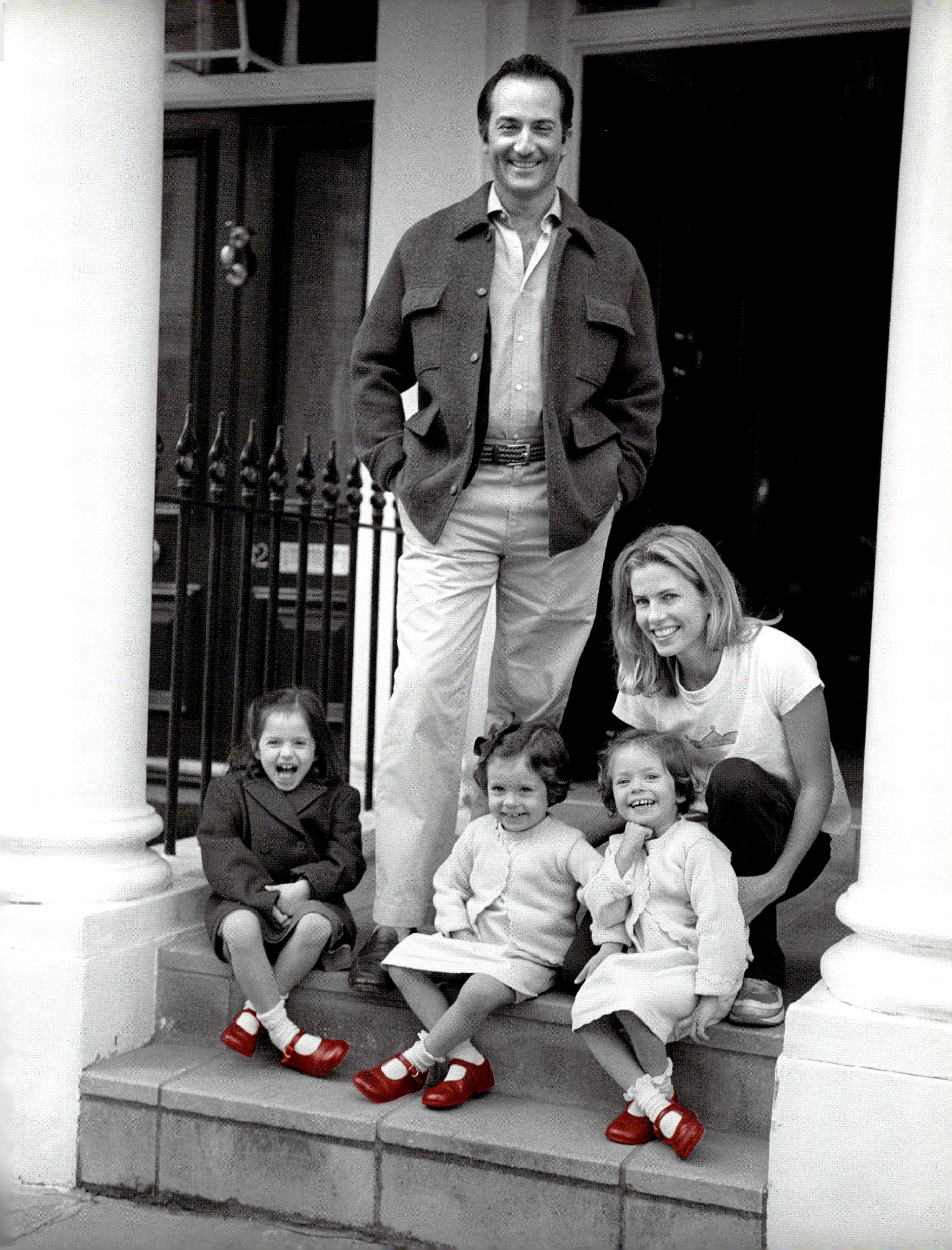

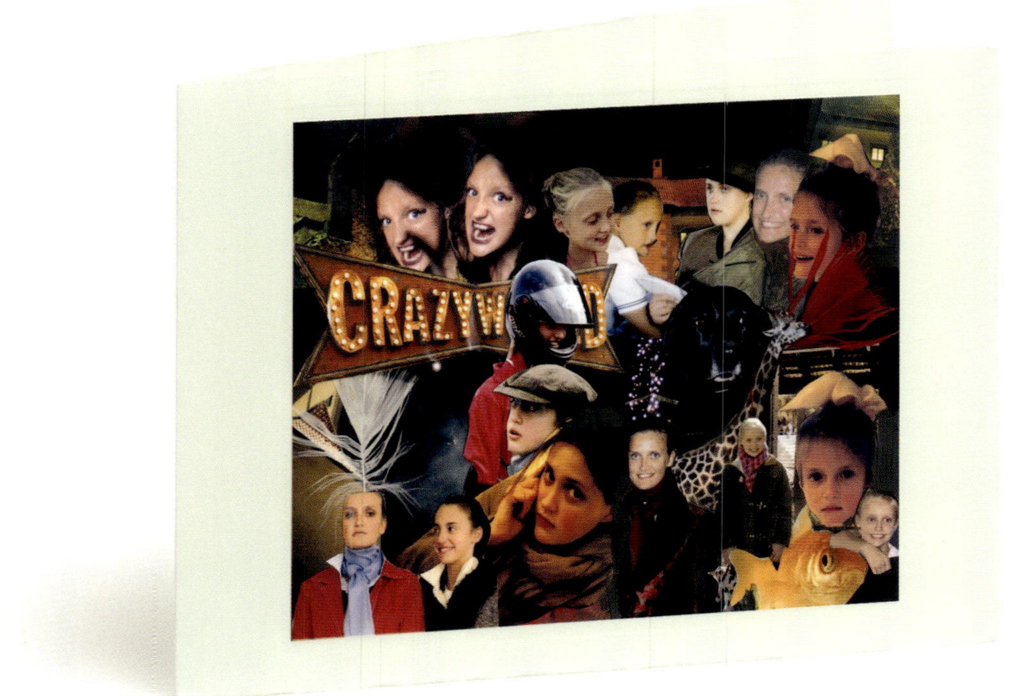

Anna Theresa Gräfin Arco, Margherita Gräfin Arco, Olympia Gräfin Arco, Maximiliana Gräfin Arco, Marie Gabrielle Gräfin Arco & Giorgiana Gräfin Arco, 2003

Photographs by S.H. & I.k.u.k.H. GRAF UND GRÄFIN ARCO-ZINNEBERG

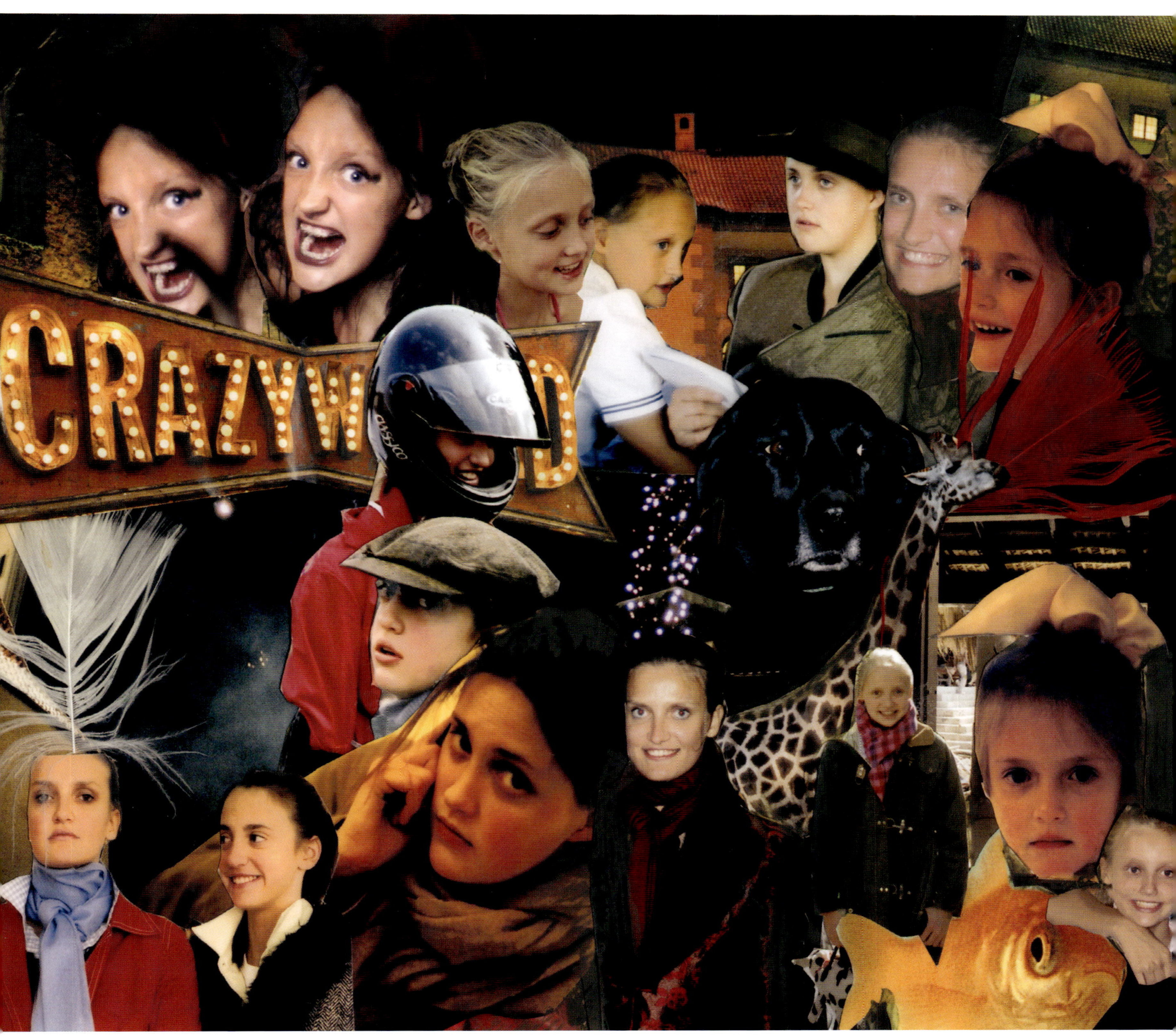
CRAZYW

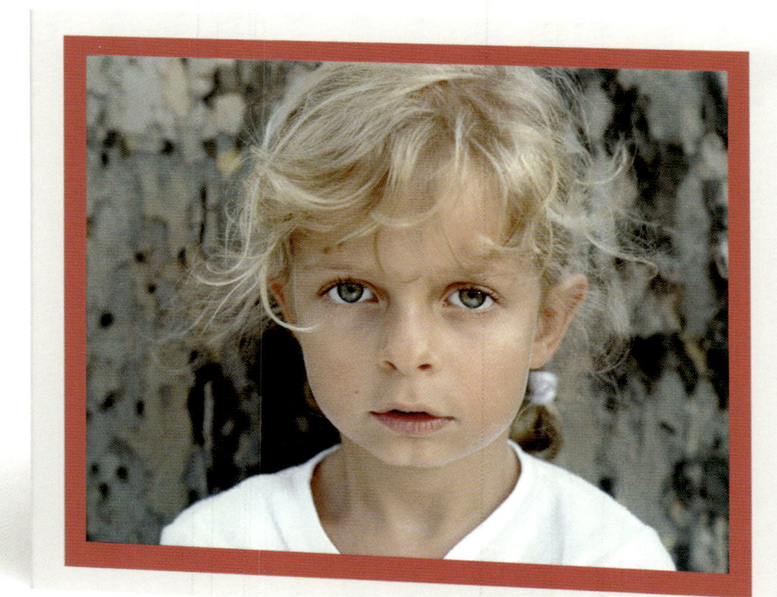

Marina Gelardin, 2002

Photograph by MARITZA CHATEAU

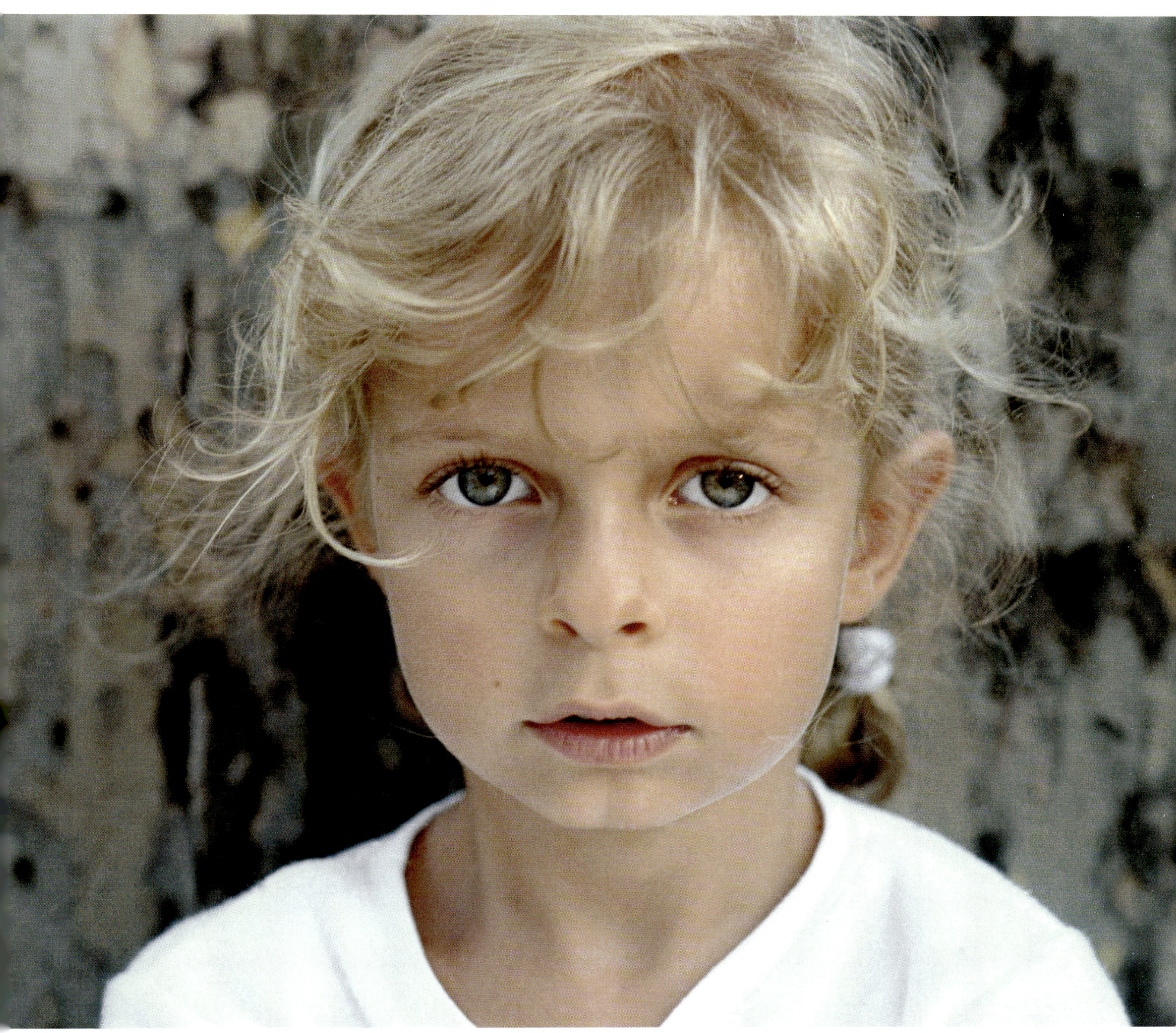

76

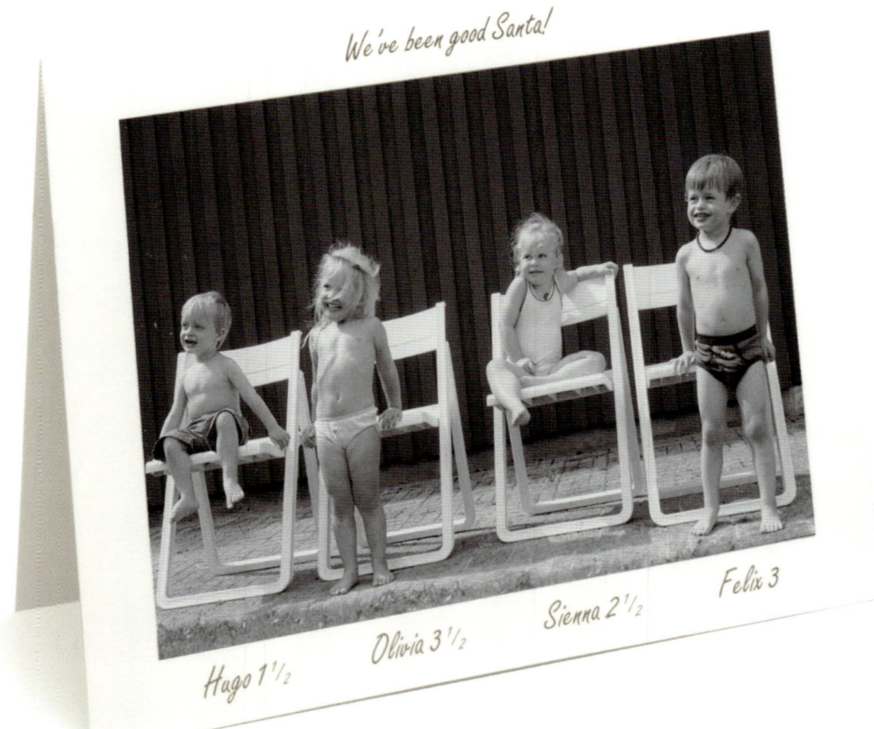

Hugo Hamilton, Olivia Linden, Sienna Linden & Felix Hamilton, 2003

Photograph by ANDREA HAMILTON

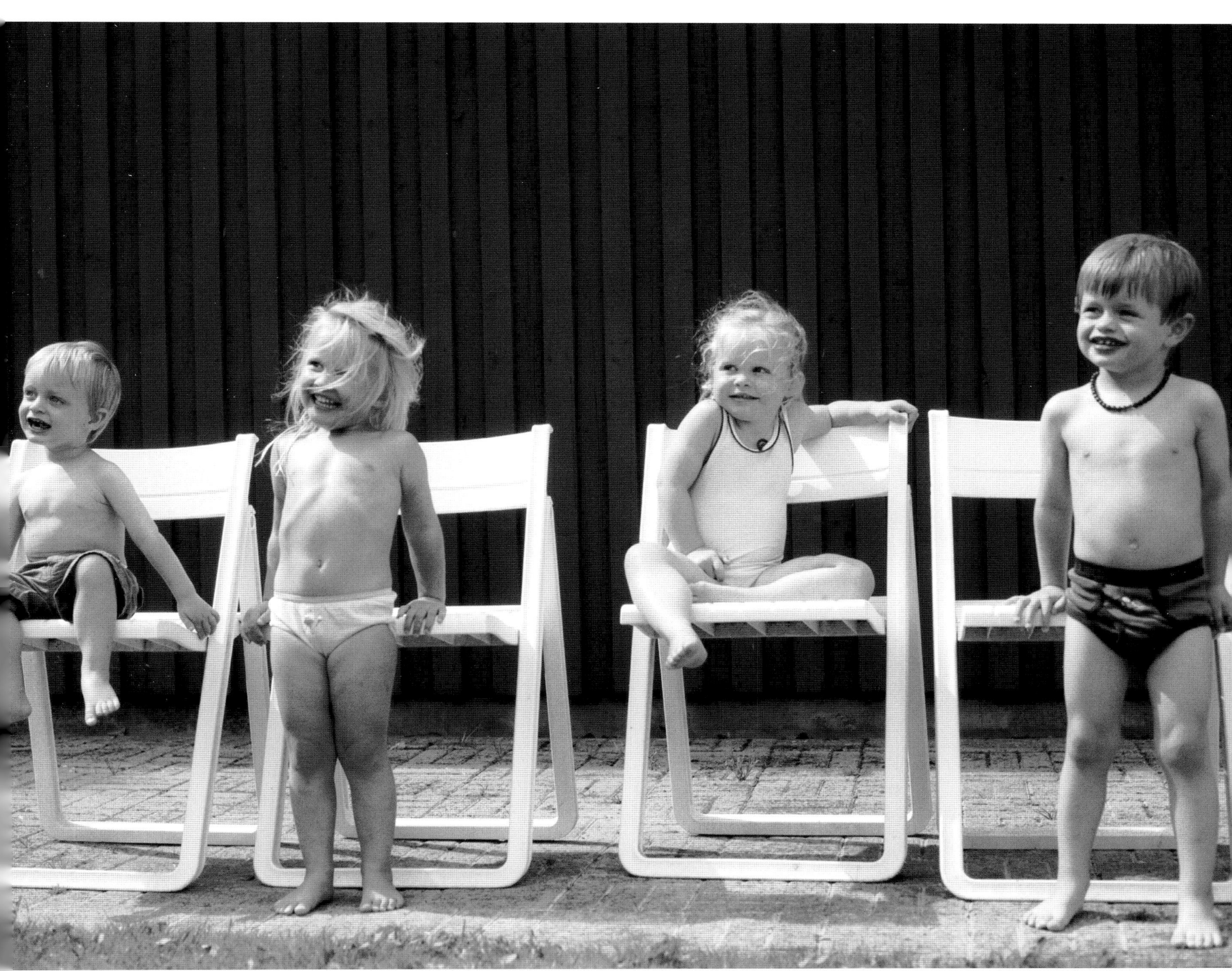

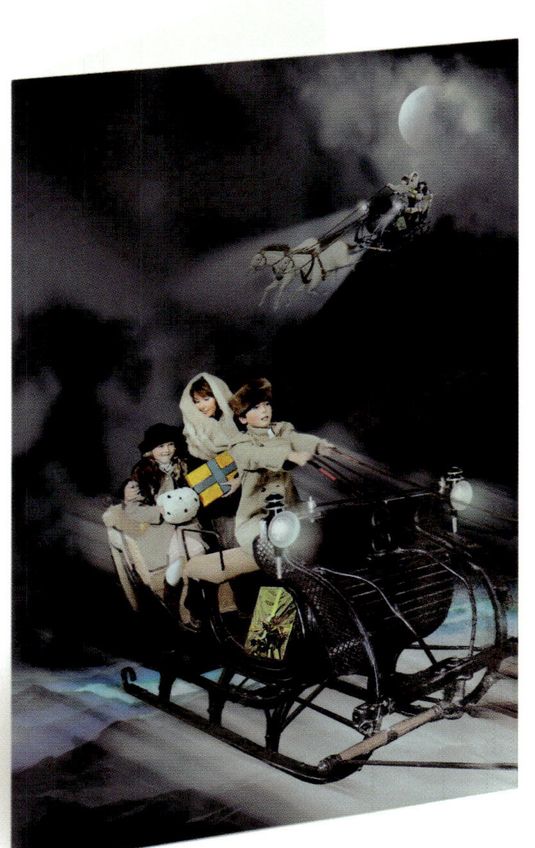

Tessa, Uli & Louis Krages, 2004

Photograph by M. PAPARA

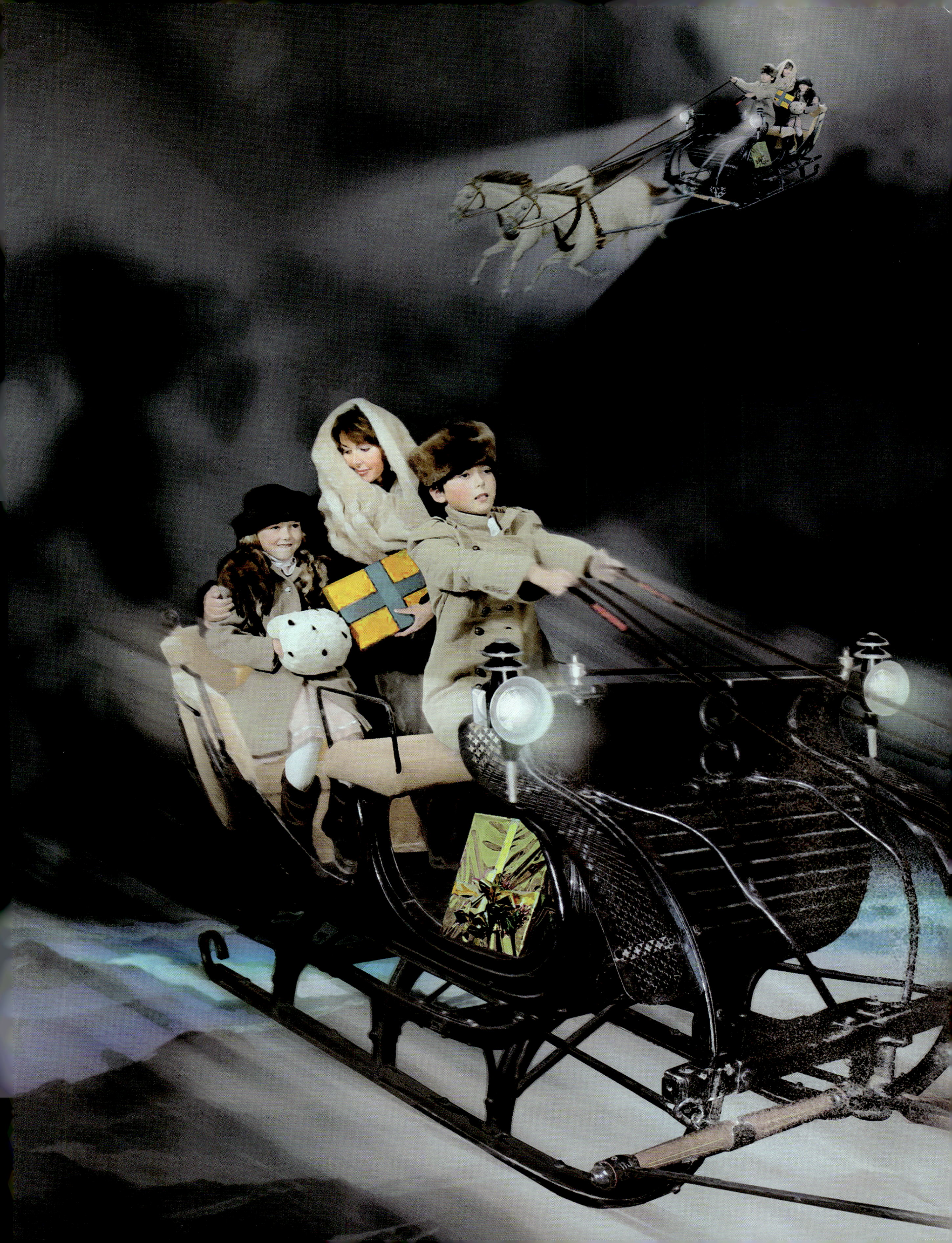

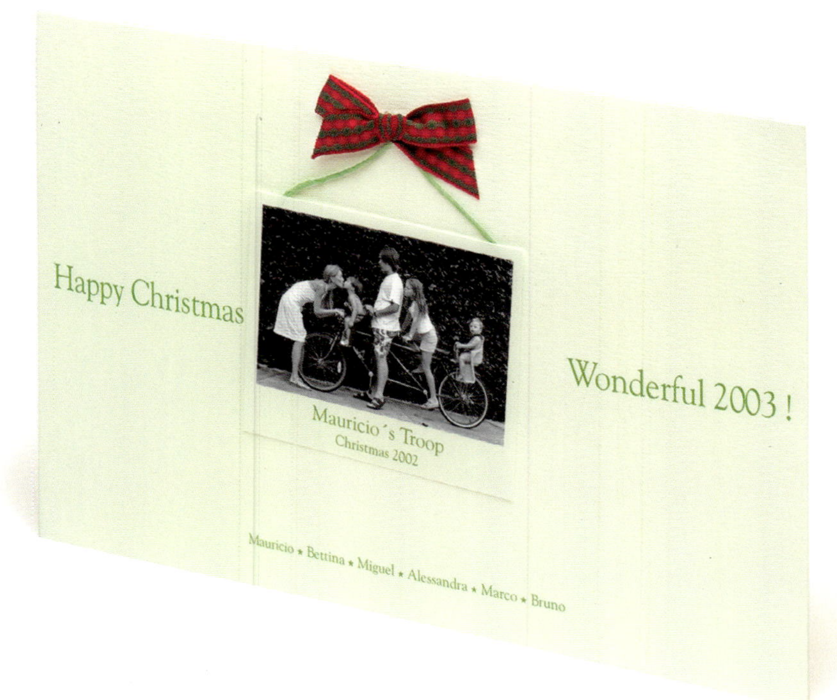

Bettina Haegler, Marco, Miguel, Alessandra & Bruno, 2002

Photograph by ISABEL BECKER

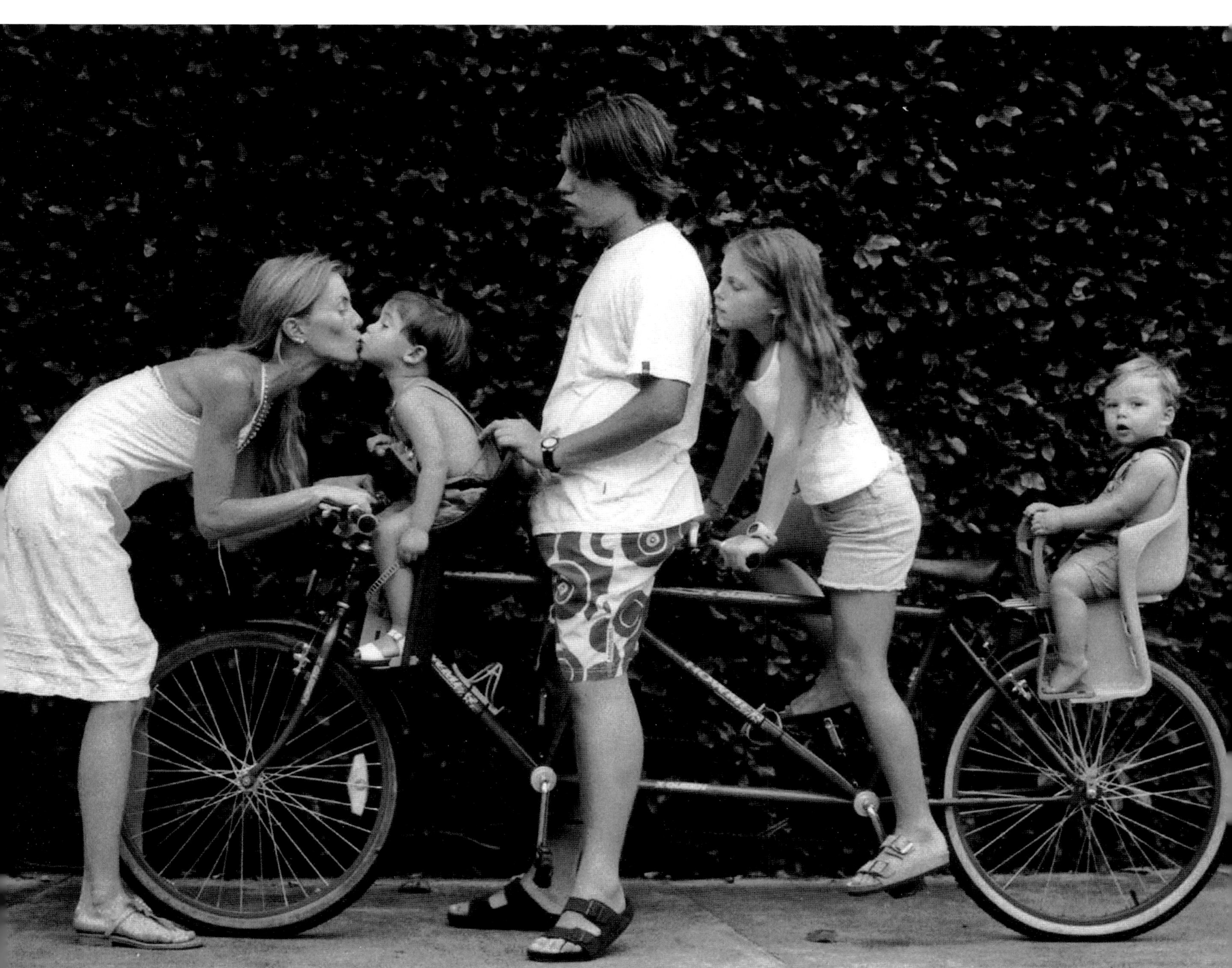

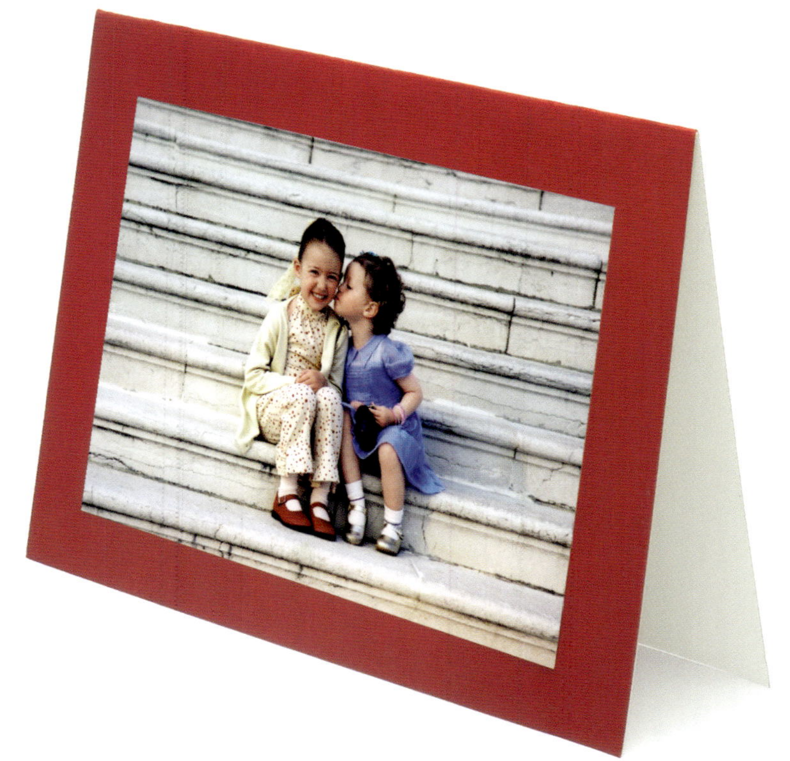

Anastasia & Antonia Ostrowsky, 2001

Photograph by KATHARINA OSTROWSKY

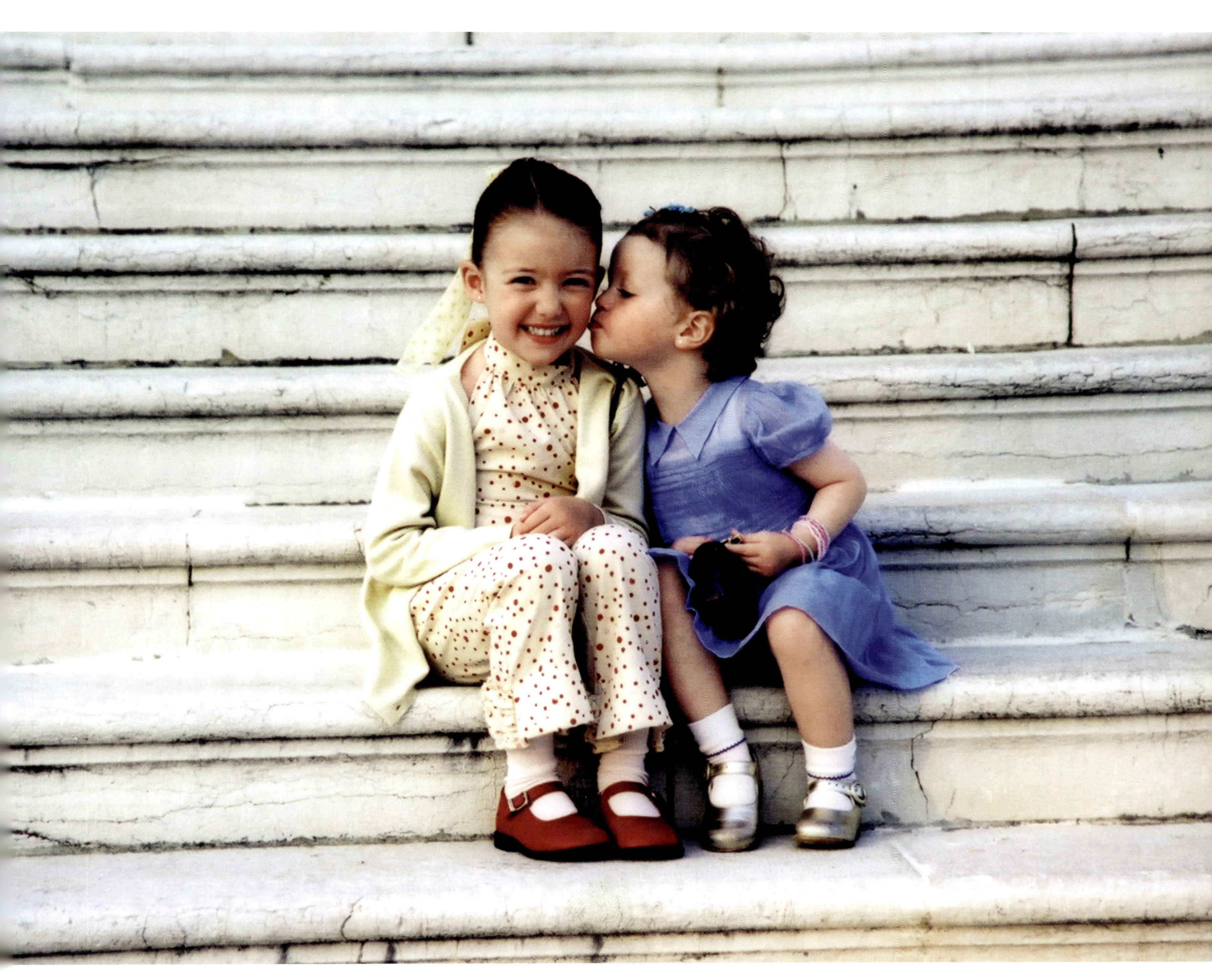

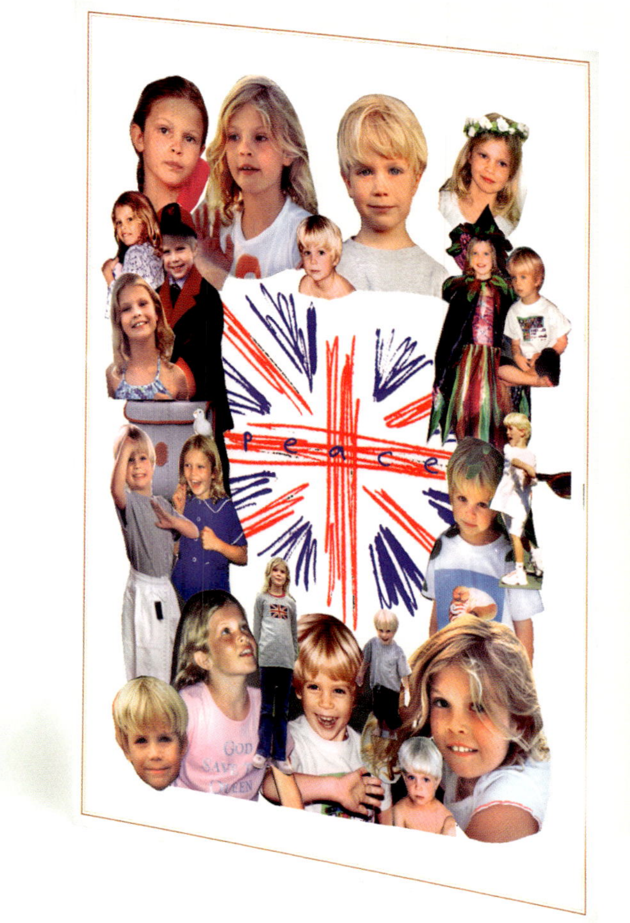

Gabriella & Nicolas de Givenchy, 2002

Photographs by CHRISTINE DE GIVENCHY

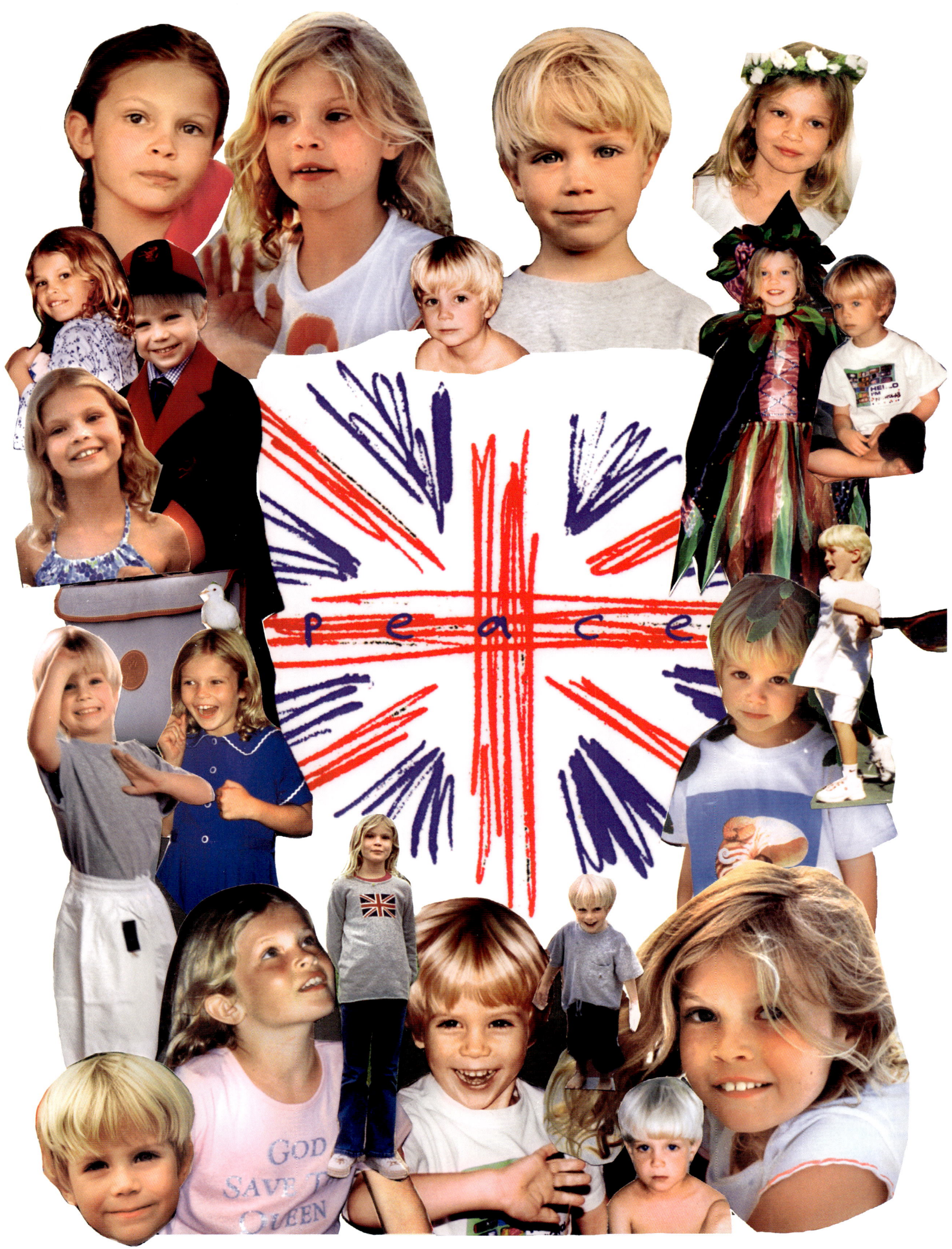
p e a c e
GOD
SAVE T
QUEEN

86

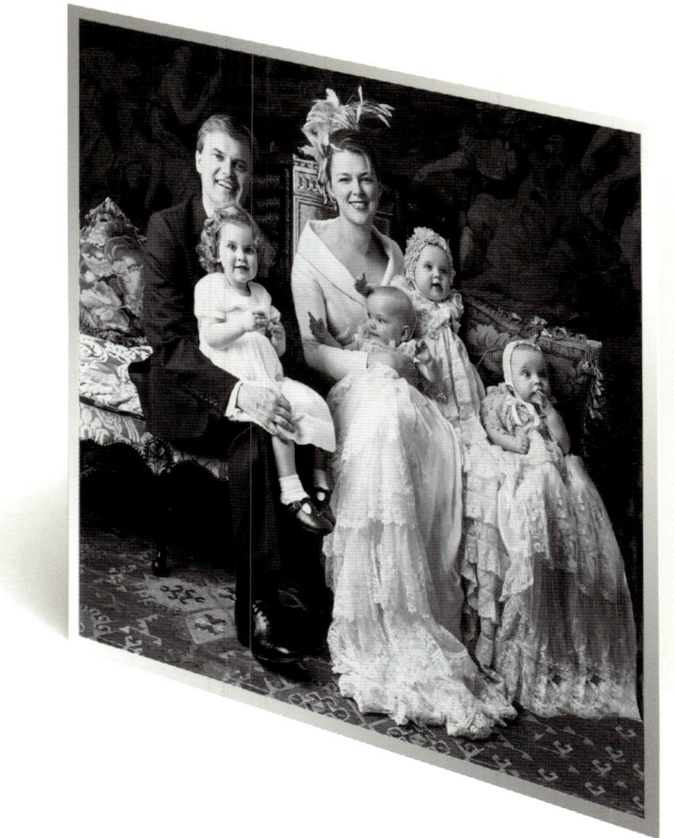

Lord & Lady Dalmeny, the Hon Marina,
the Hon Lavinia, the Hon Delphi & the Hon Celeste Primrose, 2003

Photograph by HUGO BURNAND

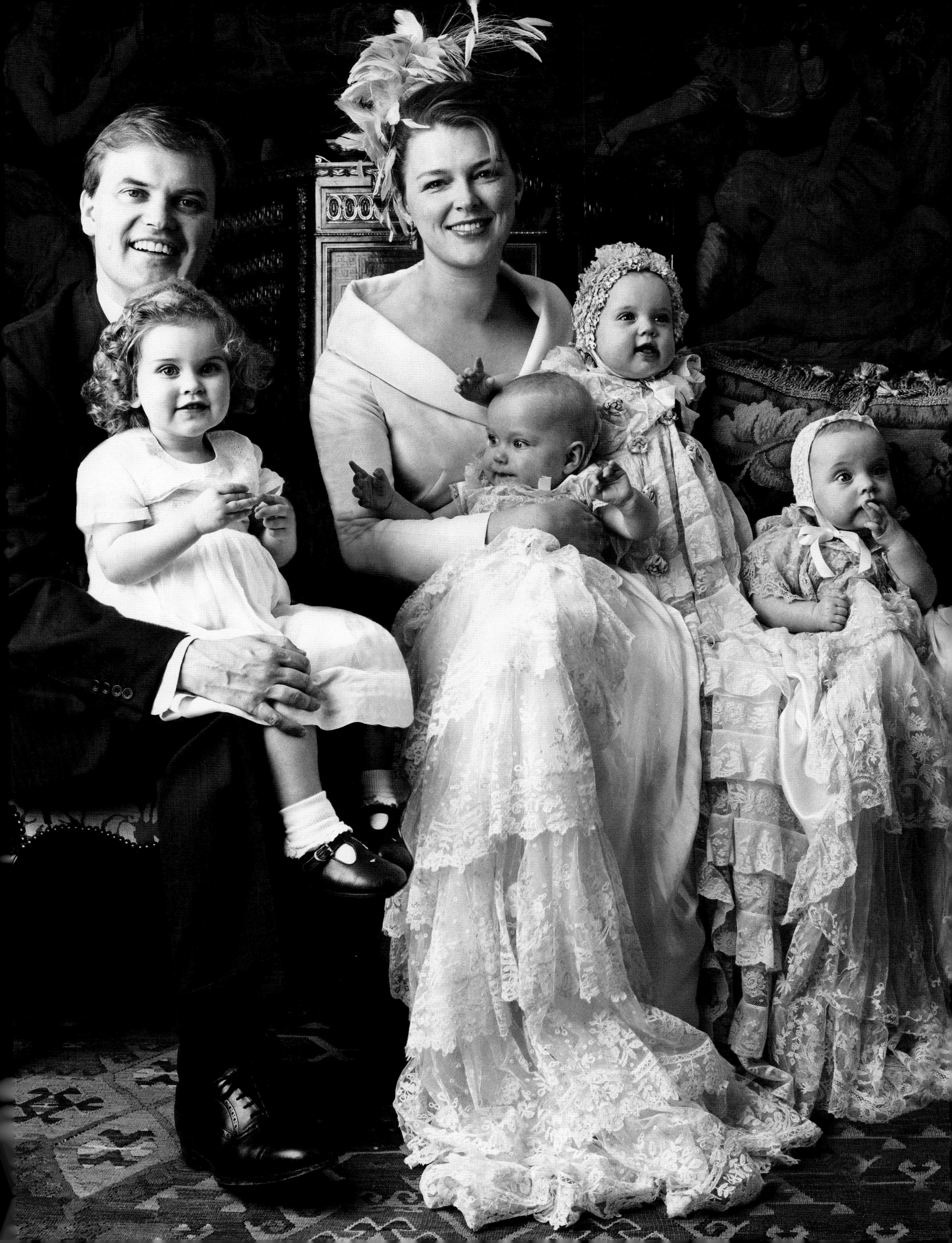

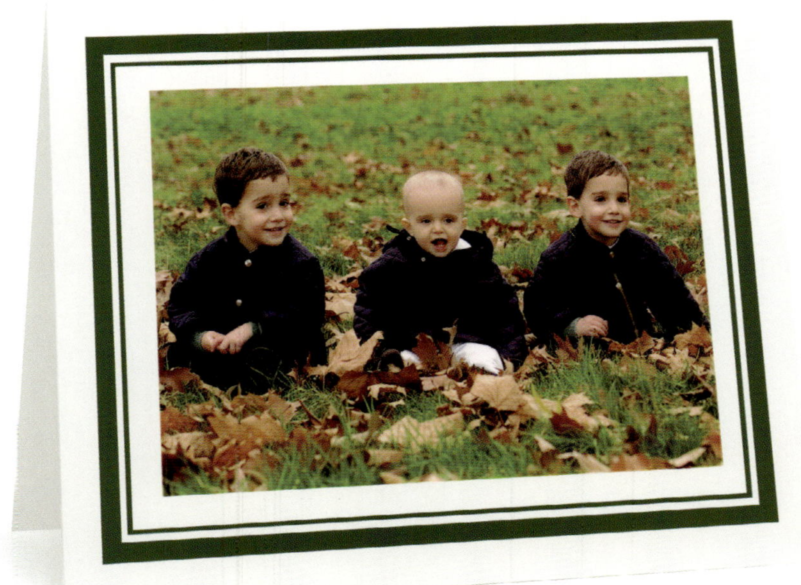

Charlie, Laith & Ramsey Gordon, 2004

Photograph by ANDREA HAMILTON

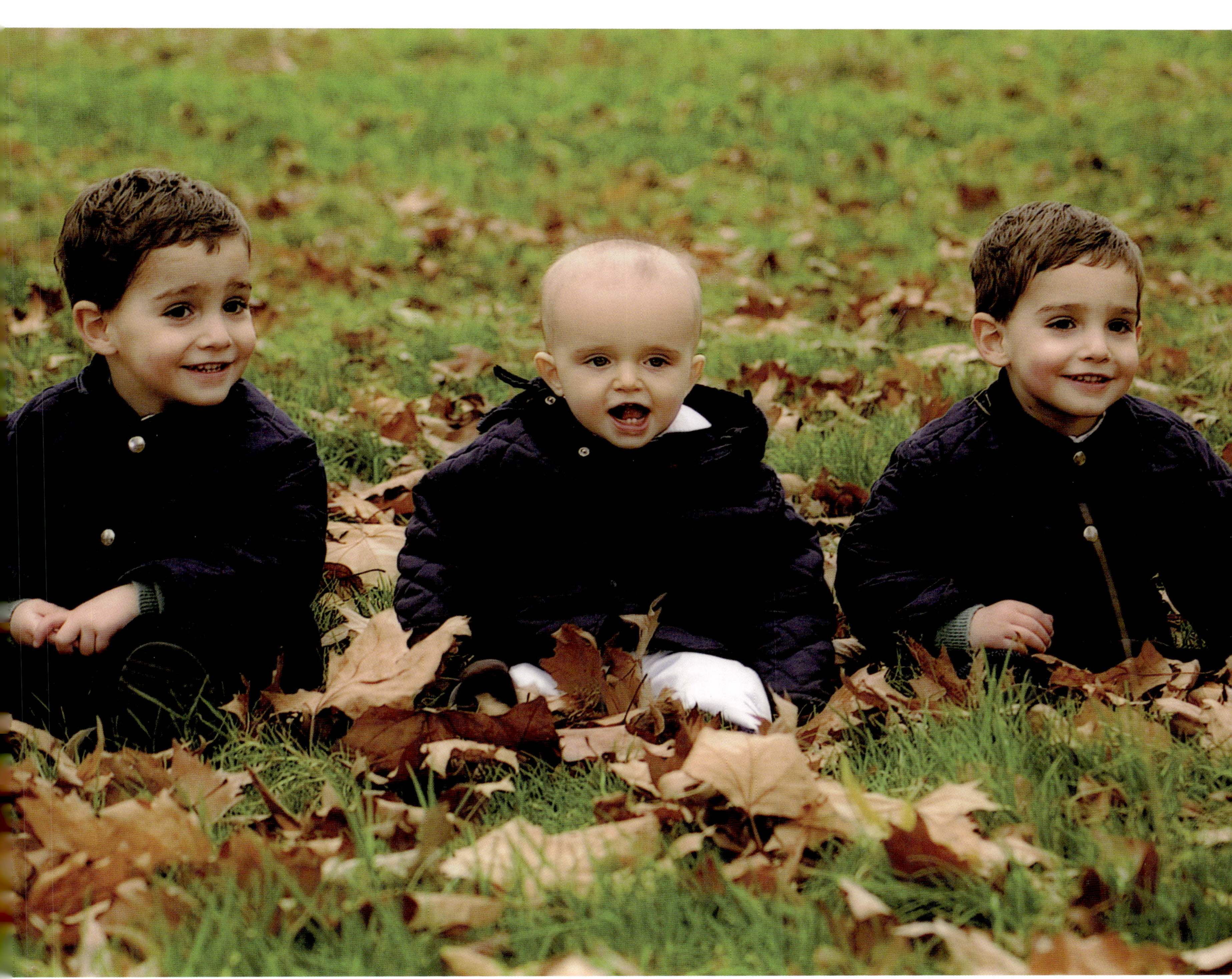

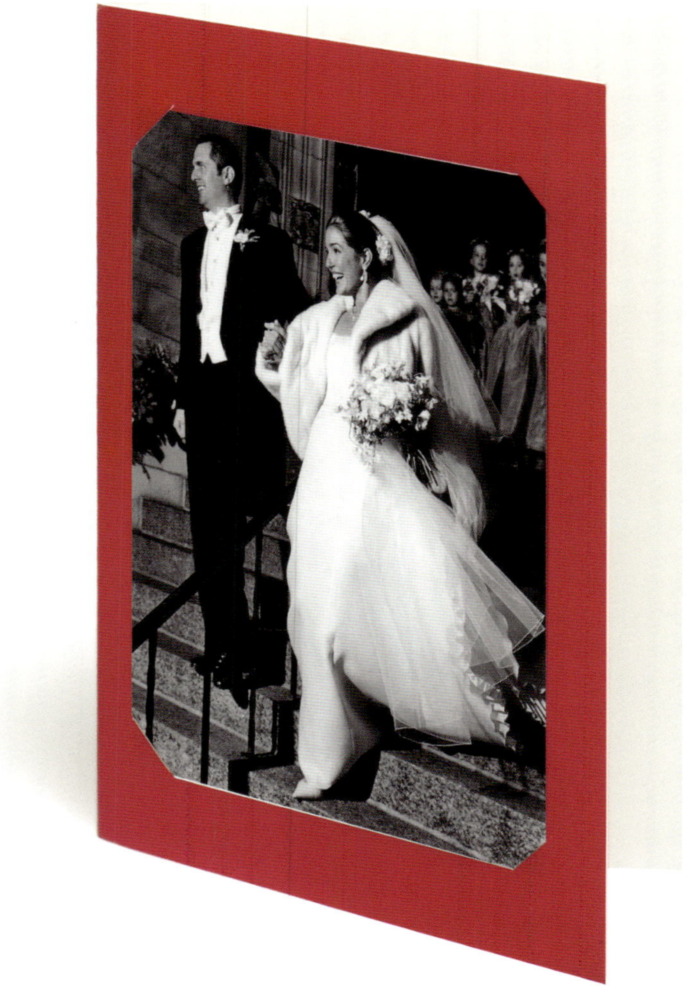

Matt & Marisa Brown, 2002

Photograph by MAURICIO DONELLI

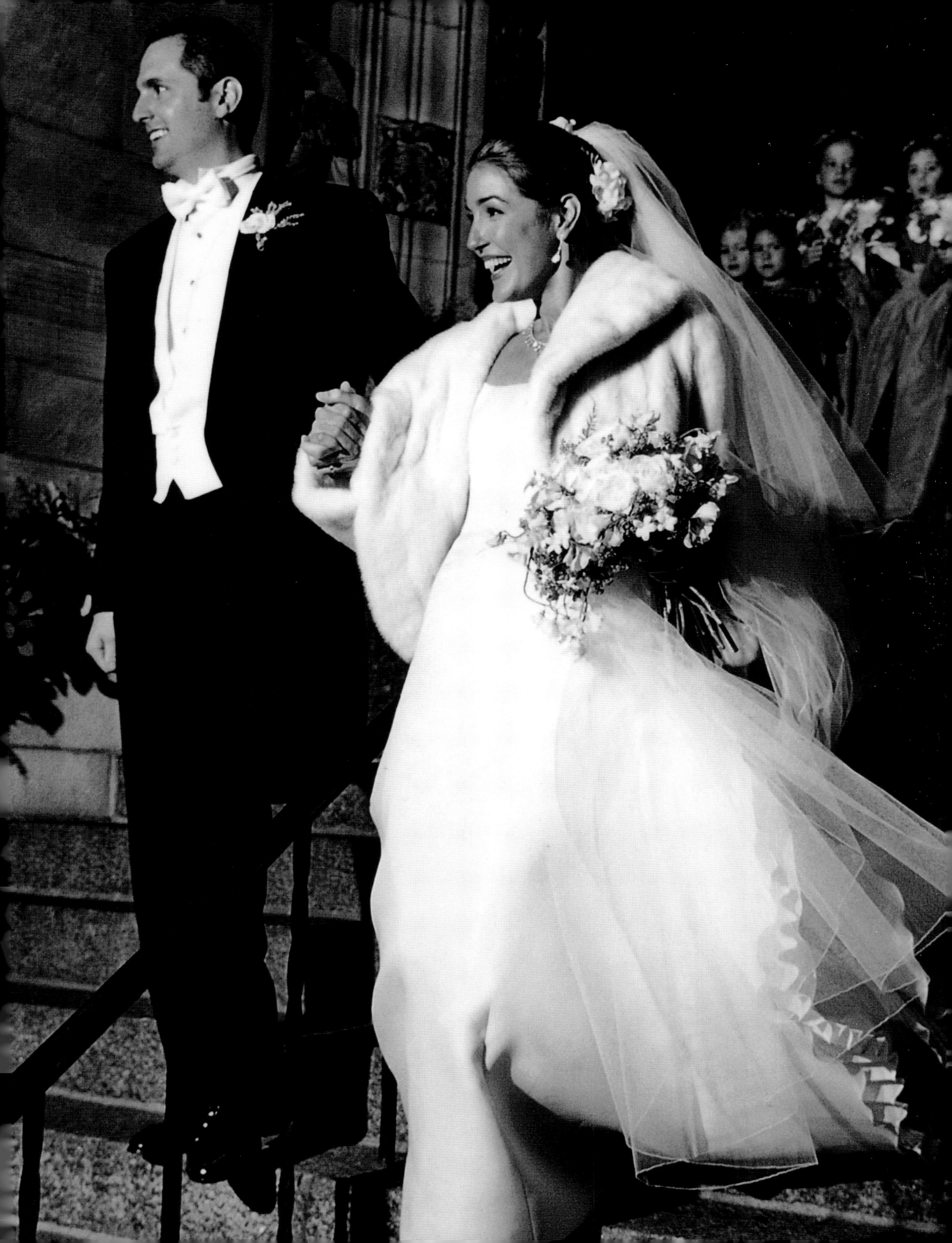

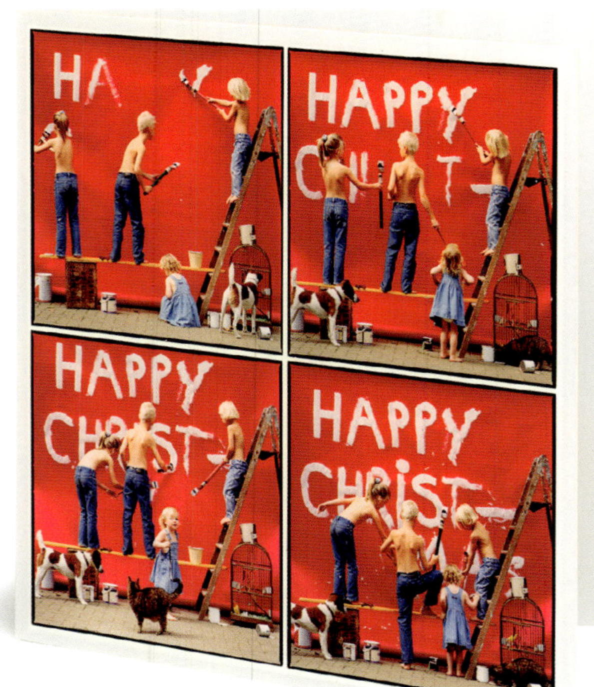

Lily, Fergus, Maya & Una Burnand, 2004

Photographs by HUGO BURNAND

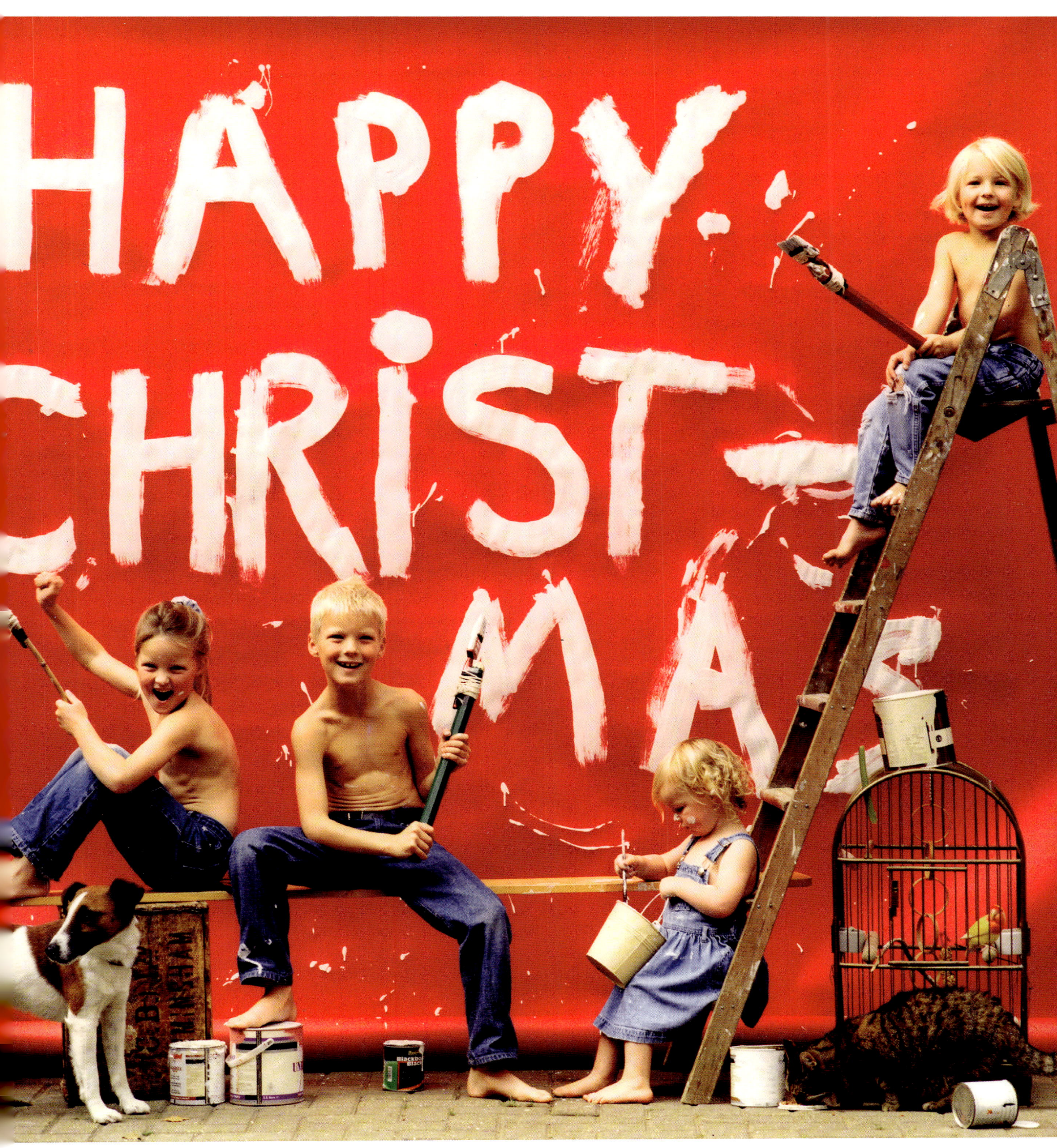
HAPPY
CHRIST
MA

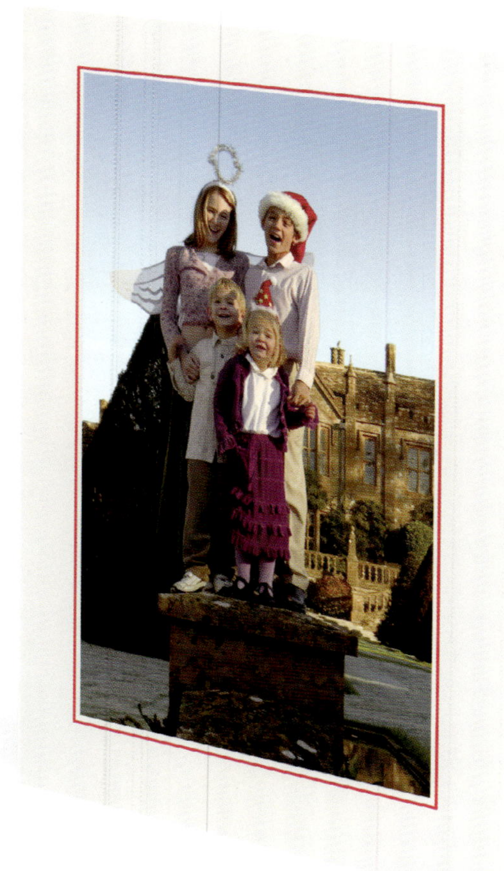

Sofia & Carlo Marsaglia,
Maximilian & Charlotte Treichl, 2004

Photograph by BRIAN NEESAM

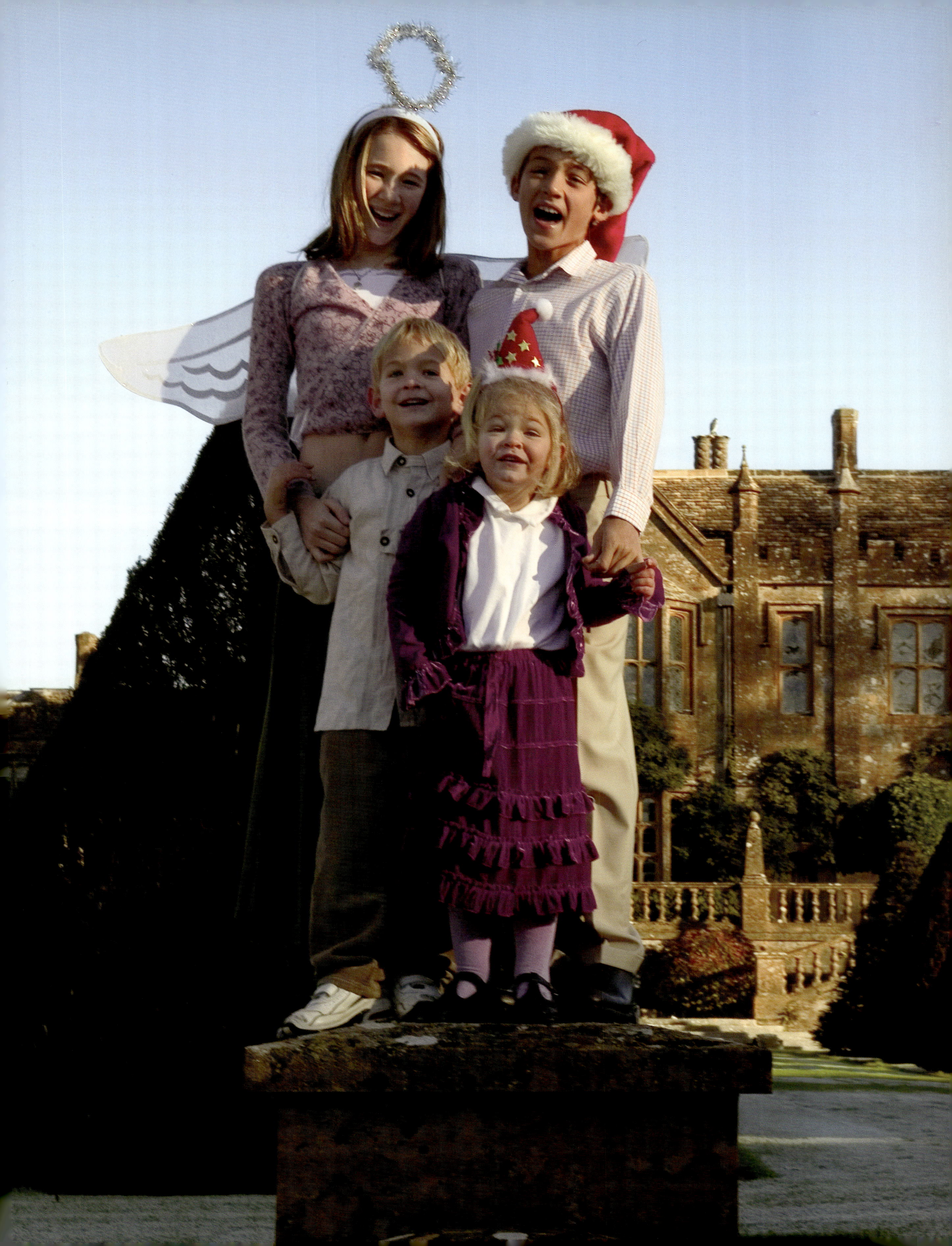

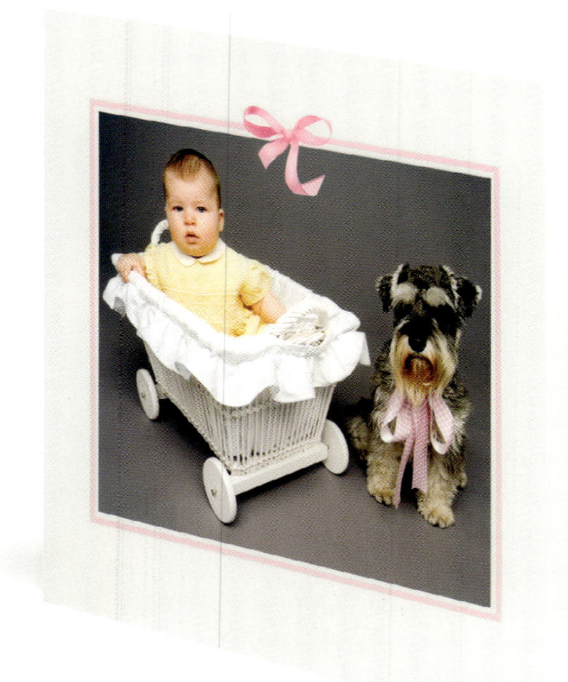

Davina Drummond, 2001

Photograph by MARTIN LEVENSON

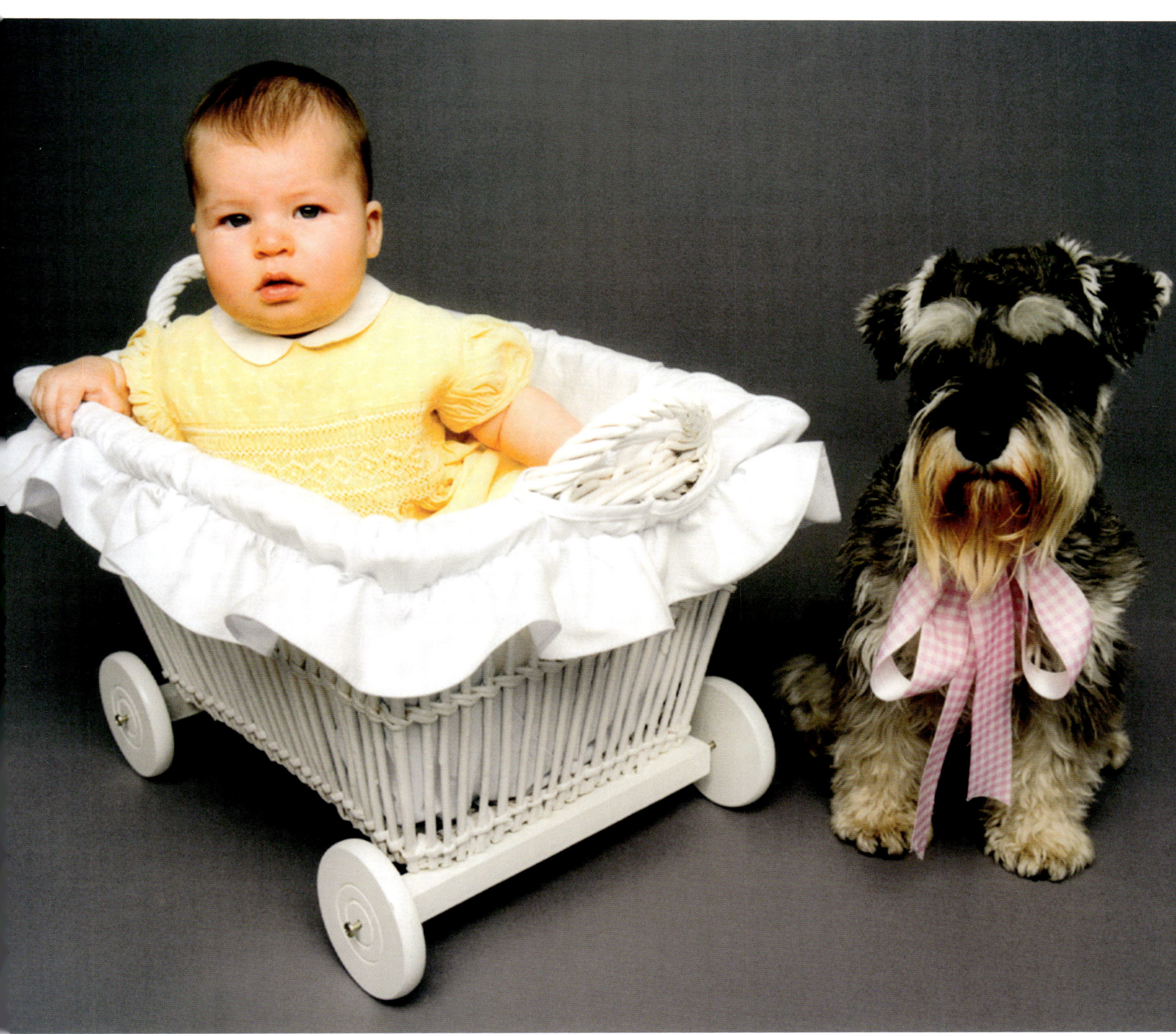

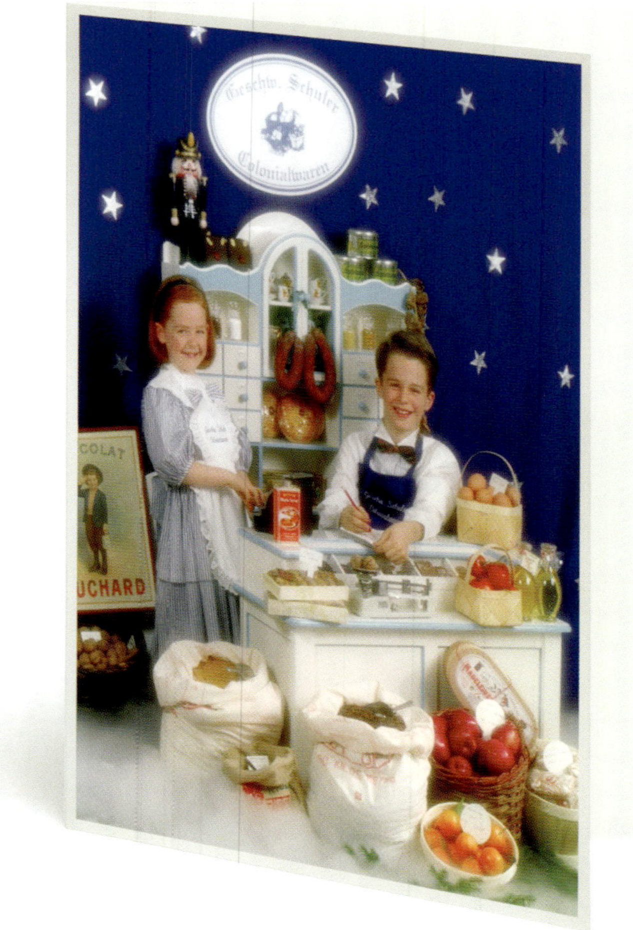

Olivia & Philip Schuler-Voith, 1992

Photograph by BIGGI SCHULER-VOITH

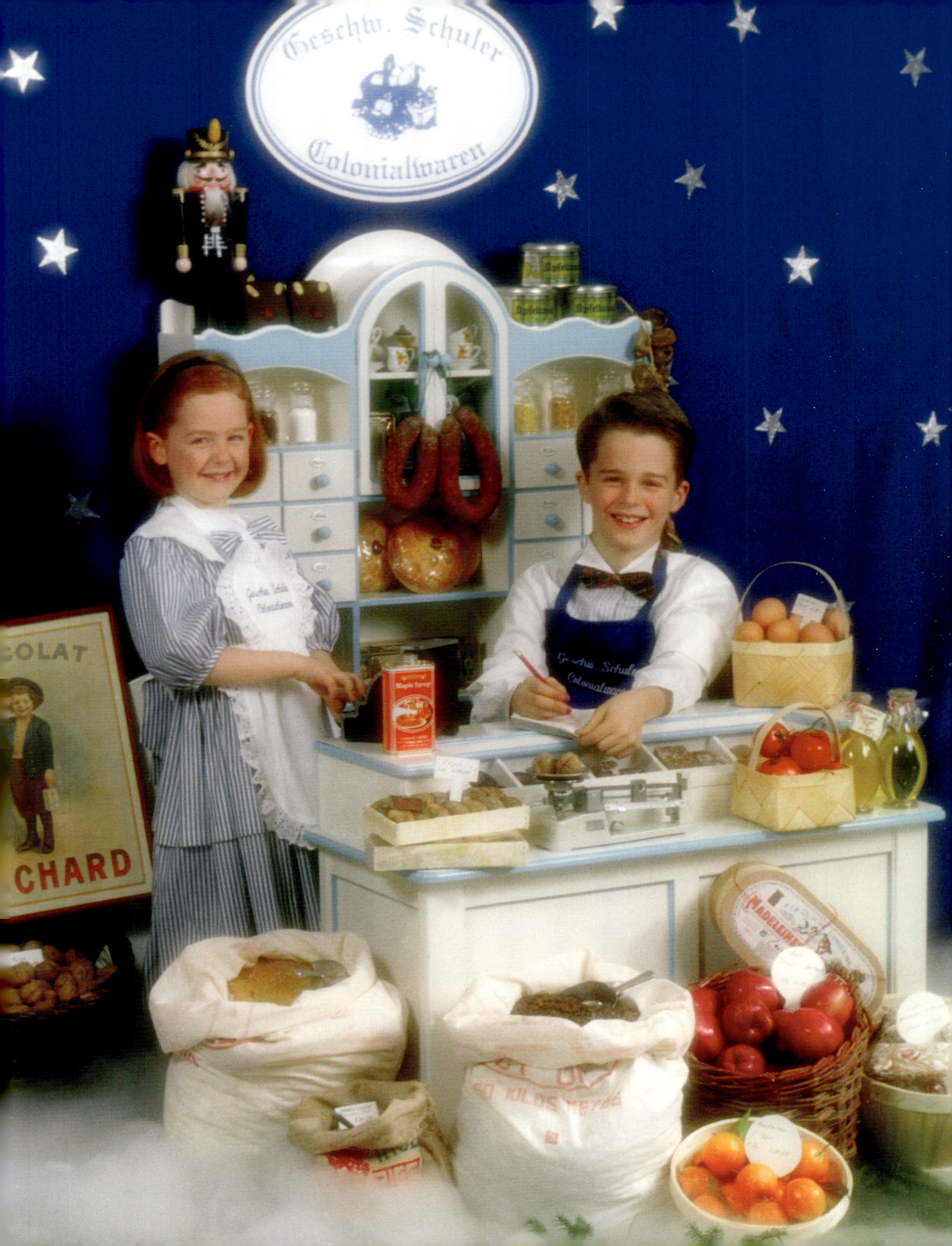
Geschw. Schuler
Colonialwaren
COLAT
CHARD
Maple Syrup
50 KILOS

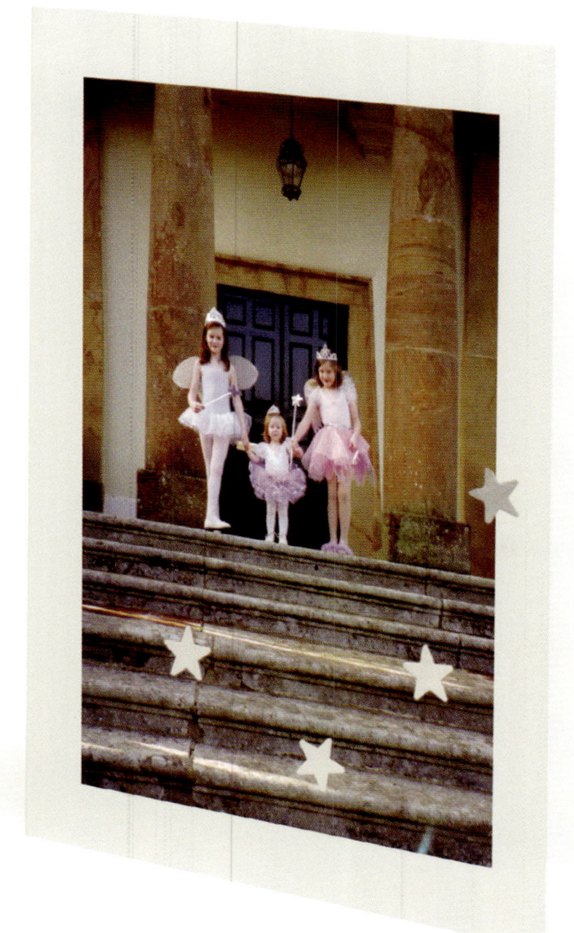

Leonora, Gabriella & Christabel Gilmour, 2004

Photograph by MARDI GILMOUR

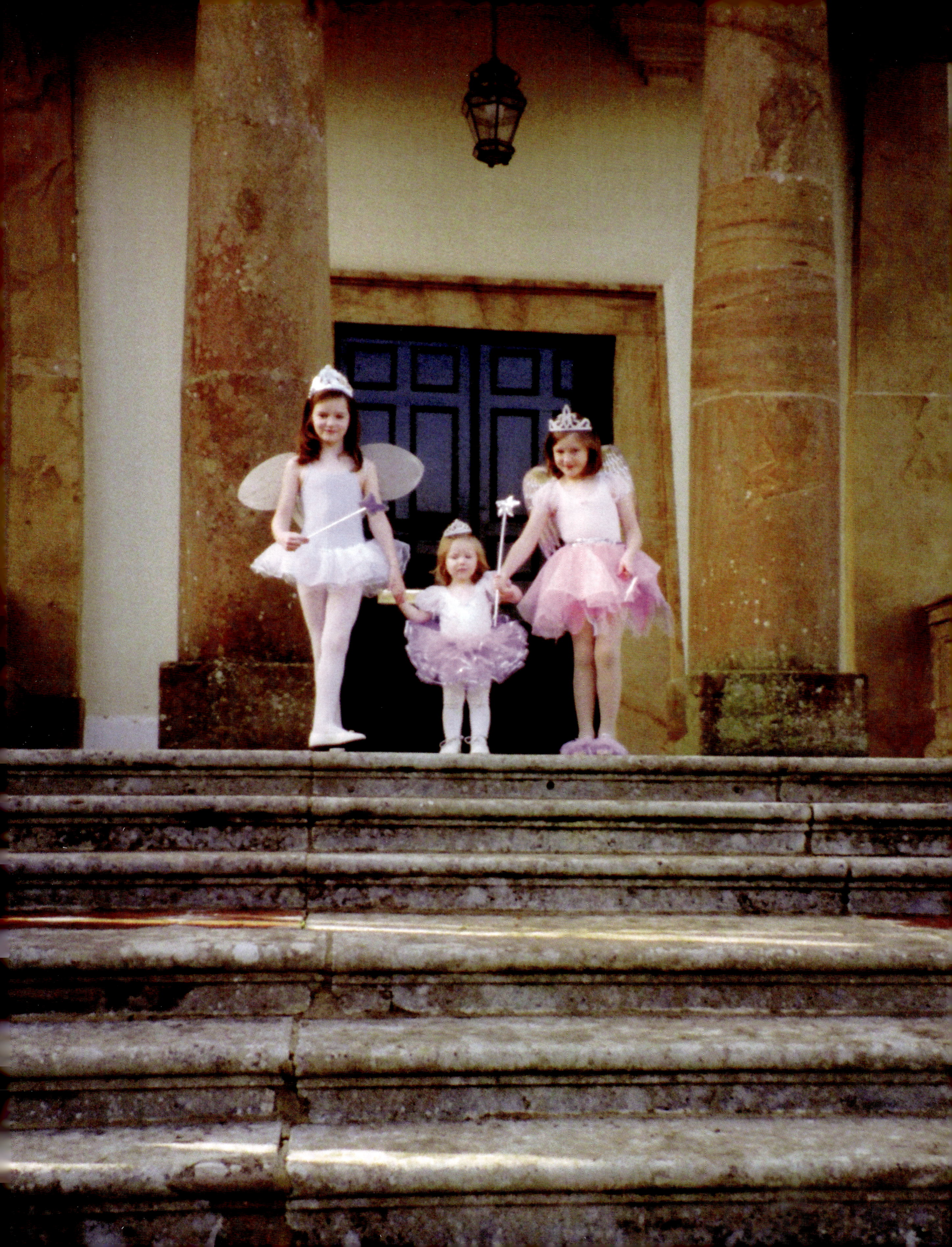

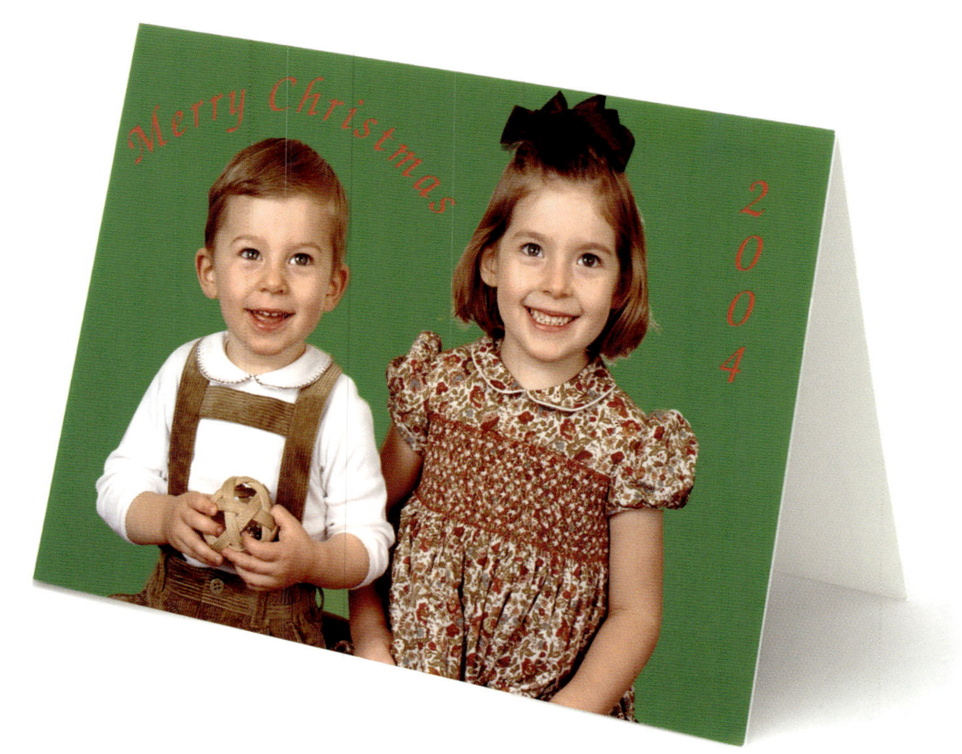

Freiherr Waldemar & Freifrau Ludmilla von Oppenheim, 2004

Photograph by STAN LENMAN

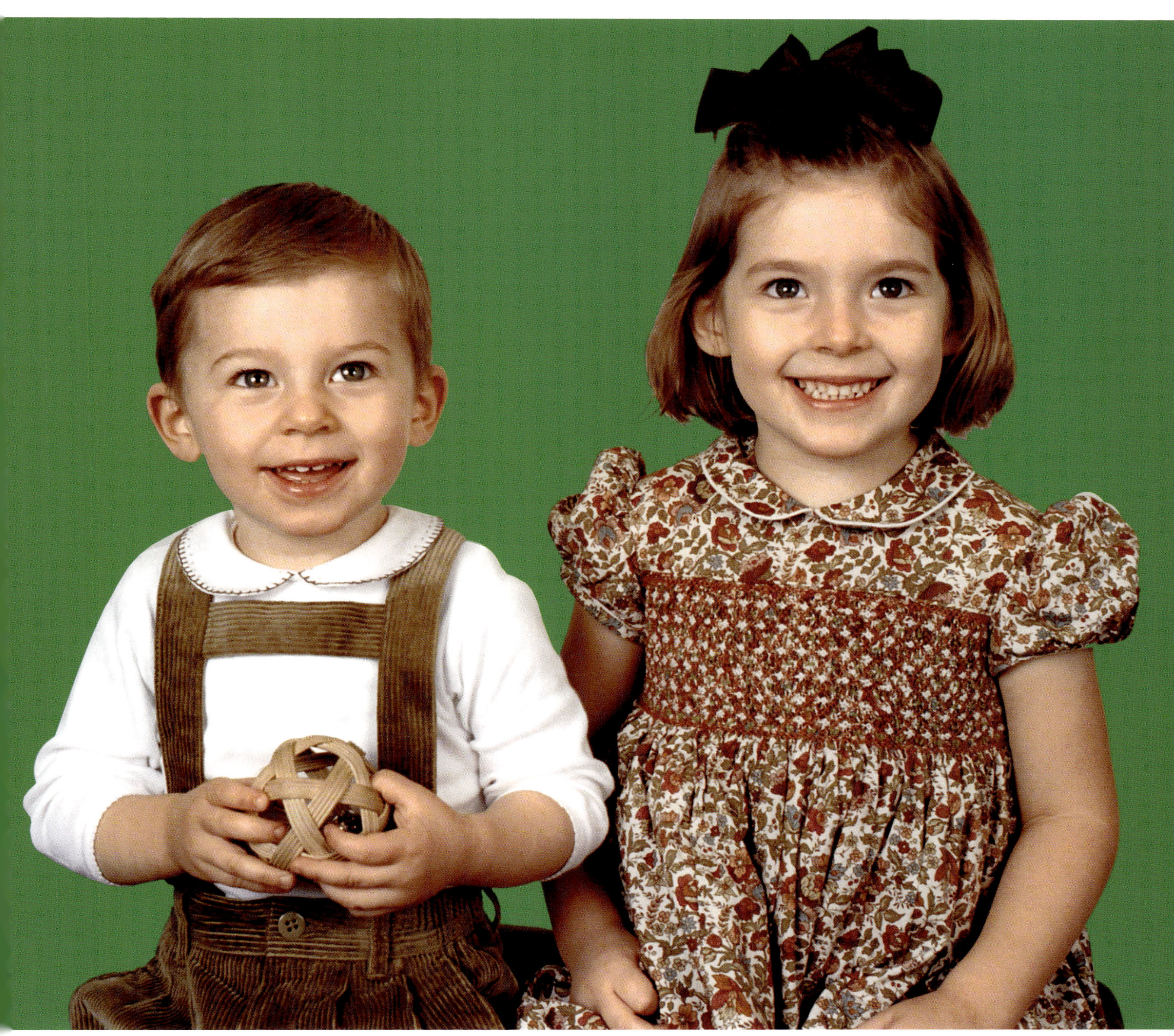

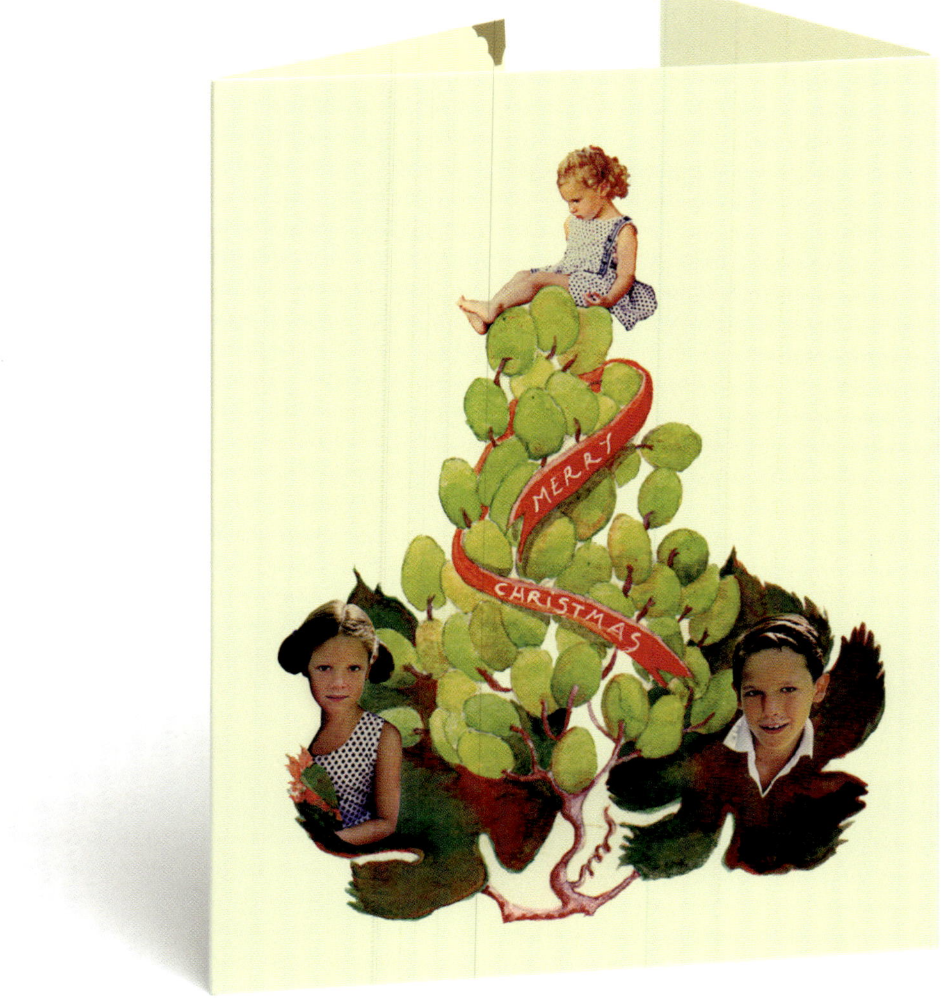

Guglielmo, Angelica & Isabella Tosato, 2002

Photographs by GIULIO PIETROMARCHI
Illustration by SOPHIE BENINI PIETROMARCHI

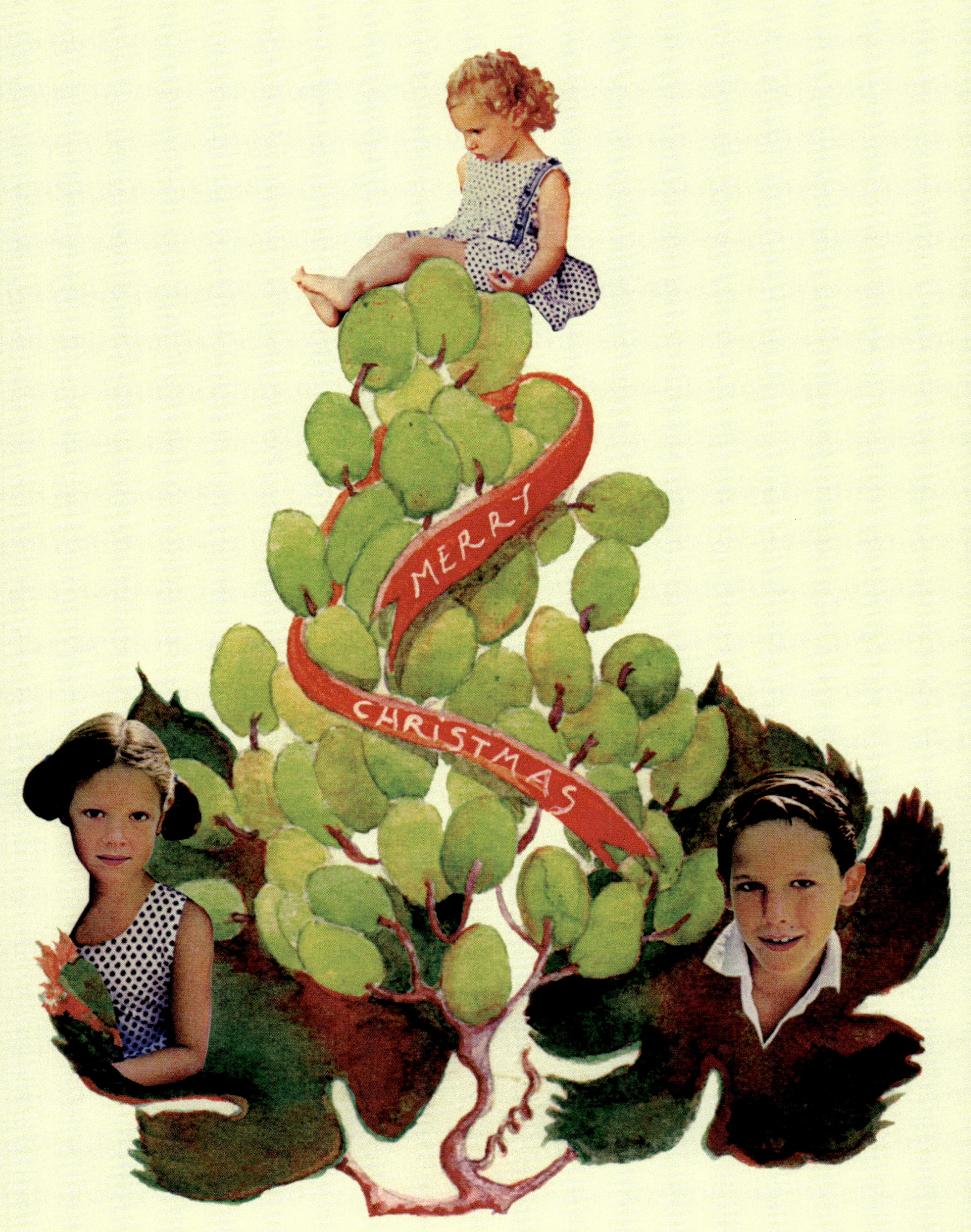
MERRY
CHRISTMAS

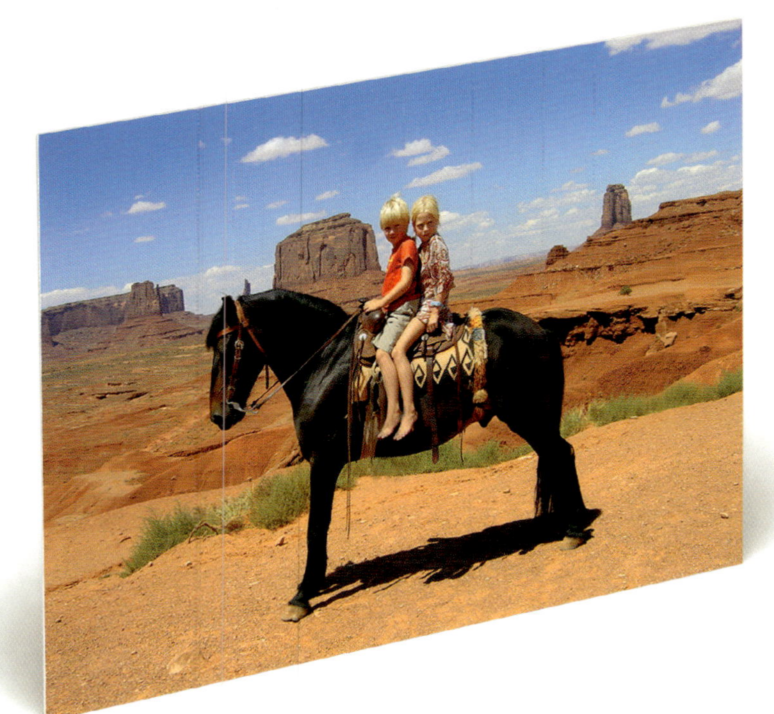

Josefa & Verus von Haeften, 2003

Photograph by HERRET VON HAEFTEN

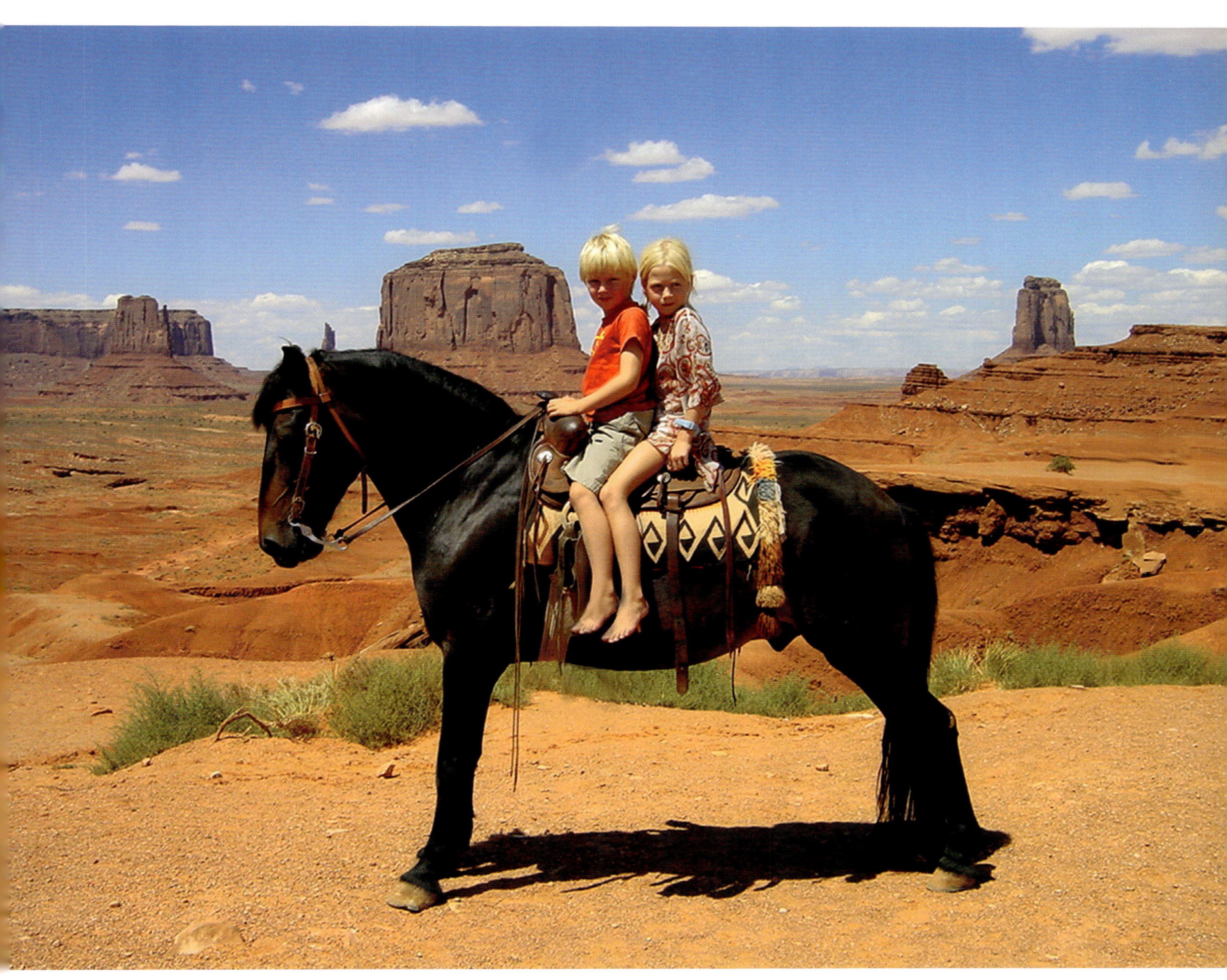

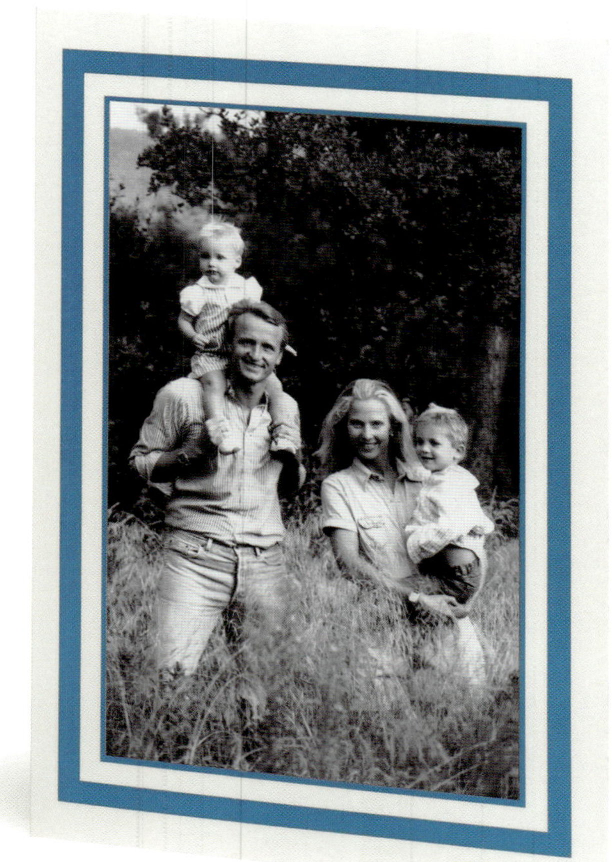

Carlota, Bart, Alexandra & Niklas Homan, 2002

Photograph by BART HOMAN

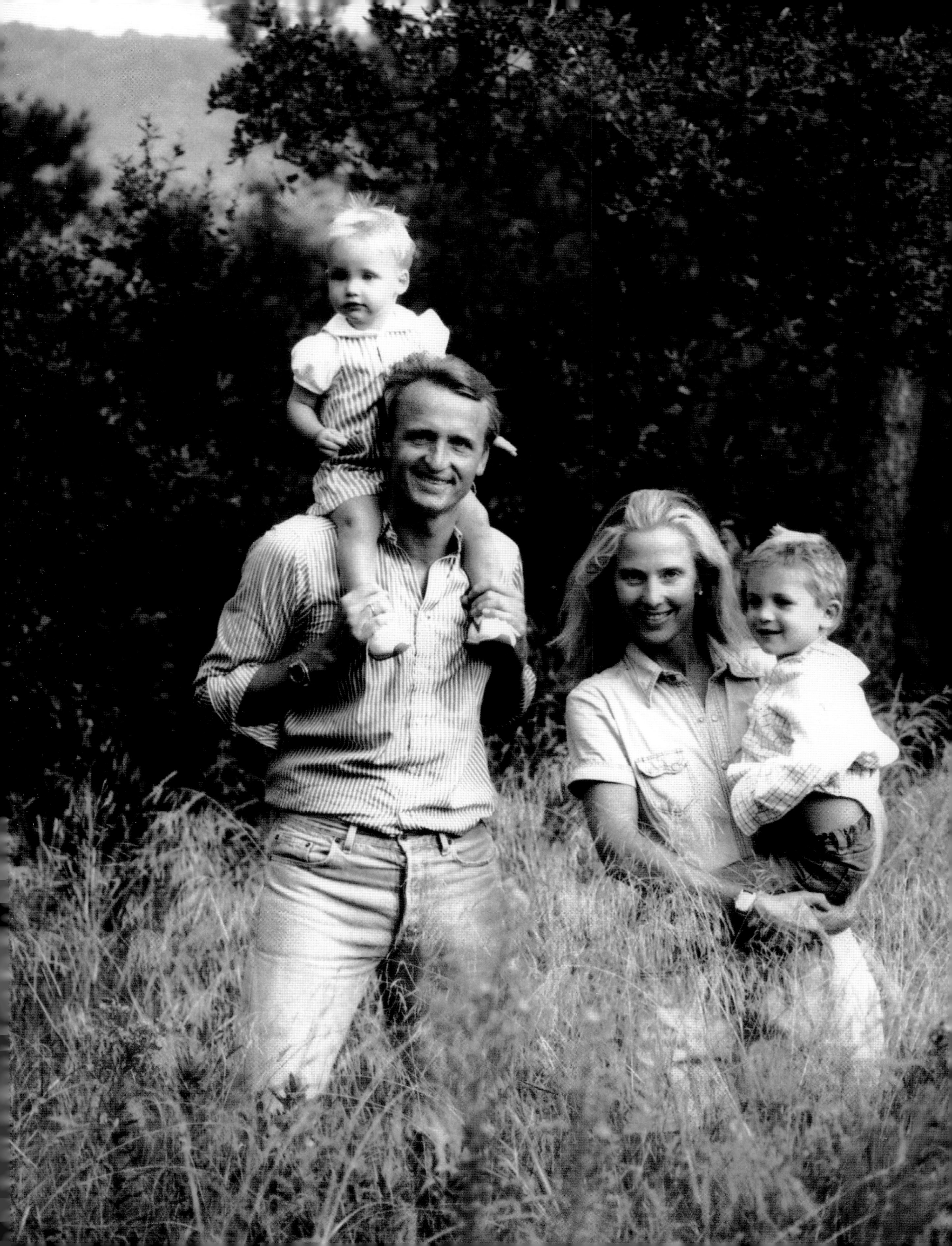

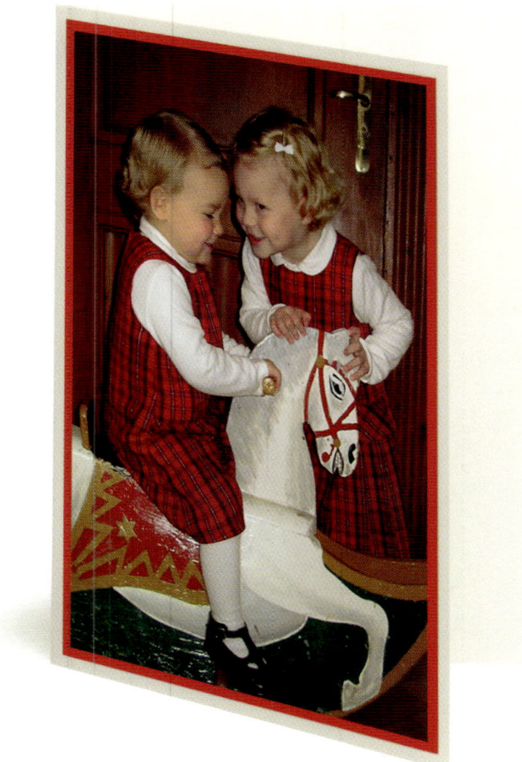

Gräfin Philippa & Gräfin Johanna von Oppersdorff, 2004

Photograph by GRÄFIN MARITA VON OPPERSDORFF

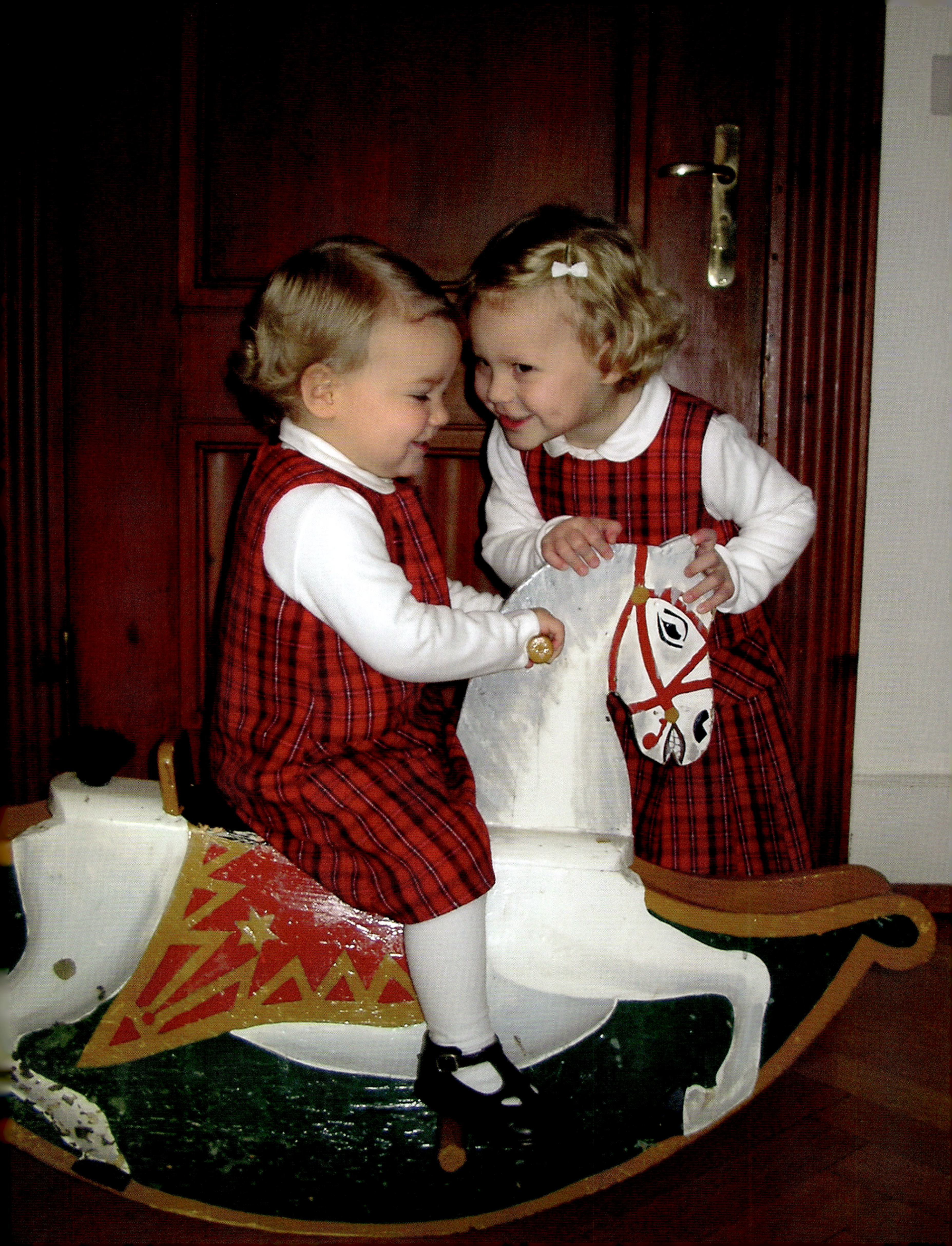

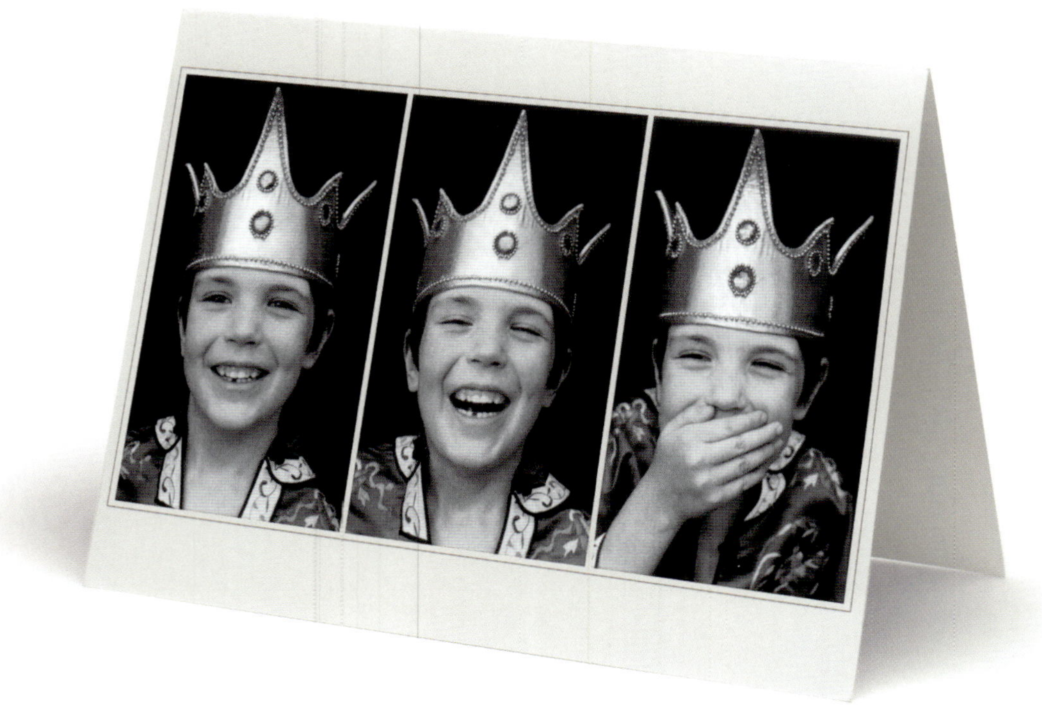

Vladimir Crasneanscki, 2003

Photographs by JAMES P GRAHAM

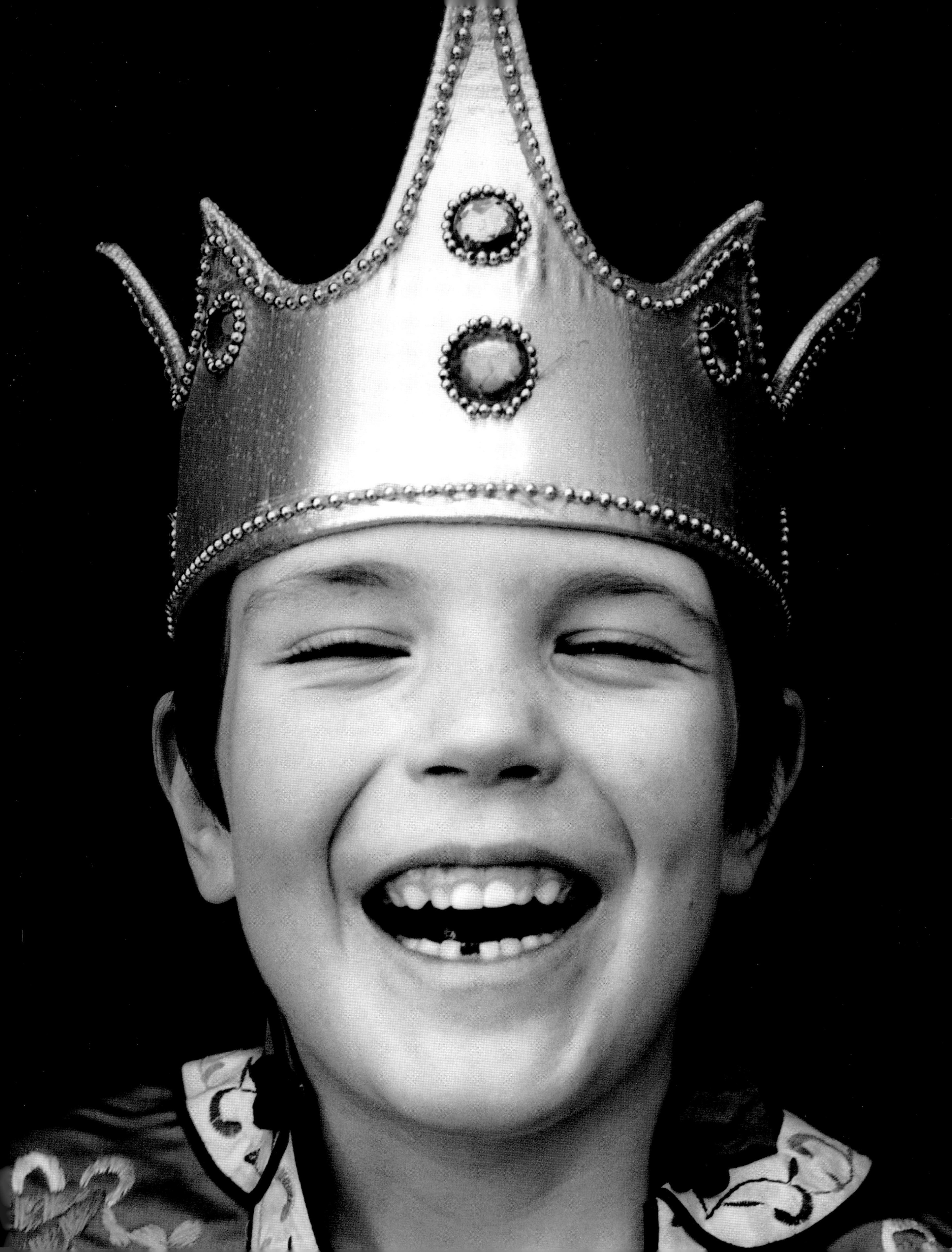

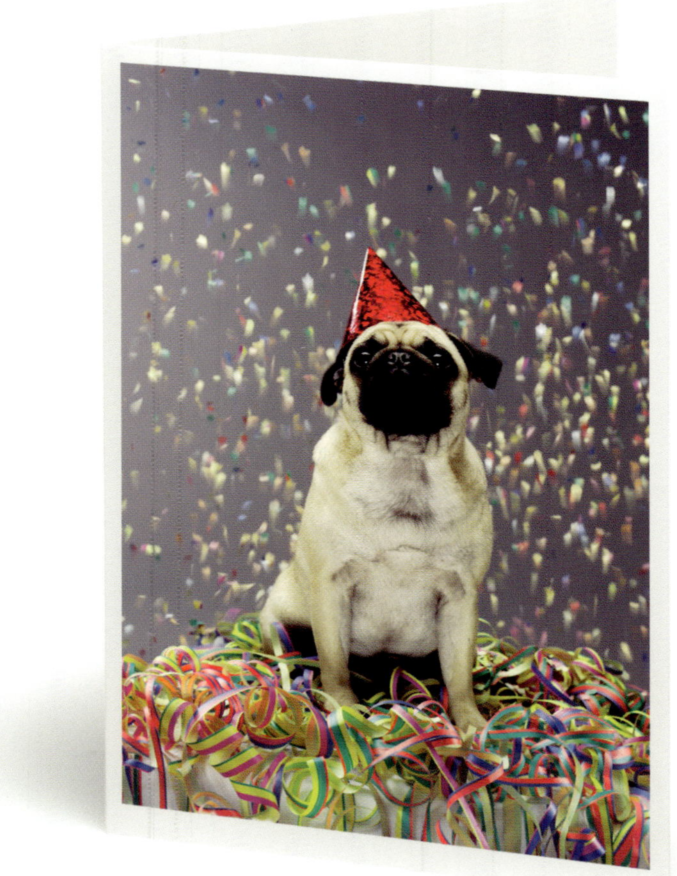

"Emily" & "Lucky" Joop, 2004

Photograph by RUSSEL PETERS

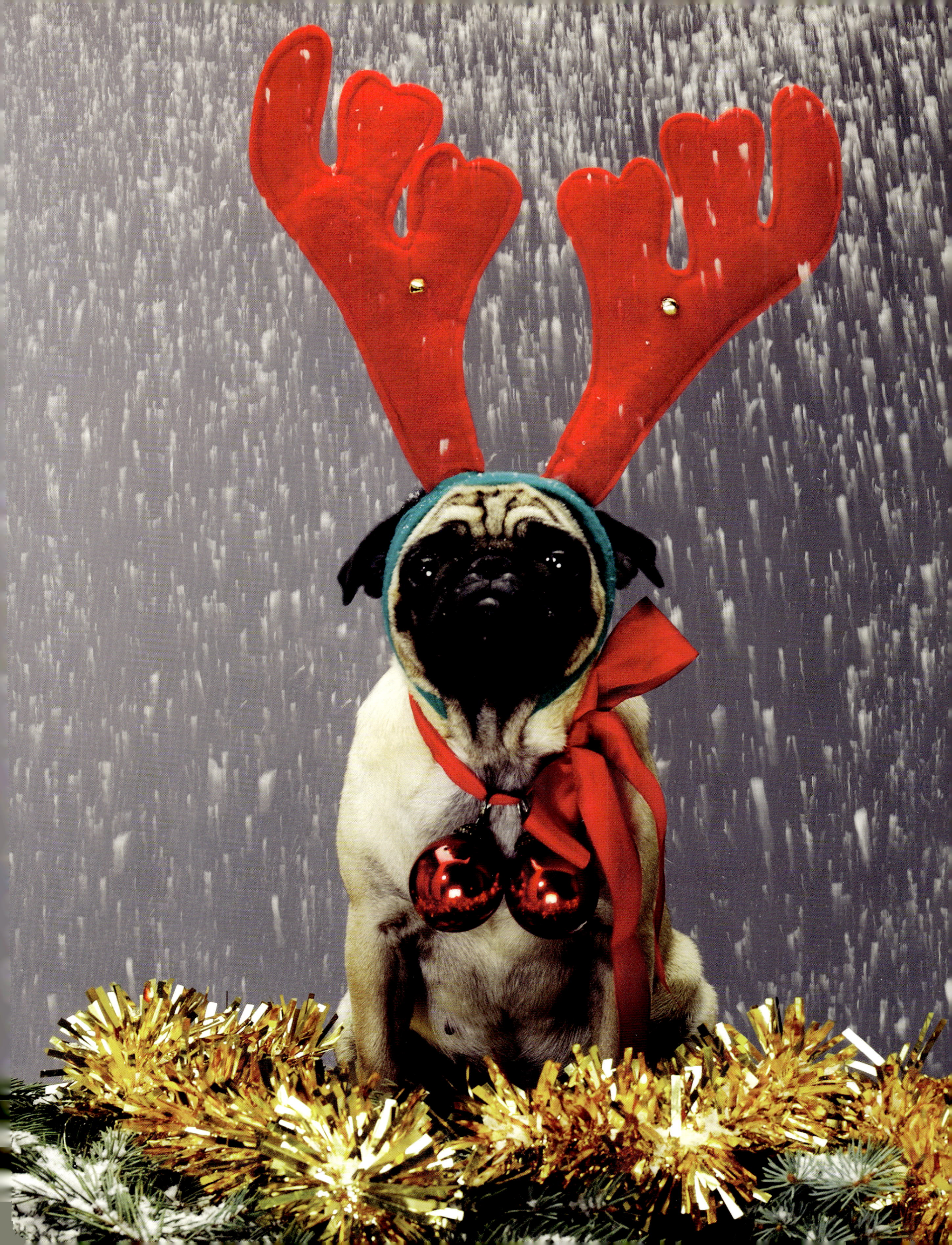

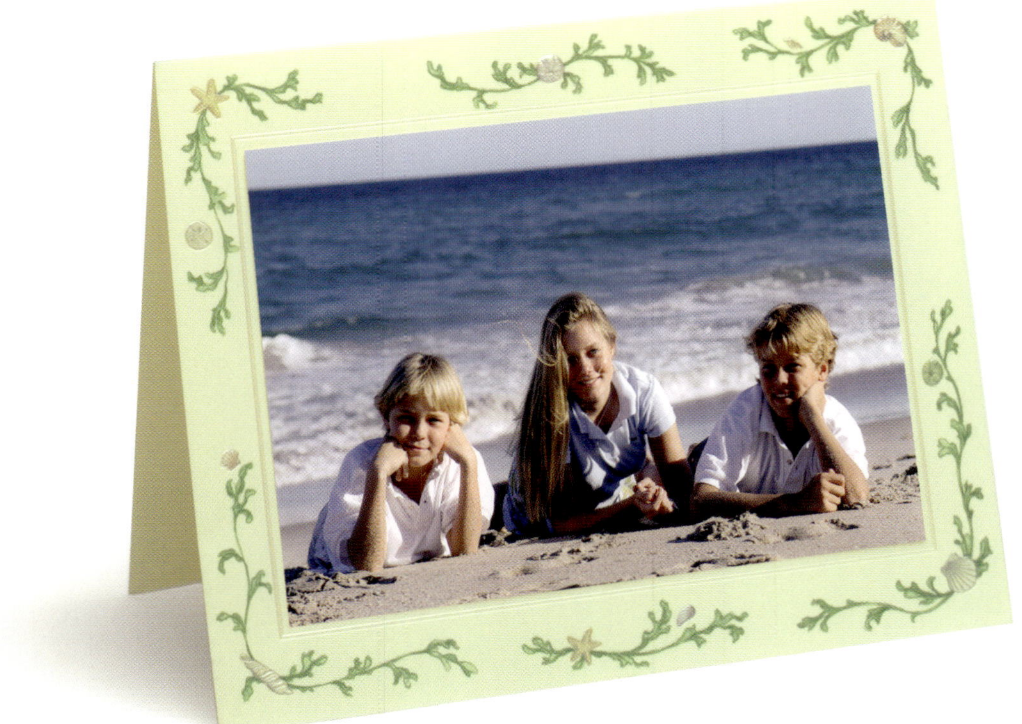

Christopher, Sabrina & Franz Burda, 2003

Photograph by BETTINA BURDA

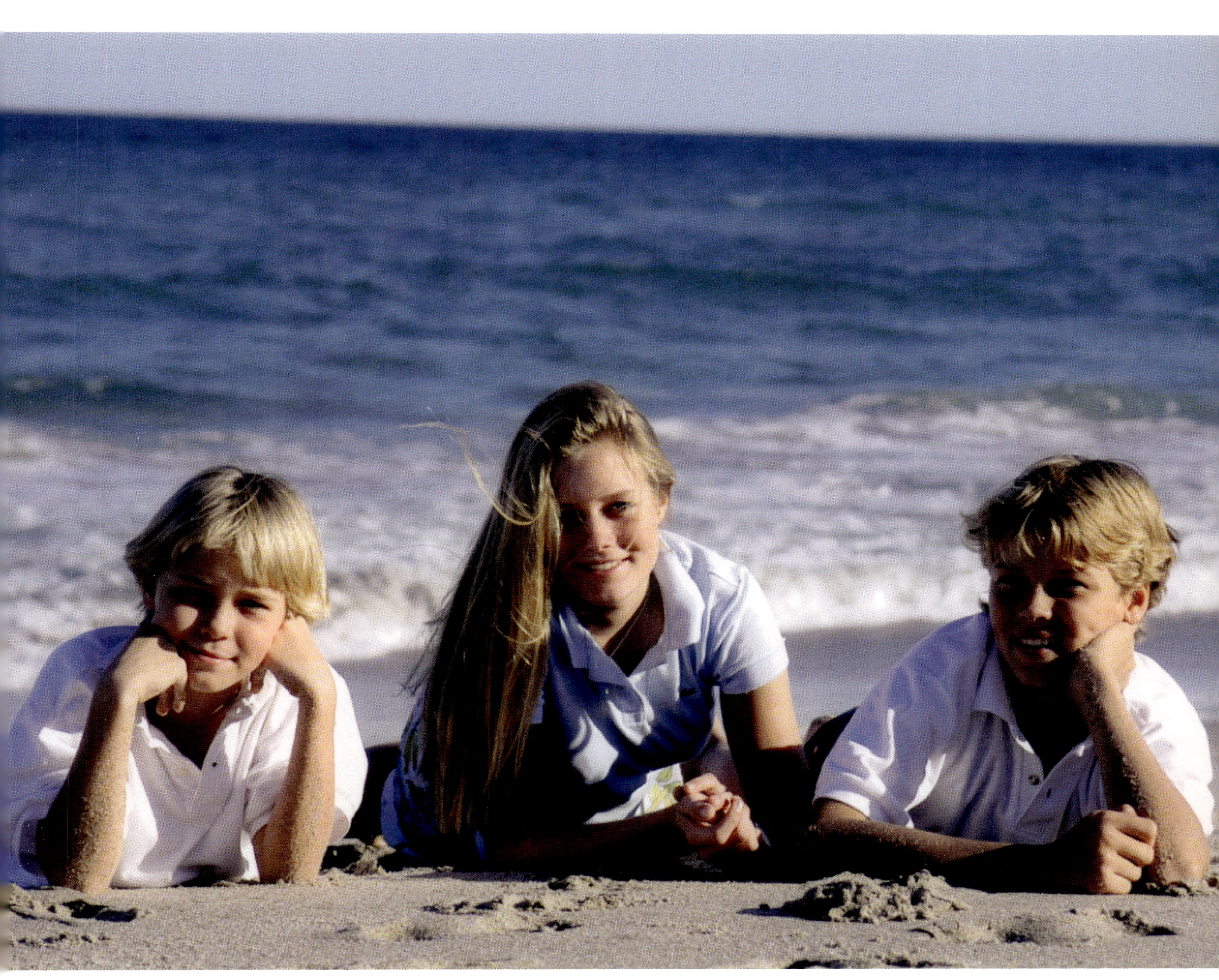

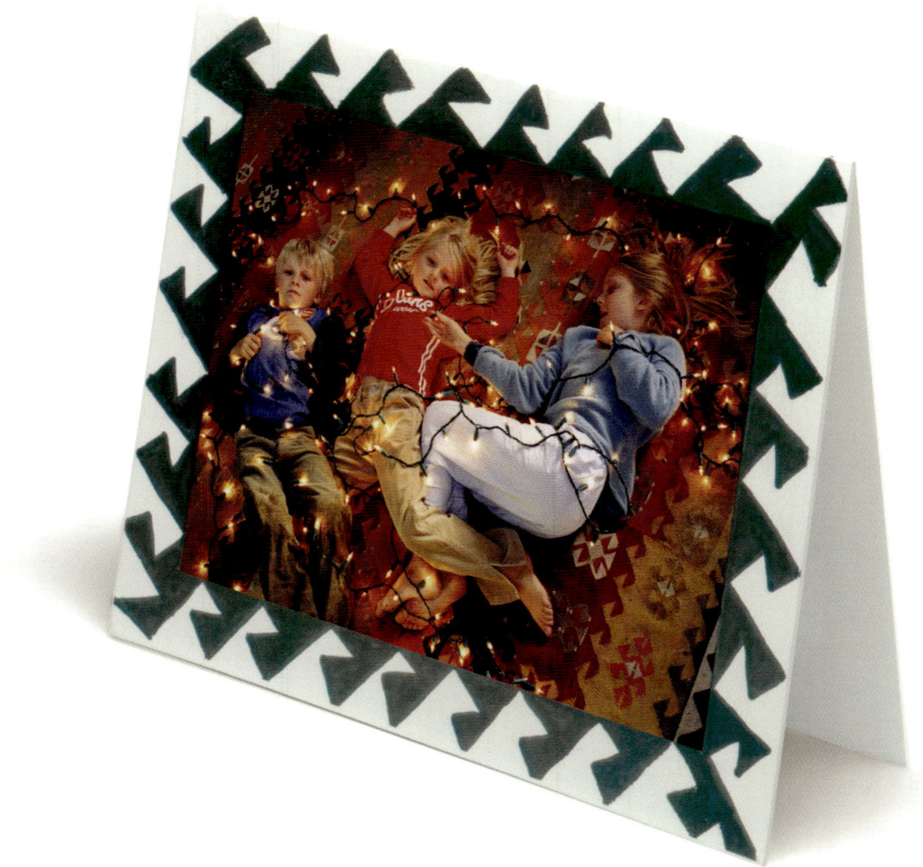

Robbie, Cressida & Alice Bullough, 2002

Photograph by EMMA HARDY

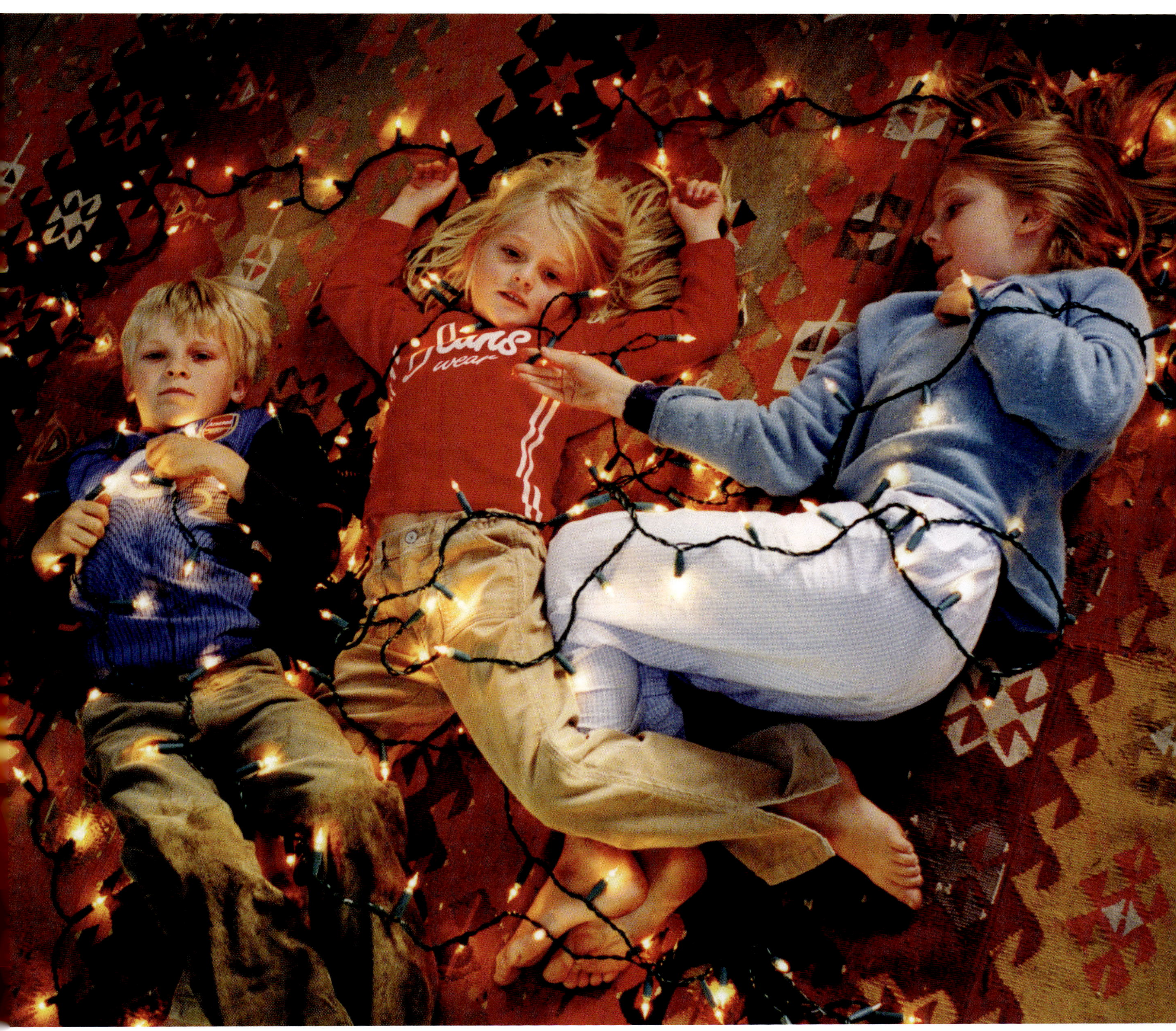
wear

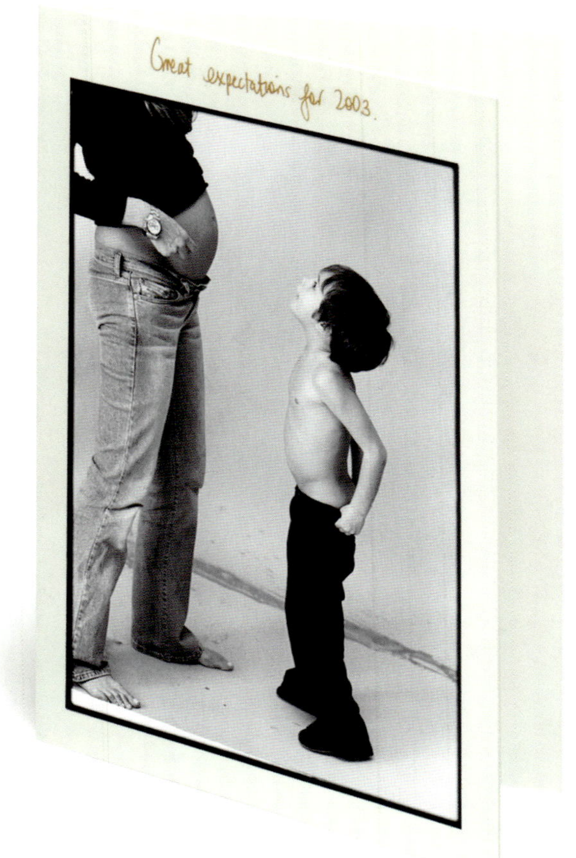

Elle Macpherson & Flynn Busson, 2002

Photograph by DAN STEVENS

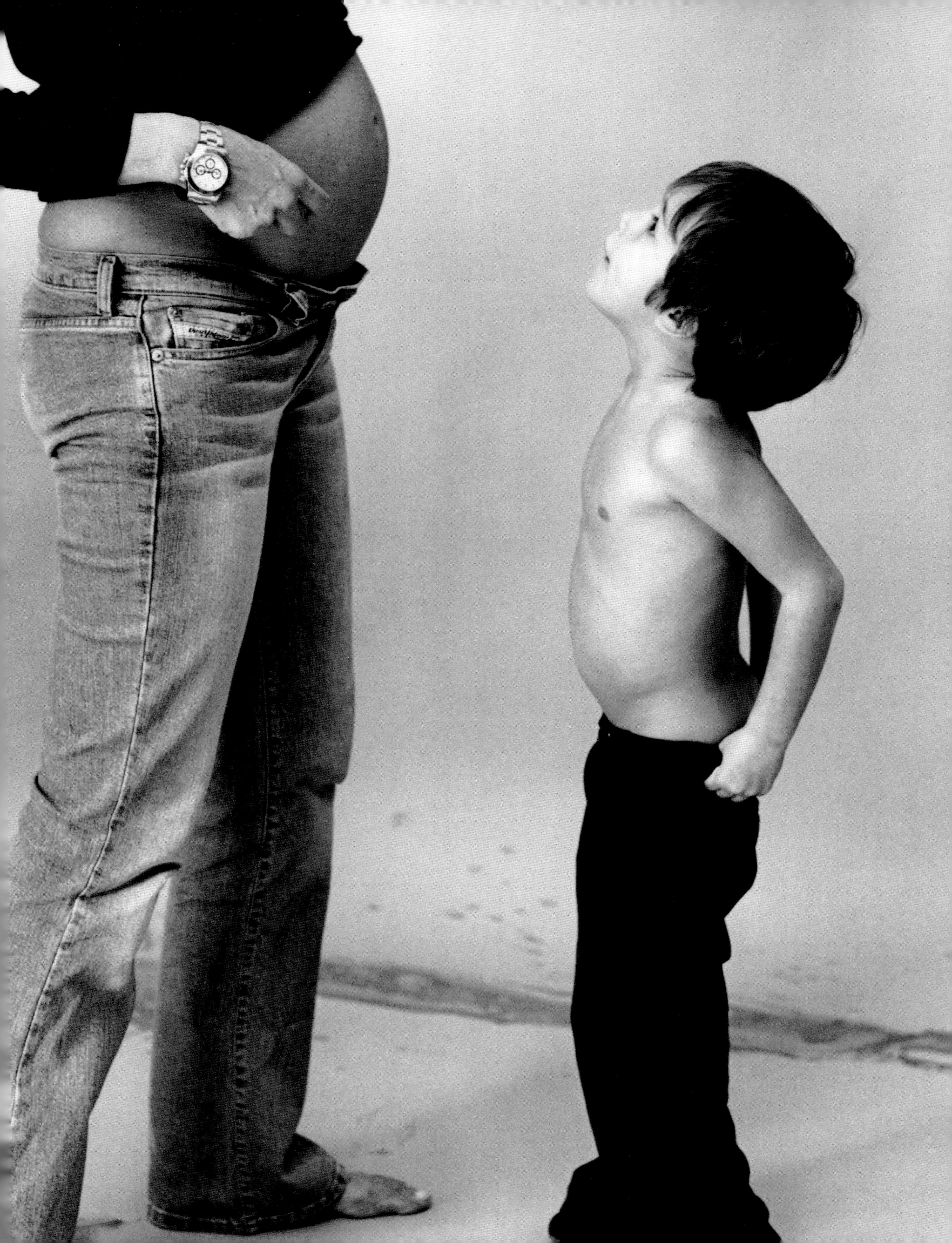

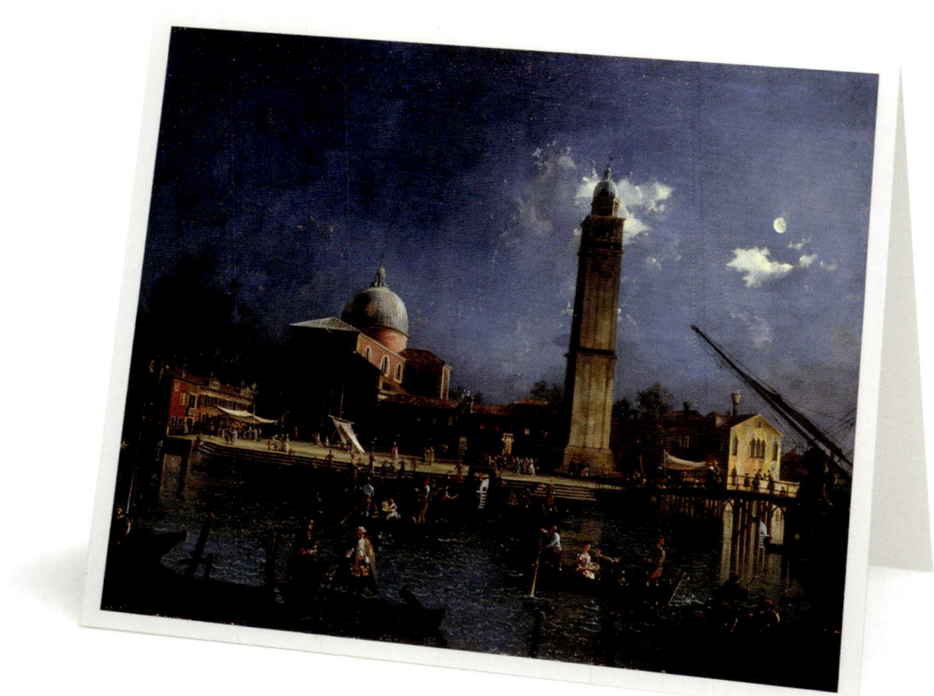

"Night Festival at San Pietro di Castello", 2003

Painting by ANTONIO CANAL, IL CANALETTO
CORINNE AND GERT-RUDOLF FLICK COLLECTION

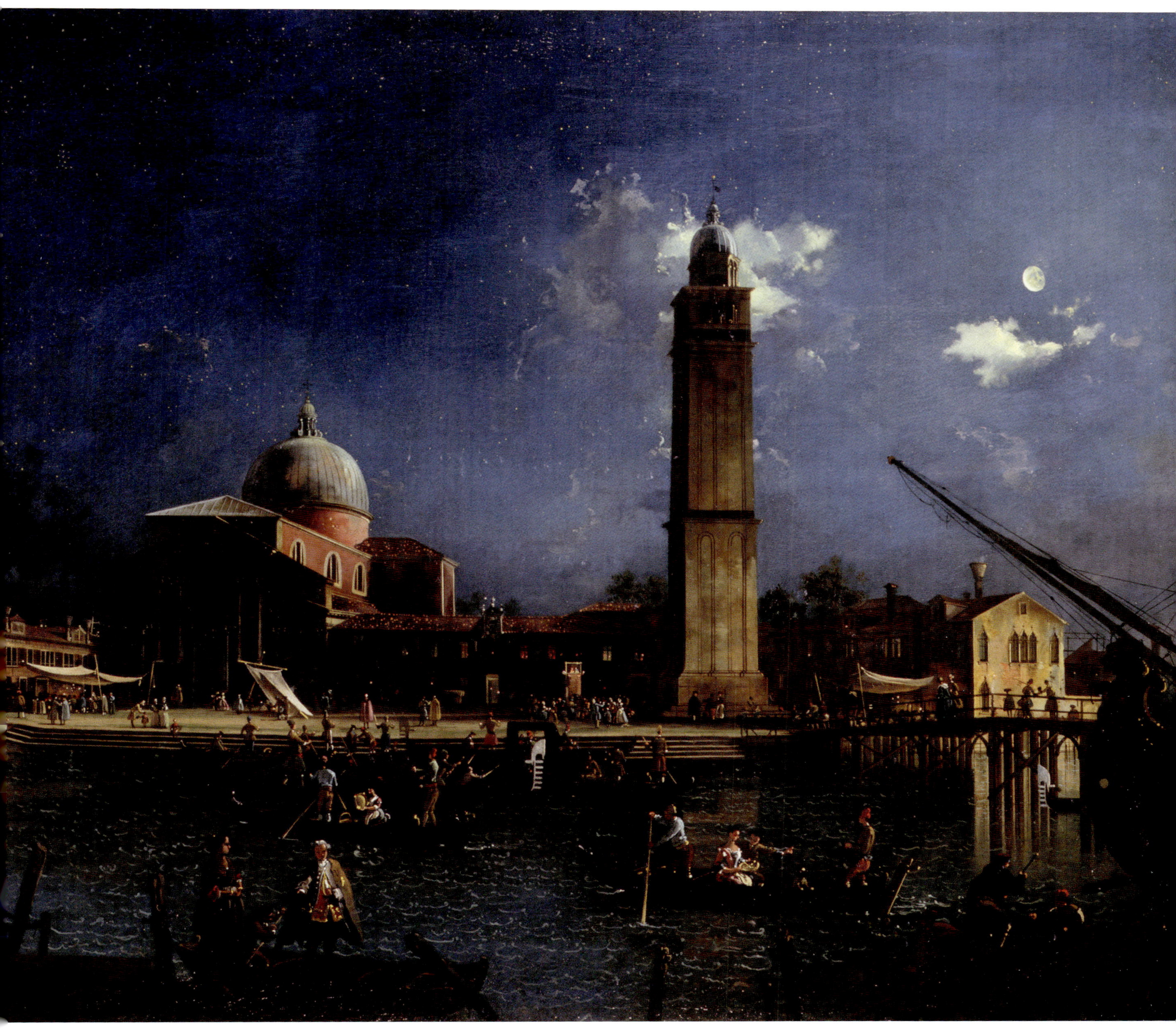

124

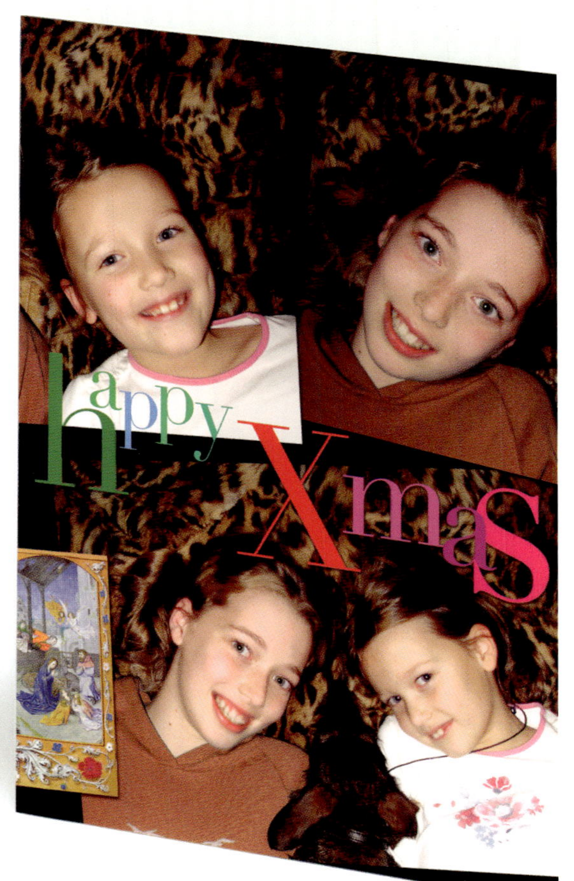

Angelica & Ambrosia Hicks, 2004

Photographs by ASHLEY HICKS

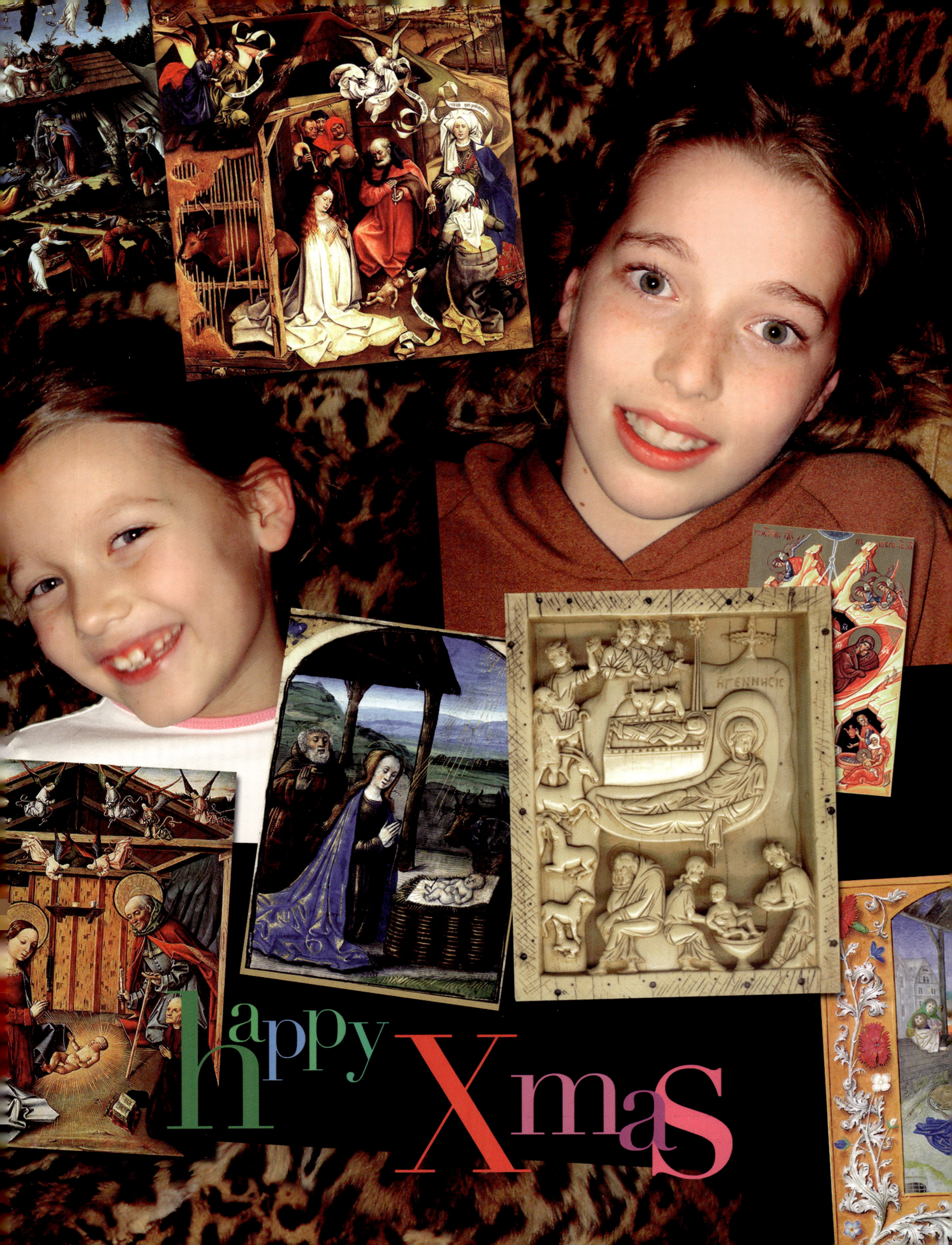

happy Xmas

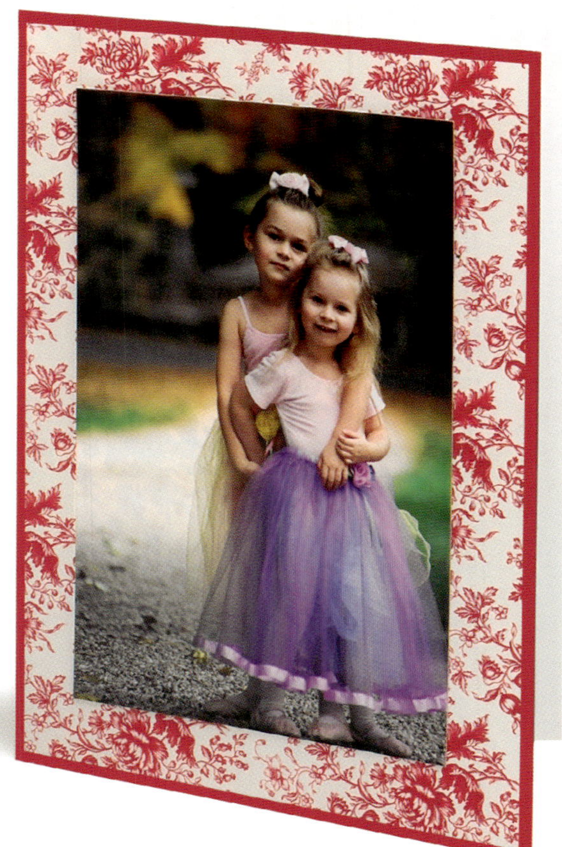

Madison & Morgan Heilshorn, 2004

Photograph by EDWARD ACKER

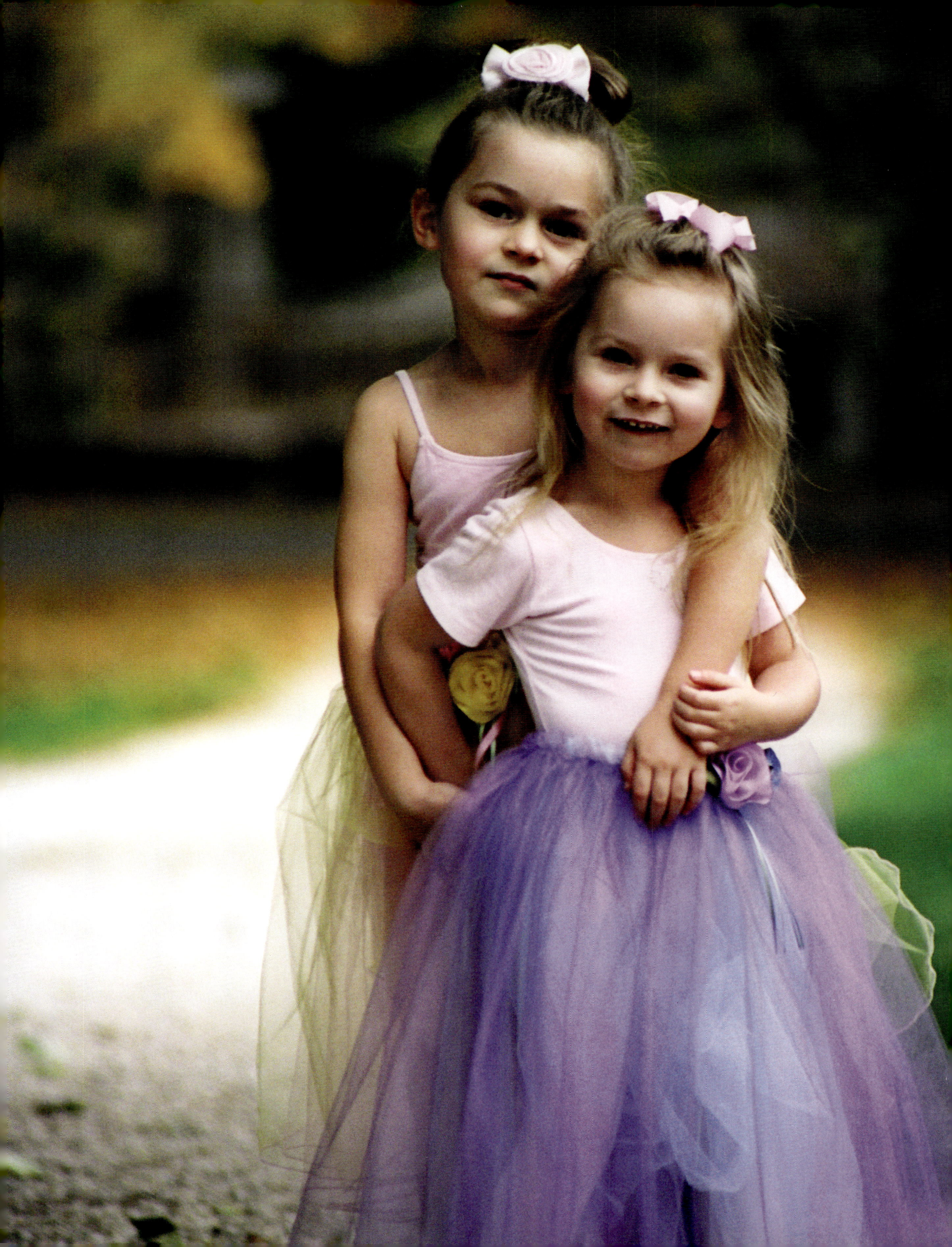

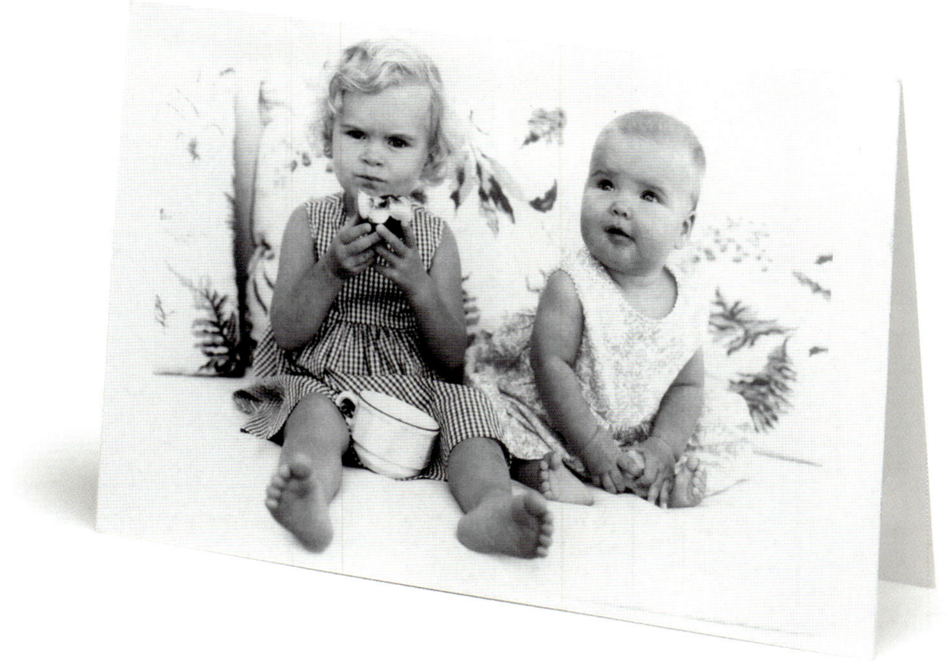

Caroline & Lara Bird Connor, 2004

Photograph by STEPHEN SIMONS

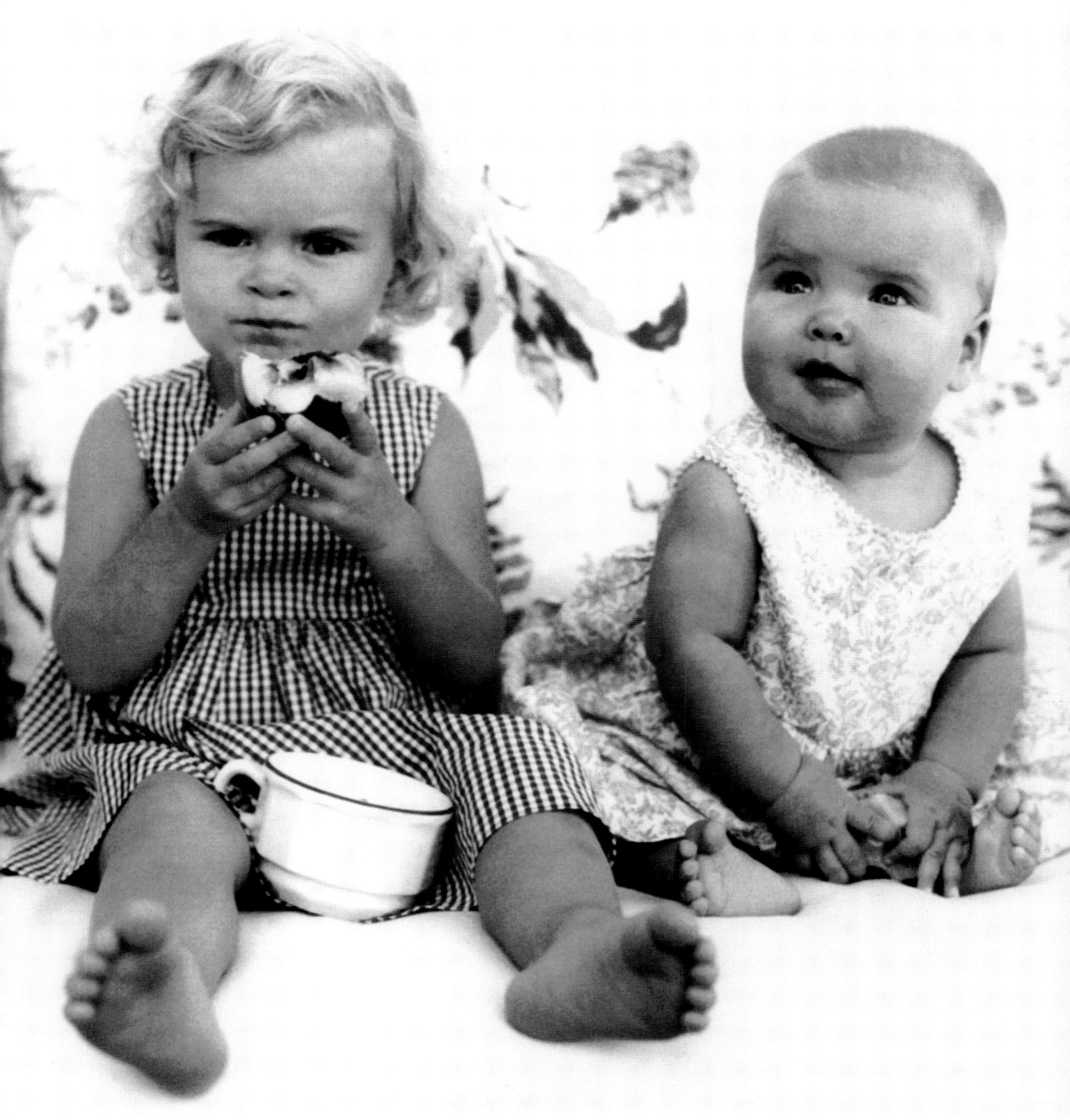

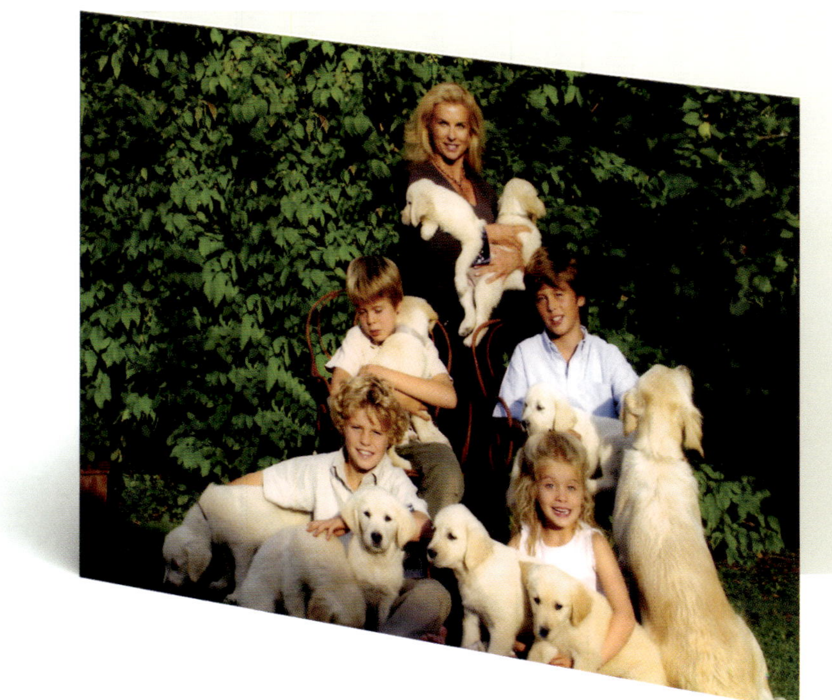

Bibi, Brandolino, Massimiliano, Lodovico & Lea Gritti, 2003

Photograph by NOUNI EISENBURGER

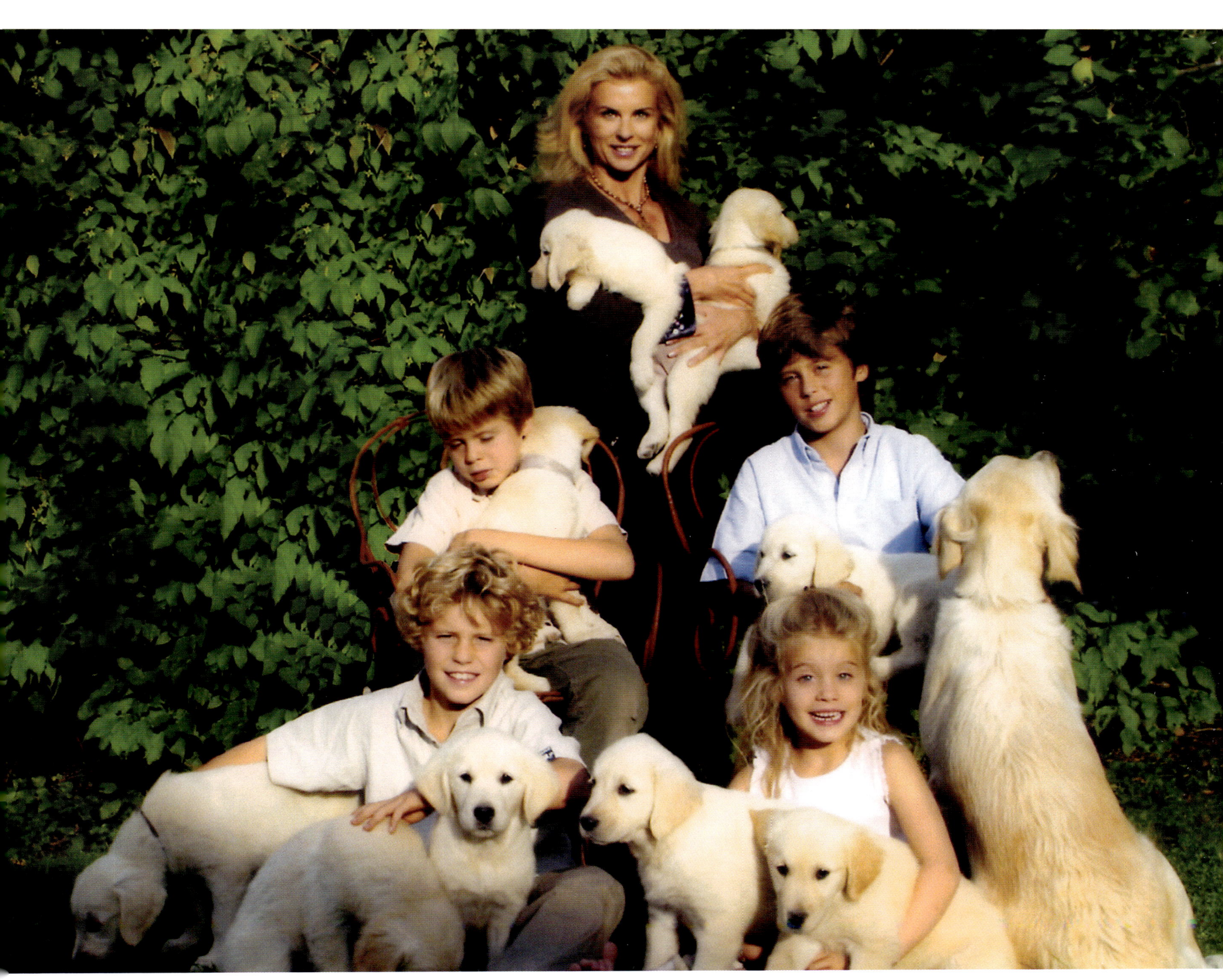

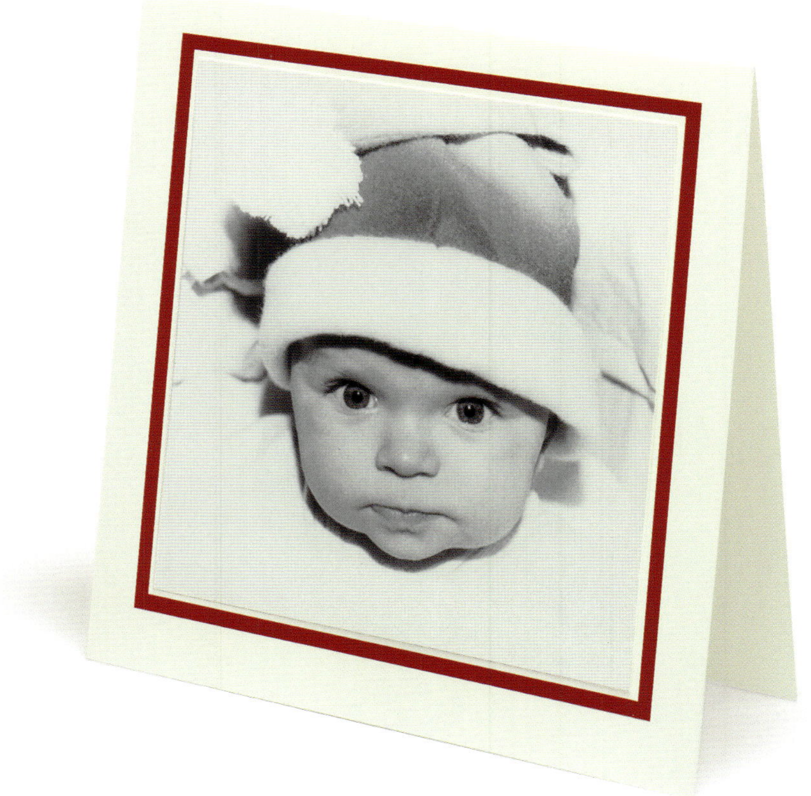

Rosa Rittweger, 2002

Photograph by ULLA SCHELLMANN

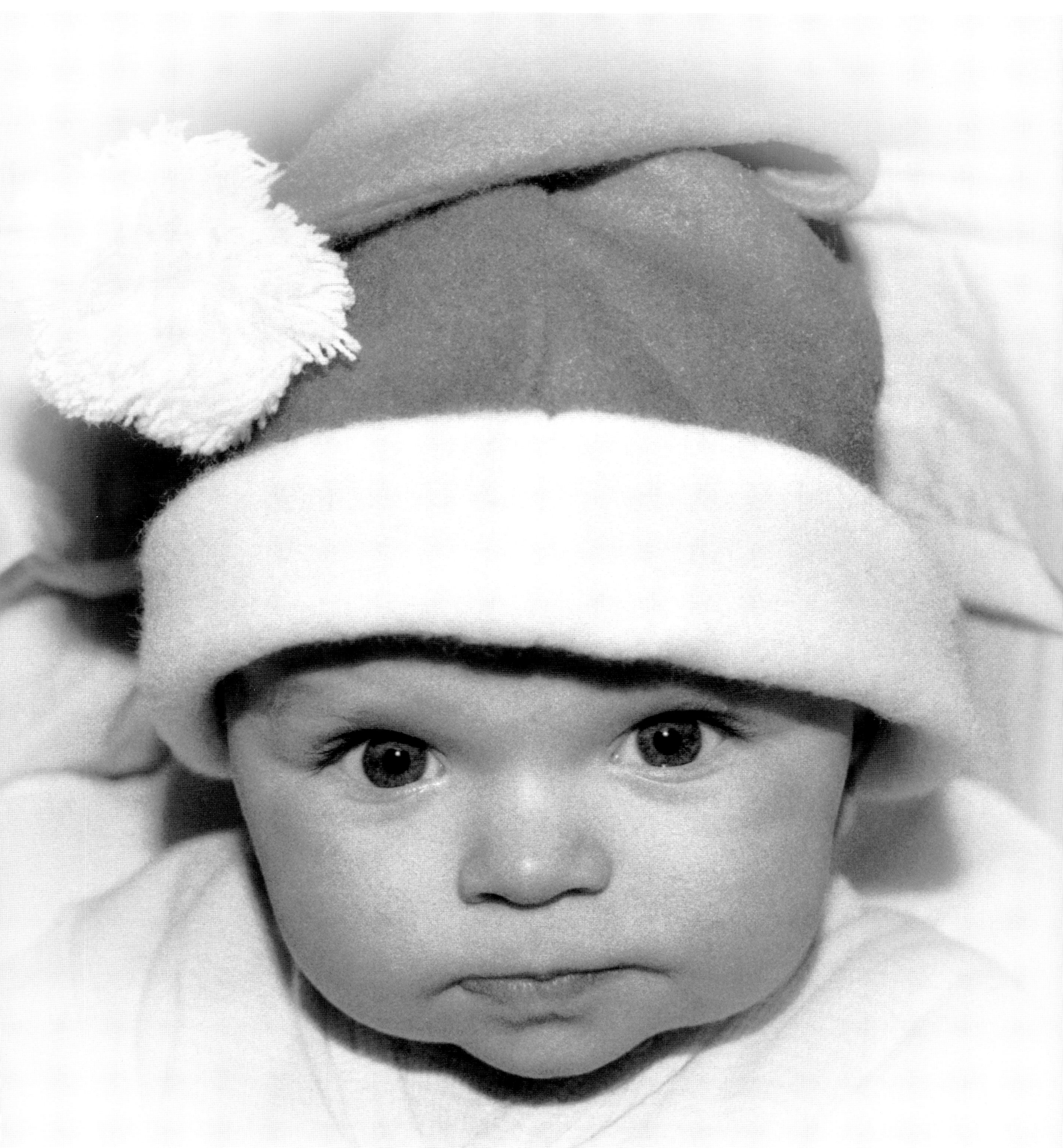

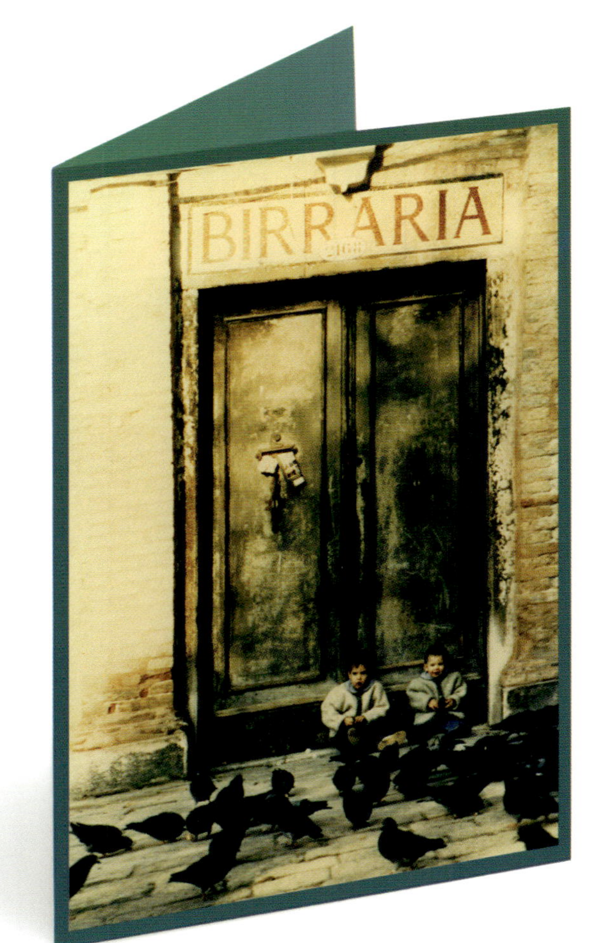

Donna Viola & Donna Vera
Arrivabene Valenti Gonzaga, 1993

Photograph by CONTESSA BIANCA ARRIVABENE VALENTI GONZAGA

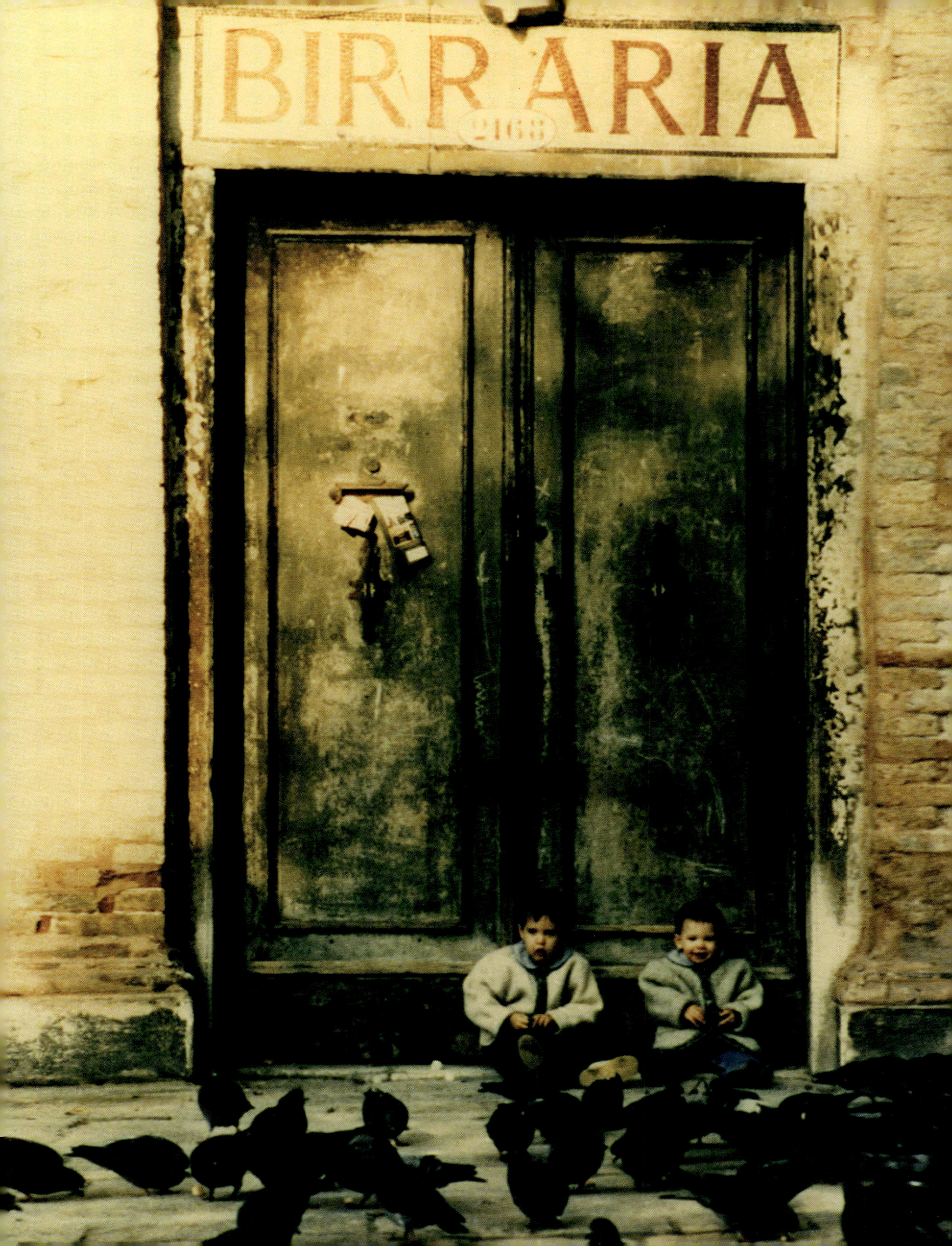
BIRRARIA
2168

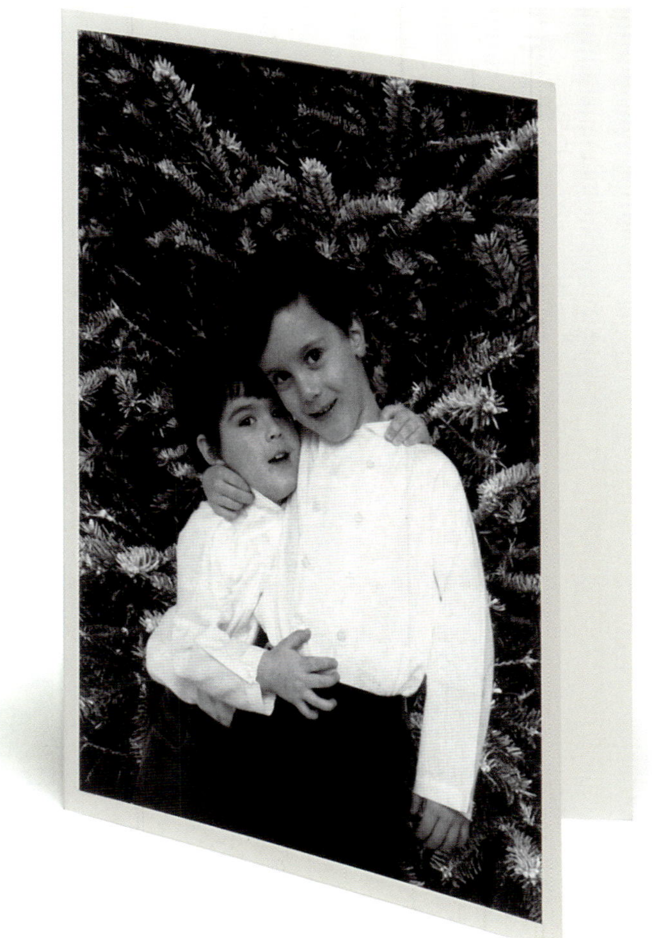

Vicomte Léopold & Vicomte Ferdinand de Biolley, 2004

Photograph by SOLINA GUÉDROÏTZ

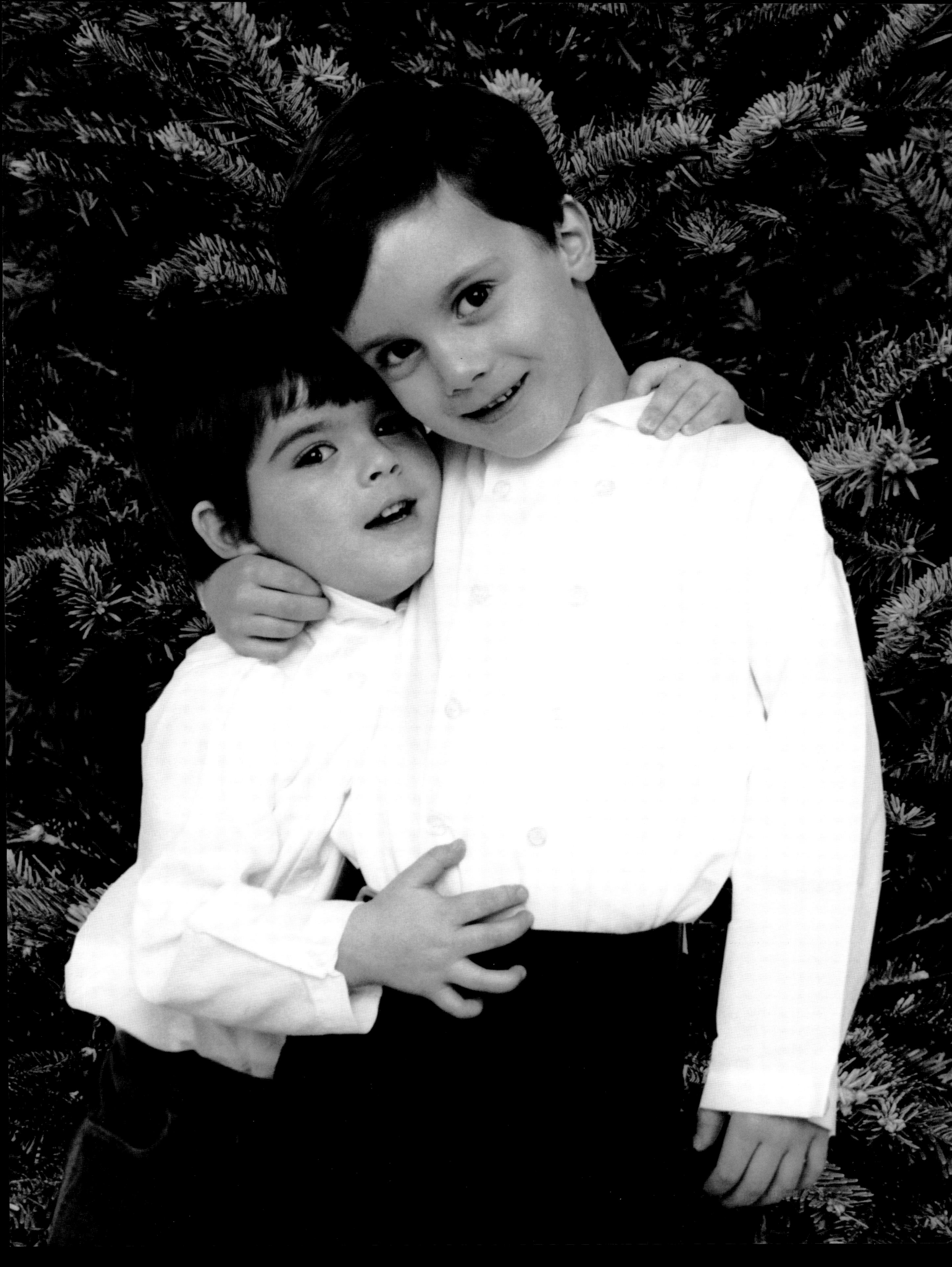

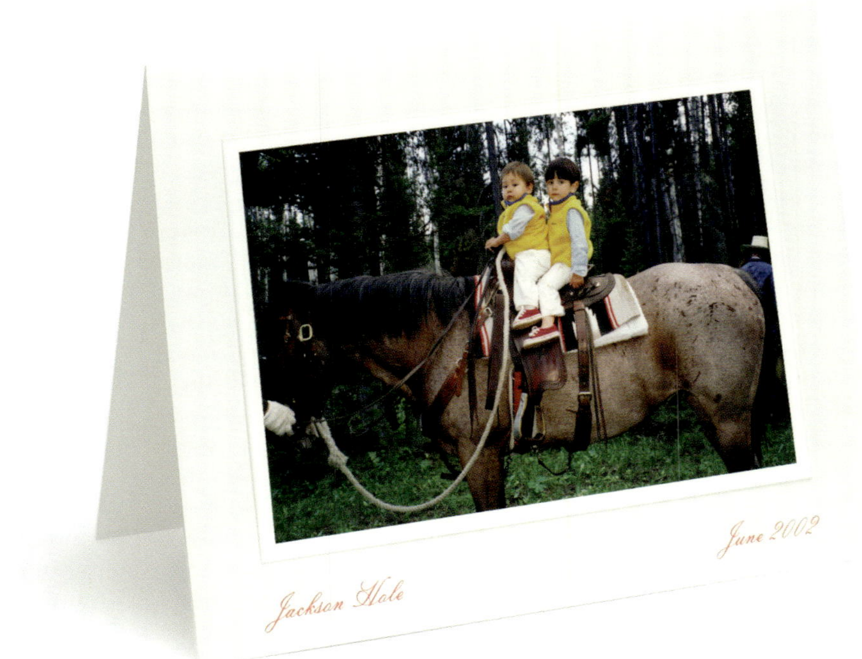

Freiherr Sebastian & Freiherr Frederick von Stauffenberg, 2002

Photograph by FREIFRAU LILLIAN VON STAUFFENBERG

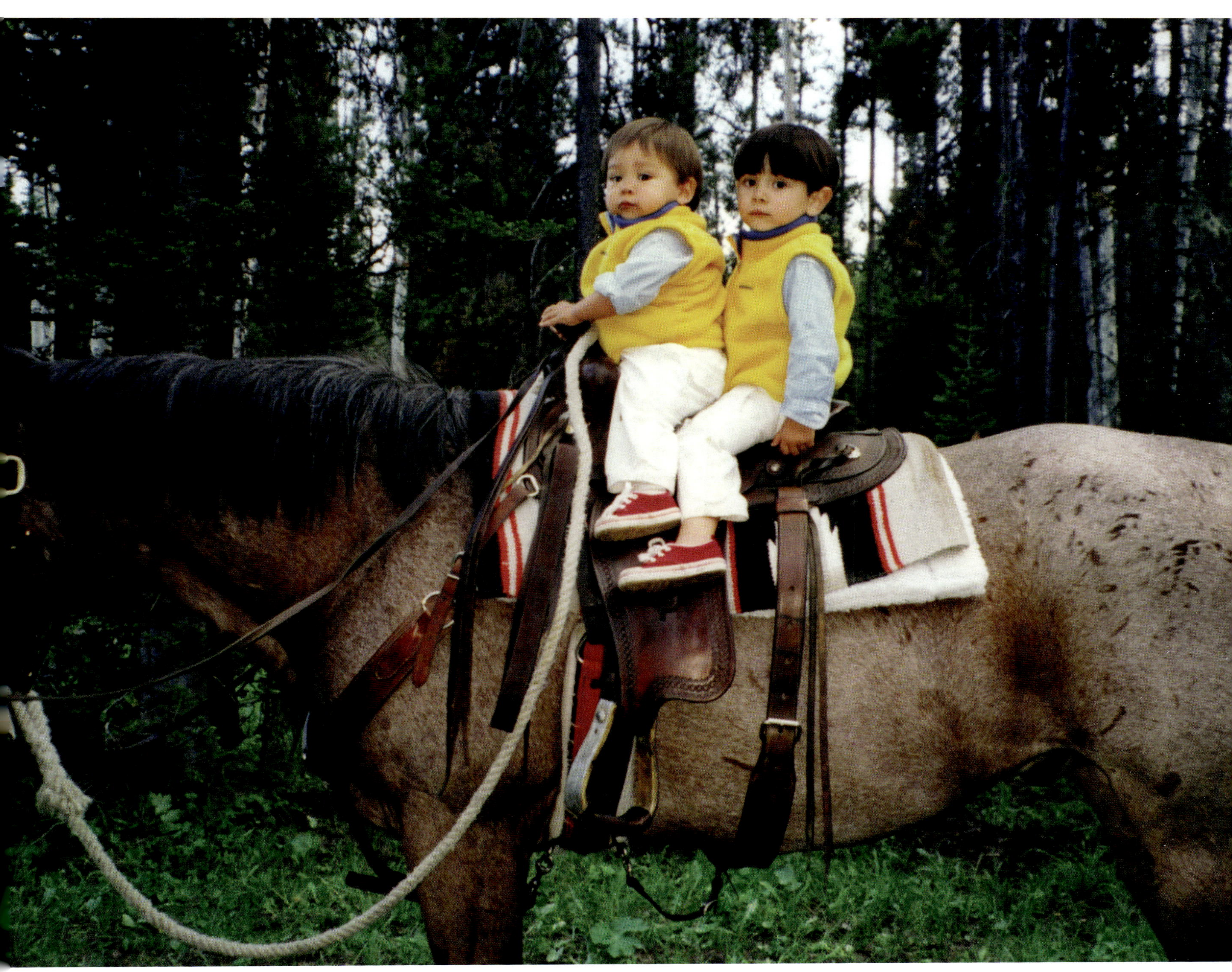

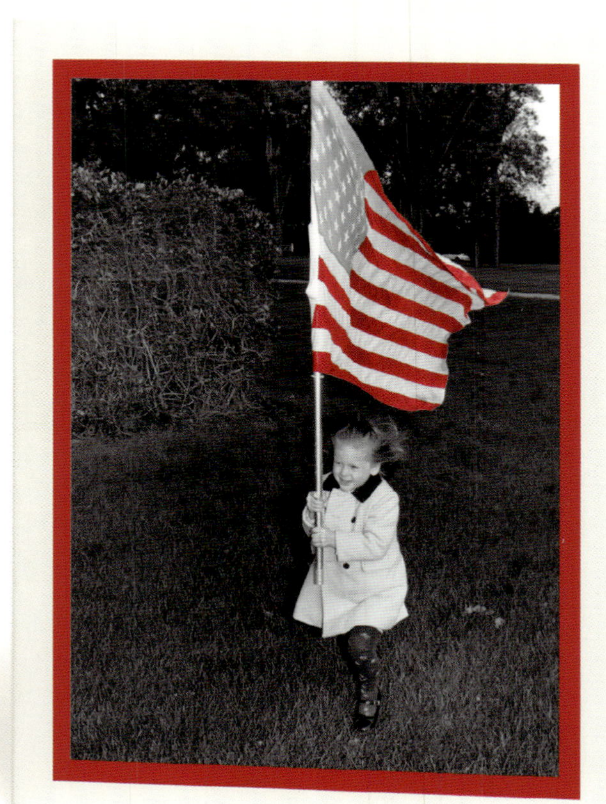

Olympia Davison, 2003

Photograph by MIA MATHESON

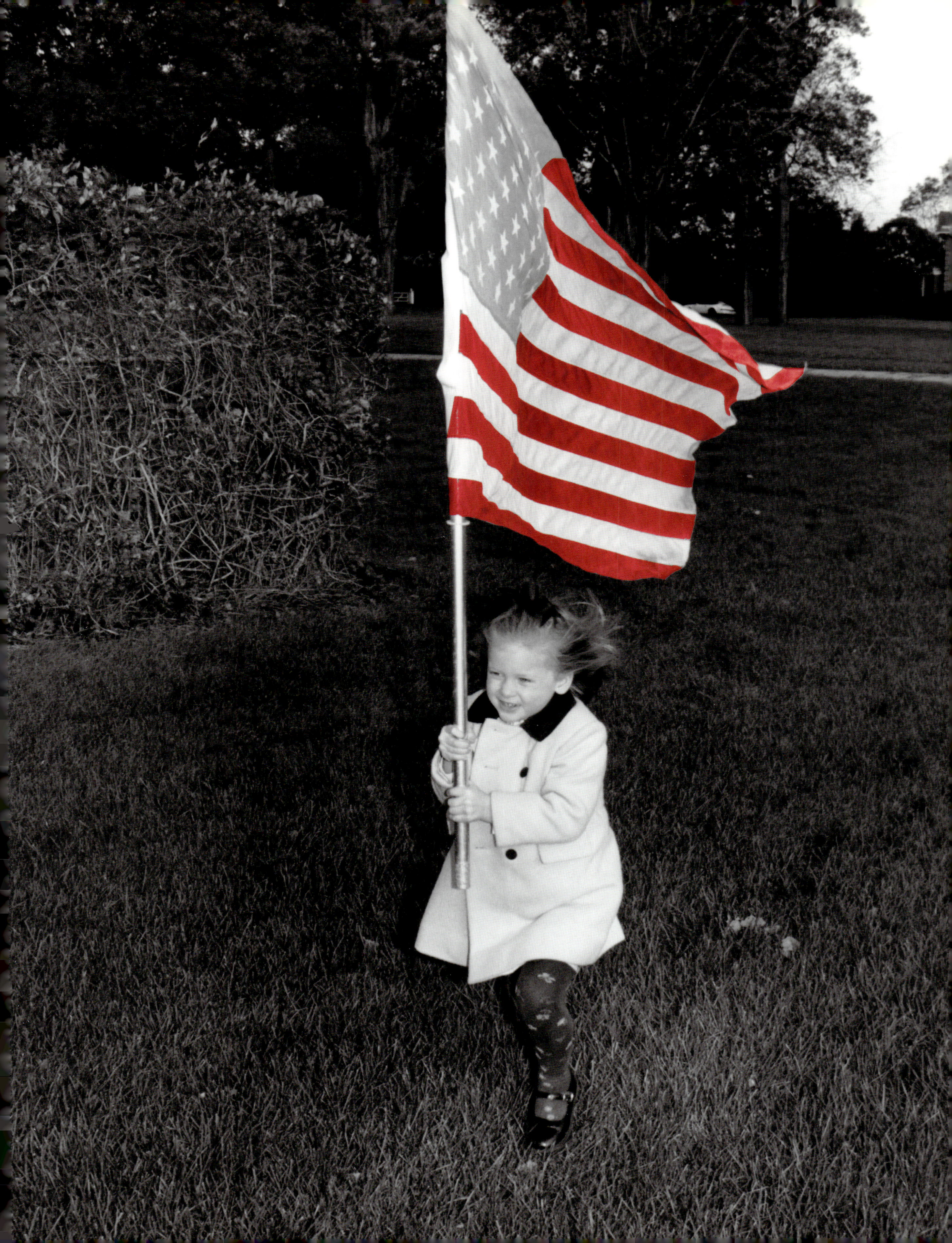

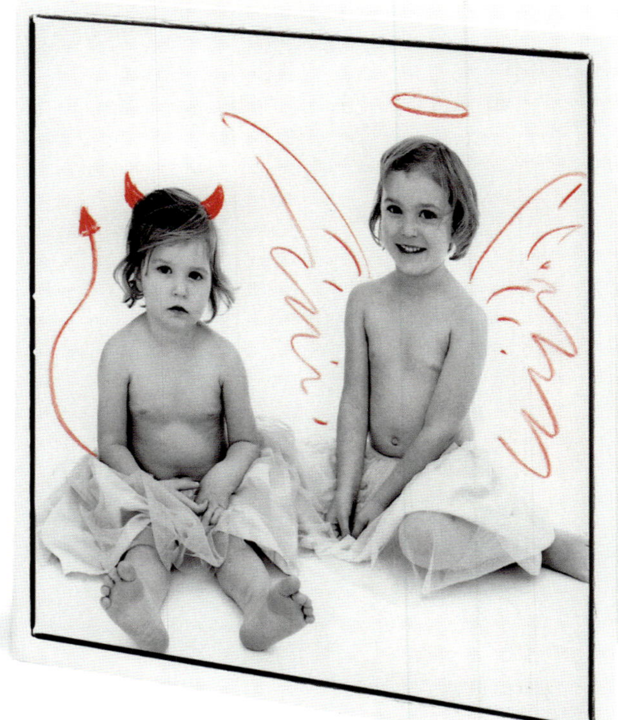

Rosie & Lily Hearn, 2003

Photograph by HUGO BURNAND

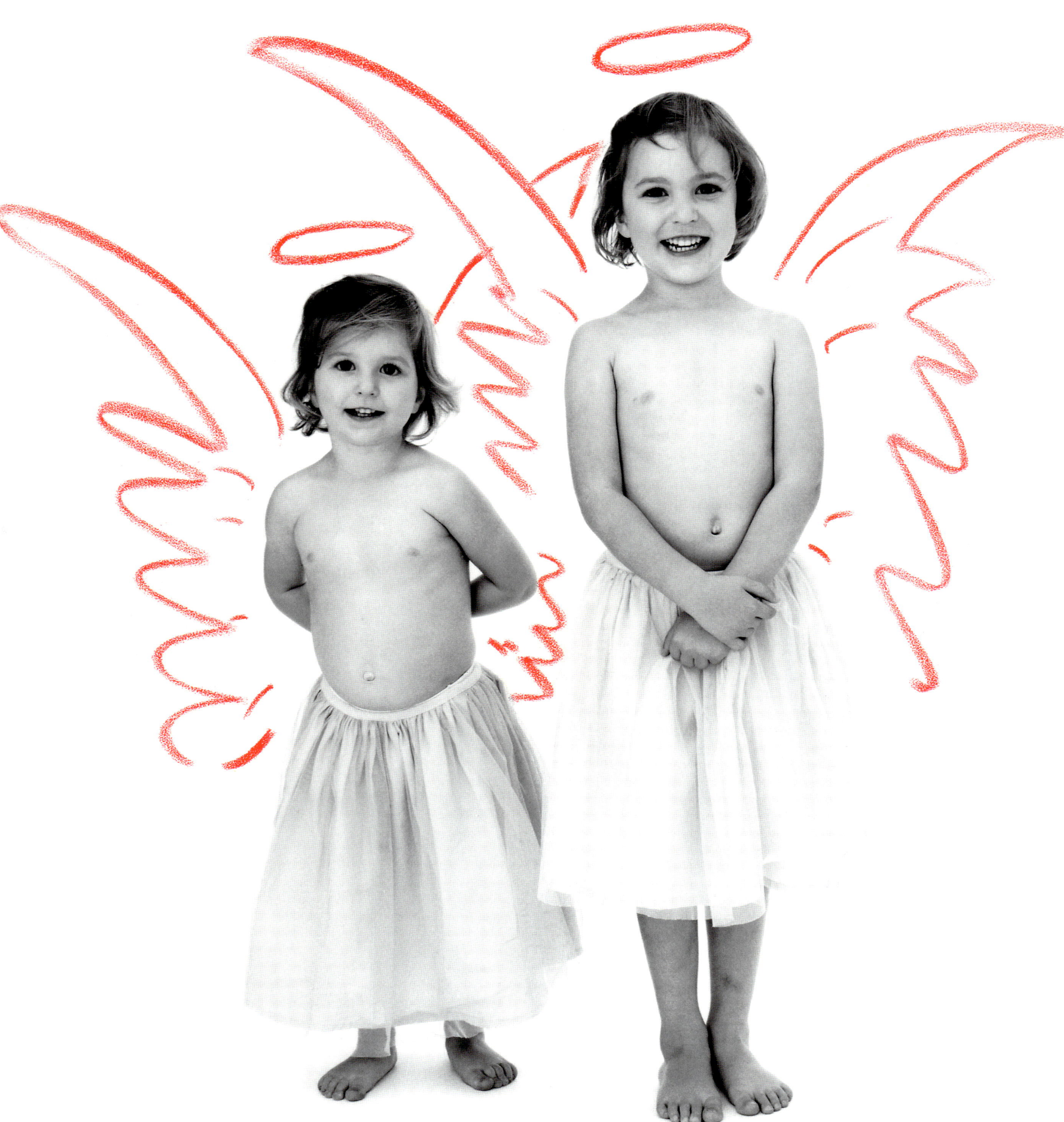

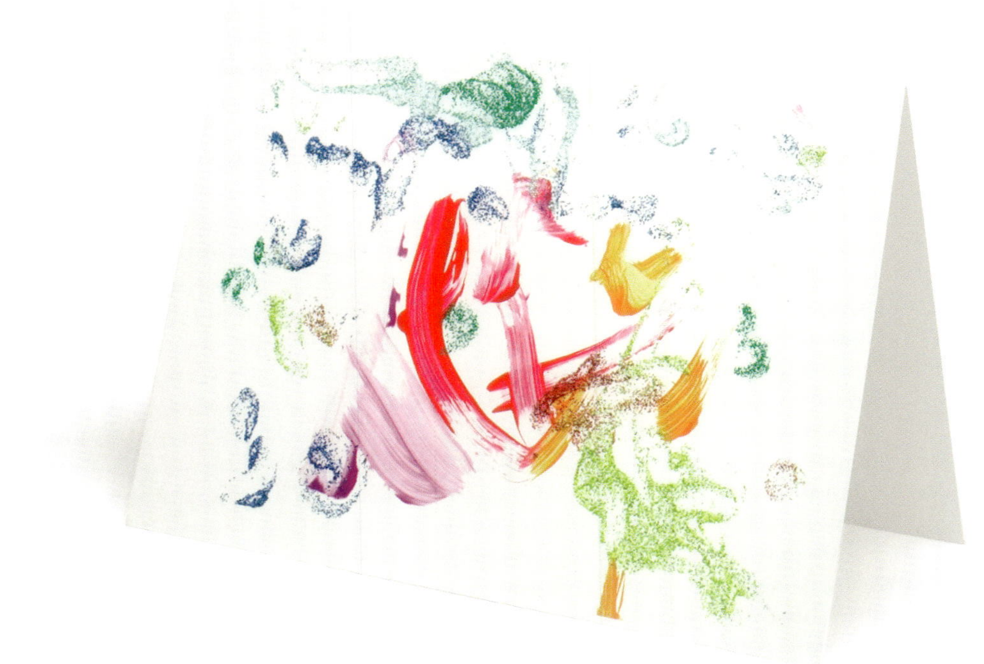

"Aryana's Christmas" , 2003

Illustration by ARYANA SHEIBANI

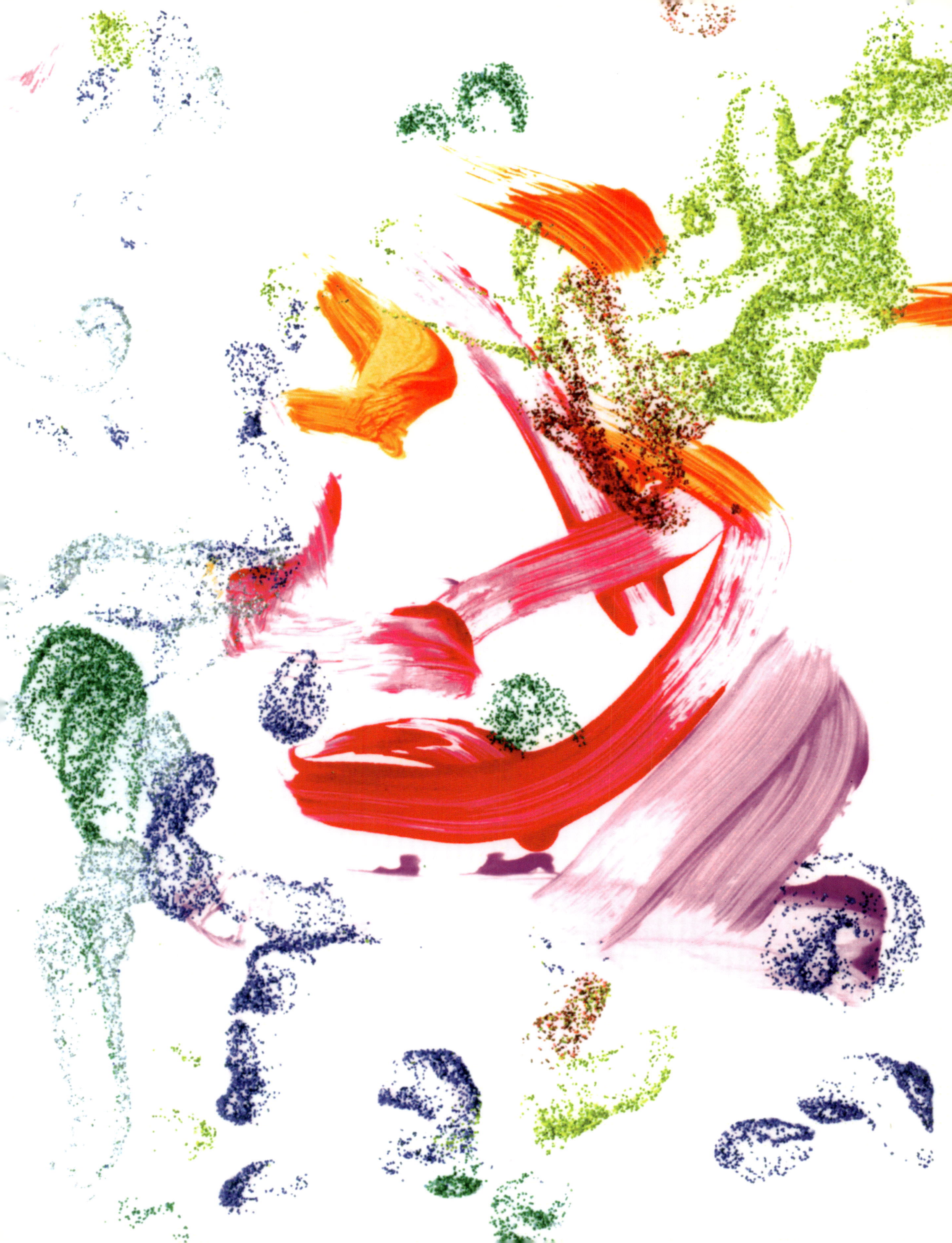

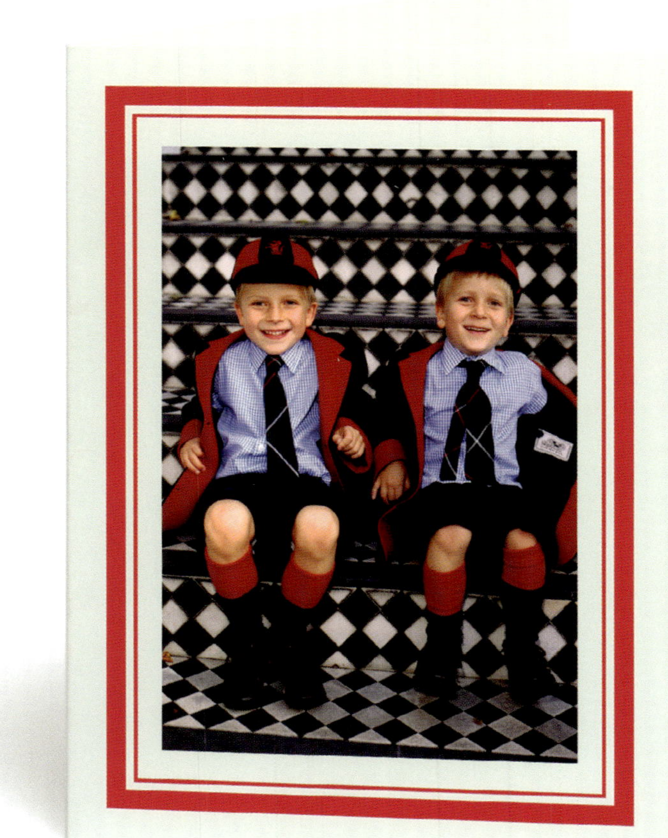

Paul & Johannes Henkel, 2002

Photograph by RICHARD GREENLY

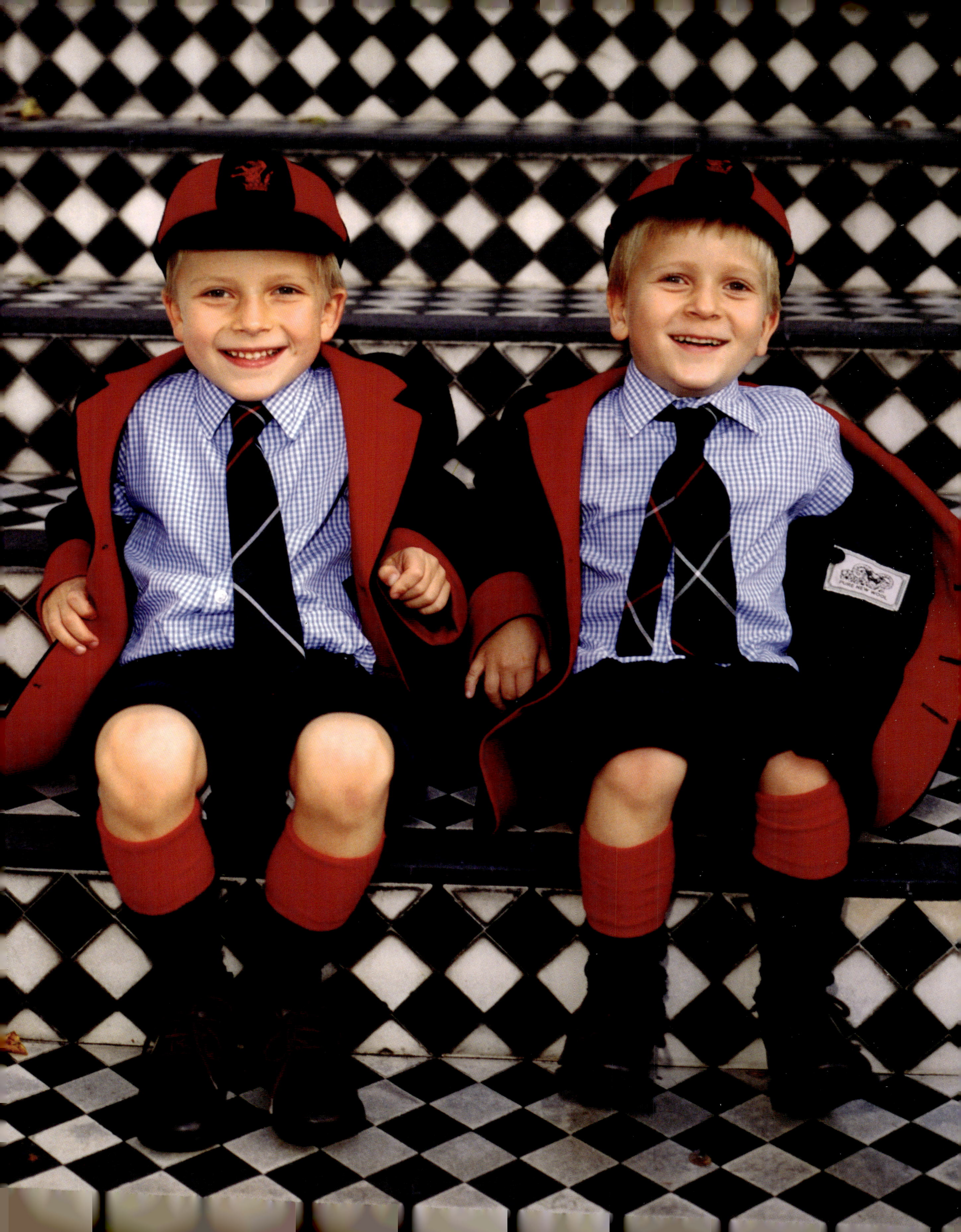

148

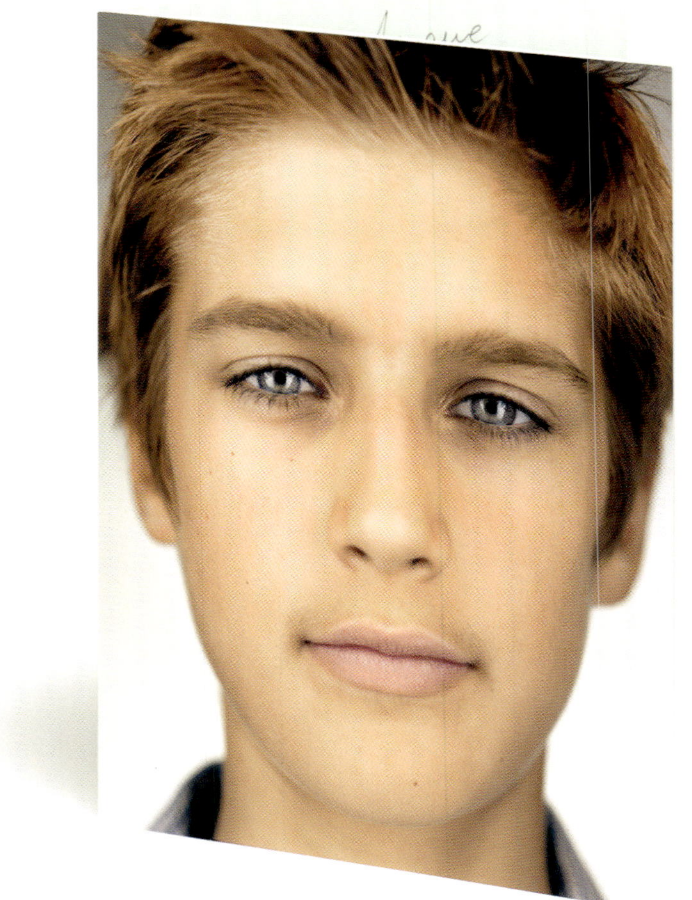

Julian teNeues, 2004

Photograph by MARTIN SCHOELLER

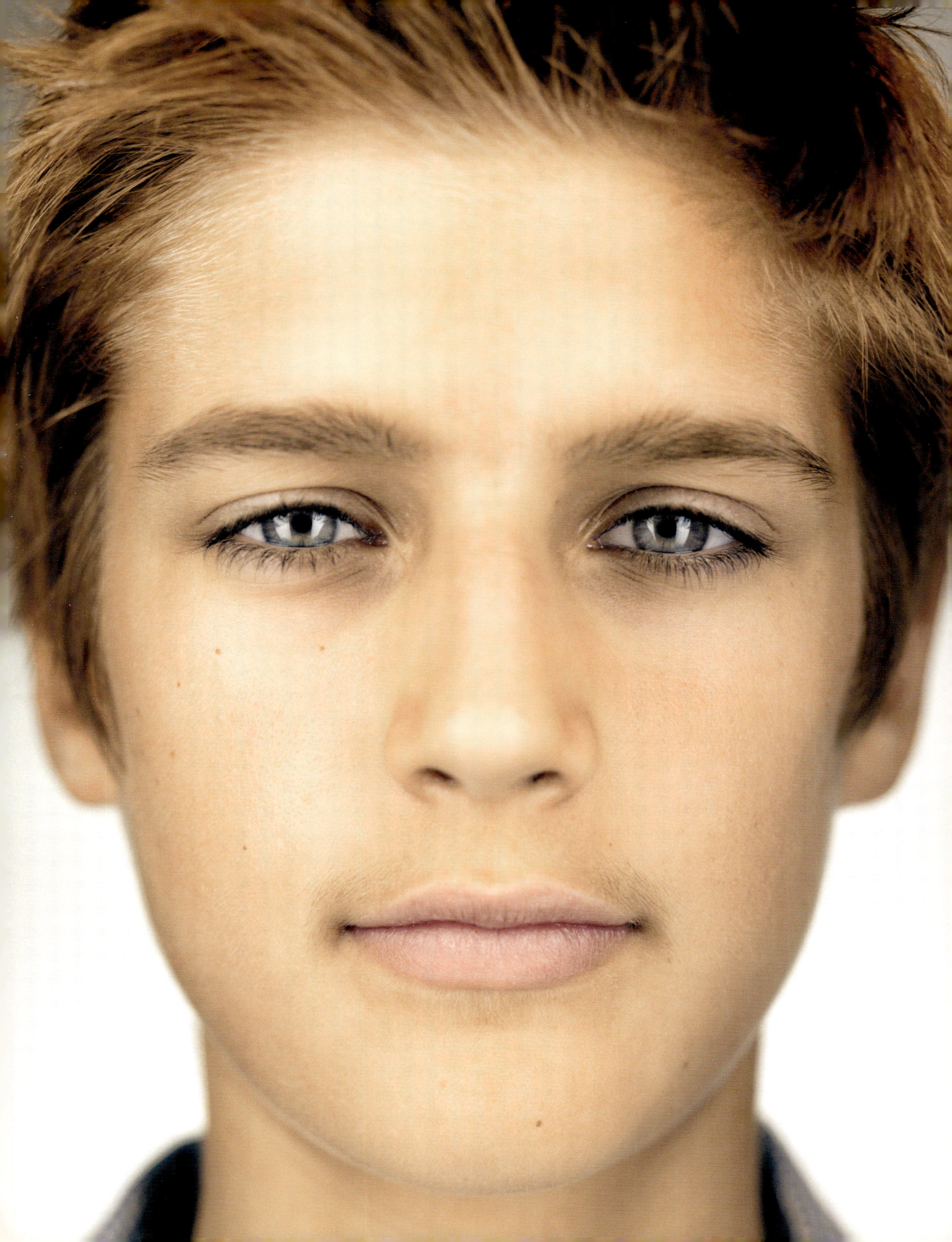

150

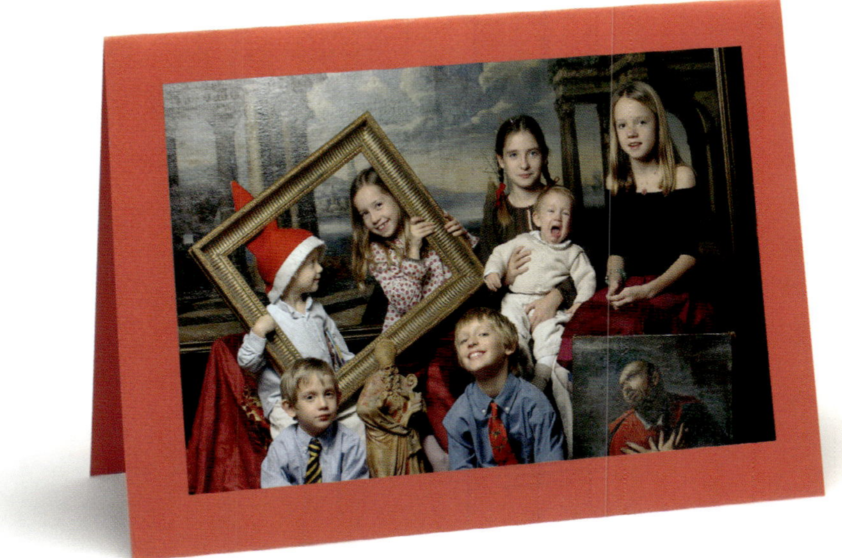

Don Henryk, Donna Nikita, Donna Luia, Don Conrad, Donna Mariuka, Don Cino & Don Cosimo Corsini, 2004

Photograph by MARCHESE VITTORIO RAPPINI DI CASTELDELFINO

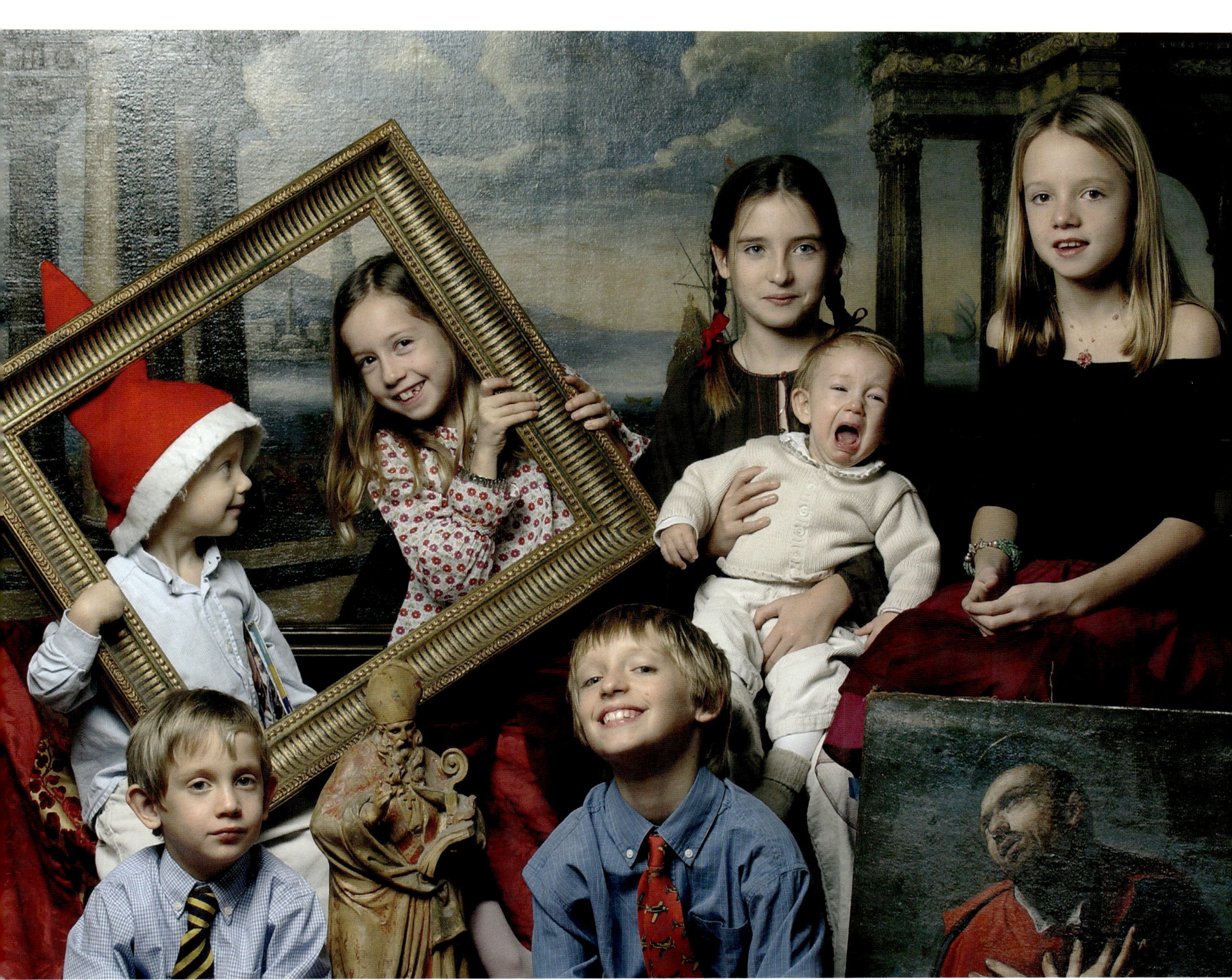

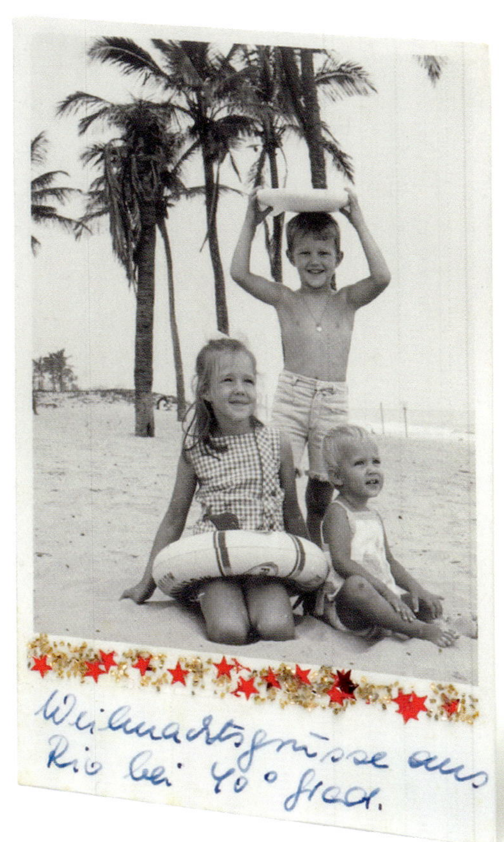

The author and her elder siblings, Rio, 1971

Afterword

Thanks to my wonderful mother I fell in love with Christmas cards very early in my life. Together with my elder siblings we played with them building houses and tunnels and creating new ones by posing in front of imaginary cameras. Having about 3500 cards from various collections including my own, from all over Europe and the US, did not make the selection an easy task.
These cards do not follow any particular criteria–except for being beautiful, fun and original, each conveying their very own Christmas spirit.
The lifetime of a Christmas card is that short period of conspicuous display from its arrival just before Christmas to Twelfth Night, when, according to tradition, all Christmas cards and other festive decorations should be cleared away. Then the cards generally disappear into complete oblivion, staying undisturbed for a very long time or sometimes forever. Nobody can examine them, discuss or enjoy them or shamelessly criticize them anymore.
My aim as a collector and author of this book was to rescue the Christmas card from its oblivion and give these delightful works of art a more appreciated standing, perhaps preserving them as a small inspiration for future generations.
The most prominent motifs of Christmas cards are children. From the beginning of this project there was never a doubt in my mind that a part of the proceeds of this book should be devoted to a charity helping suffering children. This charity I found in the wonderful organisation of CLIC Sargent.
In my attempt to piece together 'the story'–it was my good fortune to find many kind helpers. In varying degrees and in various ways, they all contributed to my work.

Lady Helen Taylor showed a most encouraging and helpful interest throughout and I am particularly delighted that she has contributed the foreword to this book.

I am also greatly indebted to Mrs Hana Tiller (Senior Events Manager of CLIC Sargent) for her manifold interest and help.

I should like to express my enormous thanks to my friends and gratitude for their loans of unusual and unique Christmas cards.

I should also like to acknowledge my friend and publisher, Hendrik teNeues, whose kind advice and suggestions far exceeded the call of duty and who believed in this idea from day one.

I should also record my grateful thanks to all photographers for their gracious permission to photograph and reproduce their cards and images.

I would like to express my thanks and gratitude to Karsten Thormaehlen, my Art Director, in the actual production and design of this book–for his talent, dedication, patience and advice, and for taking most of the necessary photographs for this book.

Last but not least, I would like to thank my husband, who has lost me for months and months to a little book on Christmas cards.

Alexandra Adami

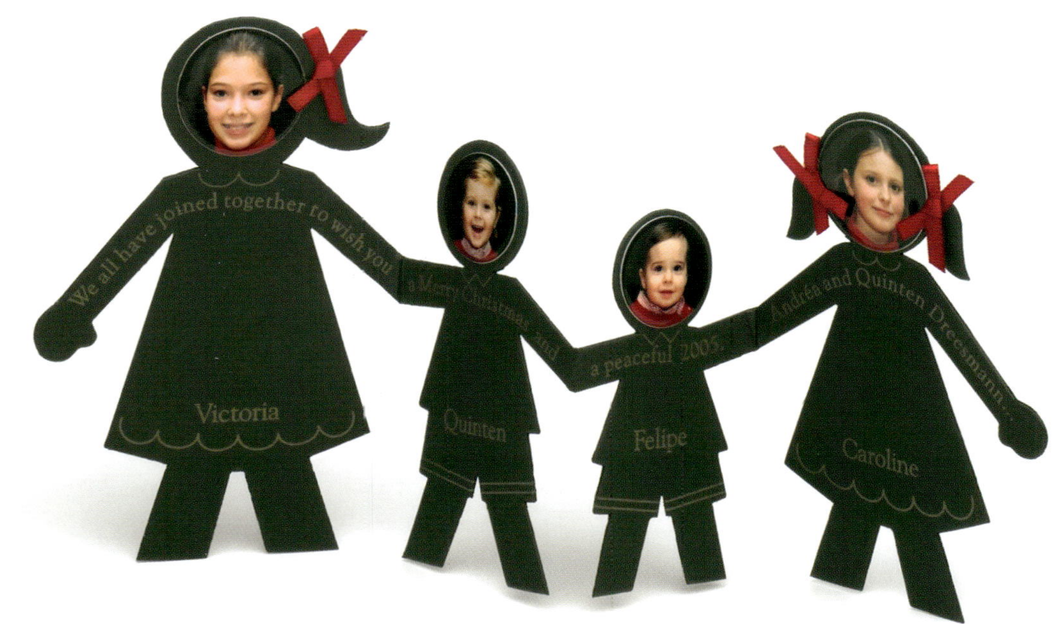

Victoria, Quinten, Felipe & Caroline
Dreesmann-de Botton, 2004

Photographs by FREDERIC FAURE

Index

d'Abo, Anouschka 50-51
d'Abo, Celina 50-51
d'Abo, Jasper 50-51
Adami, Allegra 54-55, 156
Adami, Camilla 54-55
Arco, Gräfin
Anna Theresa 72-73
Arco, Gräfin Giorgiana 72-73
Arco, Gräfin Margherita 72-73
Arco, Gräfin
Marie Gabrielle 72-73
Arco, Gräfin Maximiliana 72-73
Arco, Gräfin Olympia 72-73
d'Arenberg, Princesse
Aliénor 34-35
d'Arenberg, Princesse
Dorothée 34-35
d'Arenberg, Princesse
Lydia 34-35
Arrivabene Valenti Gonzaga,
Donna Vera 134-135
Arrivabene Valenti Gonzaga,
Donna Viola 134-135
Bamford, "Fudge" 26-27
Bamford, "Jasper" 26-27
Bamford, "Minnie" 26-27
Bamford, "Pansy" 26-27
de Biolley, Vicomte
Ferdinand 136-137
de Biolley, Vicomte
Léopold, 136-137
von Bohlen und Halbach,
Eckbert 8, 62-63
von Bohlen und Halbach,
Heinrich 8, 62-63
von Bohlen und Halbach,
Tassilo 8, 62-63
Booth-Clibborn, Céleste 24-25
Booth-Clibborn, Edwina 24-25
Booth-Clibborn, Evelyn 24-25
Booth-Clibborn, Gisèle 24-25
Brown, Marisa 90-91
Brown, Matt 90-91
Bullough, Alice 118-119
Bullough, Cressida 118-119
Bullough, Robbie 118-119
Burda, Christopher 116-117
Burda, Franz 116-117
Burda, Sabrina 116-117
Burnand, Fergus 92-93
Burnand, Lily 92-93
Burnand, Maya 92-93
Burnand, Una 92-93
Busson, Flynn 120-121
Connor, Caroline 128-129
Connor, Lara Bird 128-129
Corsini, Don Cino
150-151, cover
Corsini, Don Conrad
150-151, cover
Corsini, Don Cosimo
150-151, cover
Corsini, Don Henryk
150-151, cover
Corsini, Donna Luia
150-151, cover
Corsini, Donna Mariuka
150-151, cover
Corsini, Donna Nikita
150-151, cover
Crasneanscki, Vladimir
10, 112-113
Dalmeny, Lady 86-87
Dalmeny, Lord 86-87
The Hon Celeste Primrose 86-87
The Hon Delphi Primrose 86-87
The Hon Lavinia Primrose 86-87
The Hon Marina Primrose 86-87
Davison, Olympia 140-141
Dell, Maximilian 16-17
Dreesmann-Beerkens,
Amadeo 28-29
Dreesmann-Beerkens,
Marc-Anthony 28-29
Dreesmann-Beerkens,
Melchior 28-29
Dreesmann-Beerkens,
Noepy 28-29
Dreesmann-Beerkens,
Olympia 28-29
Dreesmann-Beerkens,
Rembrandt 28-29
Dreesmann-de Botton,
Caroline 42-43, 154
Dreesmann-de Botton,
Felipe 43, 154
Dreesmann-de Botton,
Quinten 43, 154
Dreesmann-de Botton,
Victoria 42-43, 154
Drummond, Davina 96-97
Dub, Romy 18-19
Eisler, Alex 40-41
Eisler, Ariana 40-41
Emo Capodilista, Conte
Filippo 20-21
Emo Capodilista, Contessa
Olimpia 20-21
Figueroa y Sayn-Wittgenstein,
Juan 38-39
Figueroa y Sayn-Wittgenstein,
Luis 38-39
Gelardin, Marina 74-75
Gilmour, Christabel 100-101
Gilmour, Gabriella 100-101
Gilmour, Leonora 100-101
de Givenchy, Gabriella 84-85
de Givenchy, Nicolas 84-85
Gordon, Charlie 88-89
Gordon, Laith 88-89
Gordon, Ramsey 88-89
Gritti, Bibi 130-131
Gritti, Brandolino 130-131
Gritti, Lea 130-131
Gritti, Lodovico 130-131
Gritti, Massimiliano 130-131
Guédroïtz, Prince
Alexis 6, 64-65
Guédroïtz, Princesse
Assia 64-65
Guédroïtz, Princesse
Sveva 6, 64-65
von Haeften, Josefa 106-107
von Haeften, Verus 106-107
Haegler, Bettina 80-81
Hamilton, Felix 76-77
Hamilton, Hugo 76-77
Hearn, Lily 142-143
Hearn, Rosie 142-143
Heather, Tara 36-37
Heilshorn, Madison 126-127
Heilshorn, Morgan 126-127
Henkel, Johannes 146-147
Henkel, Paul 146-147
Hicks, Ambrosia 124-125
Hicks, Angelica 124-125
Homan, Alexandra 108-109
Homan, Bart 108-109
Homan, Carlota 14, 108-109
Homan, Niklas 14, 108-109
Joop, "Emily" 114
Joop, "Lucky" 115
Kageneck, Graf Alexander 38-39
Kageneck, Graf Clemens 38-39
Kageneck, Gräfin Helena 38-39
Krages, Louis 78-79
Krages, Tessa 78-79
Krages, Uli 78-79
de Liedekerke, Comte
Raoul 30-31
Linden, Olivia 76-77
Linden, Sienna 76-77
Macpherson, Elle 120-121
Marsaglia, Carlo 94-95
Marsaglia, Sofia 94-95
teNeues, Julian 148-149
de Ocampo, Brooke 70-71
de Ocampo, Emilio 70-71
de Ocampo, Inés 70-71
de Ocampo, Isabel 70-71
de Ocampo, Marina 70-71
von Oppenheim,
Freifrau Ludmilla 102-03
von Oppenheim,
Freiherr Waldemar 102-103
von Oppersdorff,
Gräfin Johanna 110-111
von Oppersdorff,
Gräfin Philippa 110-111
Ostrowsky, Anastasia 82-83
Ostrowsky, Antonia 82-83
Reuther, Ferdinand 66-67
Reuther, Leopold 66-67
Reuther, Marie 66-67
Rittweger, Rosa 132-133
Sachs, Frederik 52-53
Sachs, Maryam 52-53
Sachs, Philipp 52-53
Sachs, Rolf 52-53
Sachs, Roya 52-53
Schliemann, Amalia 56-57
Schuler-Voith, Olivia 98-99
Schuler-Voith, Philip 98-99
Sodi, Brando 58-59
Sodi, Isabella 58-59
Sodi, Maximilian 58-59
Sodi, Nadia 58-59
von Stauffenberg,
Freiherr Frederick 138-139
von Stauffenberg
Gräfin Isabel 32-33
von Stauffenberg,
Gräfin Mafalda 32-33
von Stauffenberg,
Gräfin Olivia 32-33
von Stauffenberg,
Freiherr Sebastian 138-139
Swarovski-Adams,
Rigby 68-69
Tosato, Angelica 104-105
Tosato, Guglielmo 104-105
Tosato, Isabella 104-105
Taylor, Cassius 44-45
Taylor, Columbus 44-45
Treichl, Charlotte 94-95
Treichl, Maximilian 94-95
Zacharia, Alice 22-23
Zacharia, Emma 22-23
Zacharia, Sophie 22-23
Zacharia, Zoe 22-23

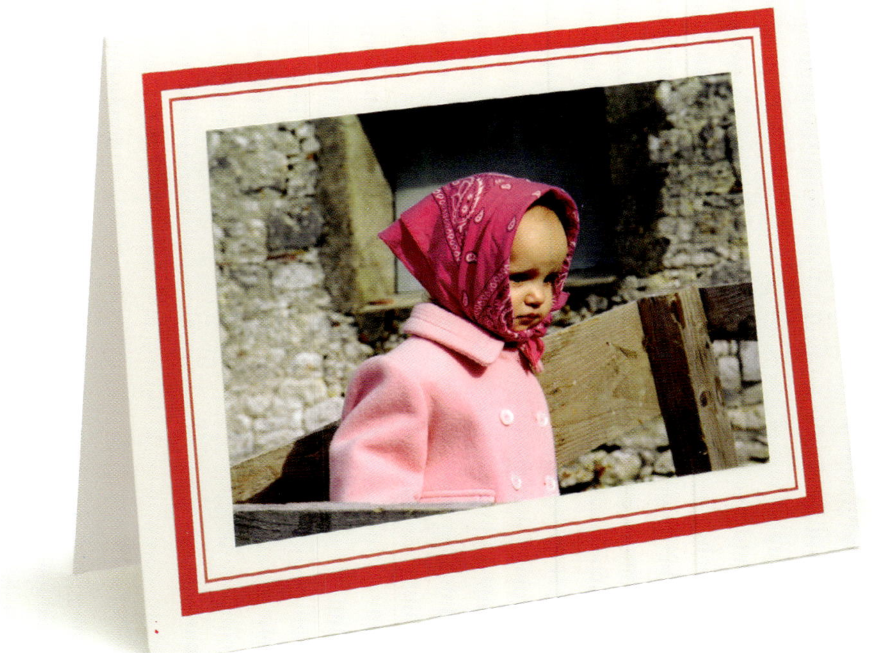

Allegra Adami, 2002

Photograph by ALEXANDRA ADAMI

Credits

d'Abo, Tatjana 50-51

Acker, Edward 126-127
Lenox, Massachusetts
EdwardAcker@earthlink.net

Adami, Alexandra 54-55, 156

Alcaide, Ricardo 24-25
alcaidericardo@hotmail.com
Layout: Phil Baines
studio@philbaines.co.uk

Arco-Zinneberg,
S. H. & I. k. u. k. H.
Graf Ripbrand und
Gräfin Maria Beatrice 72-73

Arrivabene, Contessa
Bianca Valenti Gonzaga
134-135

Becker, Isabel 80-81
mobile +21 (0)9612 0988
belbecker@uol.com.br
Layout: Just Bee Design
Rua Visconde de Piraja 414/717
Ipanema 22410-002
Rio de Janeiro, Brasil
justbee@justbee.com.br
phone +55 (0)21 2247 8878

Becker, Jonathan 70-71
phone +1 212 750 5460
office@jonathanbecker.net

Benini-Pietromarchi, Sophie
104-105
sophiebenini@libero.it
sophienow.tripod.com

Burda, Bettina 116-117

Burnand, Hugo
86-87, 92-93, 142-143
1 Powis Mews
London W11 1JN, U. K.
phone +44 (0)20 7229 2297

Canal, Antonio, Il Canaletto
122-123
painter, 1697-1768,
from the Corinne & Gert-Rudolf Flick
Collection

Chateau, Maritza 74-75

van Cleve, Joos 60-61
painter (after), c. 1485-1540/41,
from the collection of Fürsten
zu Salm

Donelli, Mauricio 90-91
www.mauriciodonelli.com

Dub, Gertrude 18-19

Du Ross, Kimberly 36-37

Eisenburger, Nouni 130-131

Eisler, Maryam 40-41
maryameisler@yahoo.co.uk

Emo Capodilista, Contessa
Madeleine 20-21

Fattal, Eliane 16-17, 32-33
phone +44 (0)20 7372 9899
mobile +44 (0)78 3155 3835

Faure, Frederic
28-29, 42-43, 154
www.faure.be
f@faure.be

Fly Pictures 52-53
phone +33 (0)49 4973070

Gilmour, Mardi 100-101de

Givenchy, Christine 84-85

Graham, James P 10, 112-113

© Richard Greenly 146-147
phone +44 (0)14 8868 5256

Guédroïtz, Solina
6, 64-65, 136-137
sguedroitz@hotmail.com

von Haeften, Herret 106-107

Hamilton, Andrea
76-77, 88-89
www.andreahamilton.com

Hardy, Emma 118-119
www.emmahardy.com

Hicks, Ashley 124-125
David Hicks 1979 Ltd.
phone +44 (0)7976 744647
www.dh1970.com

Homan, Bart 14, 108-109

Kageneck, Gräfin Theresa,
38-39

Lenman, Stan 102-103

de Lesseps, Ferdinand 30-31
phone/fax +32 (0)23746493
de.lesseps@skynet.be

Levenson, Martin 96-97
www.levenson.co.uk

Matheson, Mia 140-141
phone +1 212 721 0808
miamath@aol.com

Meinen Fotografie München
66-67
Meinen Fotografie GmbH
Schrammerstraße 3
D-80333 München
phone +49 (0)89 294949
www.foto-meinen.de

Neesam, Brian 94-95
phone/fax +44 (0)1297 34797
mobile +44 (0)7941 884017
brianneesam@btinternet.com

von Oppersdorff,
Gräfin Marita 110-111

Ostrowsky, Katharina 82-83

d'Oultremont, Ludmila
12, 34-35, 158
ludmila.doultremont@free.fr

Papara, M. 78-79
phone +49 (0)40 31797400
de@lensmagic.de

Peters, Russel 114-115
c/o Fotoformula/Milan
phone +39 0270 106775
www.russel-peters.com

Pietromarchi, Giulio 104-105

Rae, Michaela 48-49

Rappini di Castel Delfino,
Marchese Vittorio 150-151, cover

Reusse, Stephan 8, 62-63
phone +49 (0)221 418520
mobile +49 (0)173 5149836
stephanreusse@t-online.de

Schellmann, Ulla 132-133

Schliemann, Joana 56-57

© Martin Schoeller 148-149

Schuler-Voith, Biggi 98-99

Sheibani, Aryana 144-145

Simons, Stephen 128-129

Sodi, Ariane 58-59

von Stauffenberg,
Freifrau Lillian 138-139

© Dan Stevens 120-121
phone +44 (0)20 7837 3122
mobile +44 (0)79 7341 6937
www.danstevens.co.uk

Swannell, John 26-27
phone +44 (0)20 83485965

Swarovski, Nadja 68-69

© Mario Testino 44-45

Thormaehlen, Karsten
phone +49 (0)69 40898840
mobile +49 (0)172 8957687
www.karstenthormaehlen.com

Woolston, Frances 46-47

Zacharia, Mahfouz 22-23

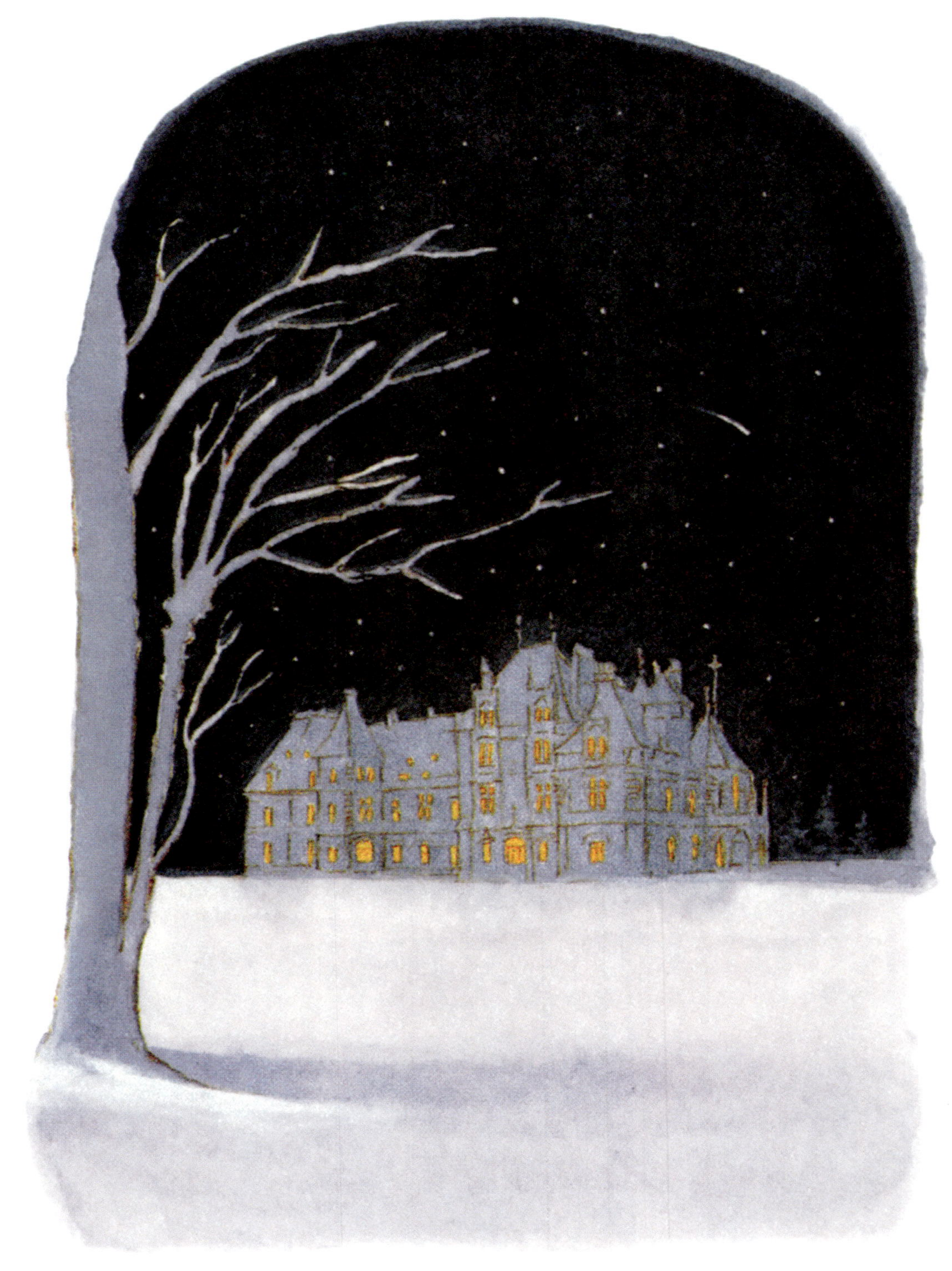

d'Arenberg, 2003

Illustration by LUDMILA D'OULTREMONT

Editor Alexandra Adami

Editorial Coordination Alexandra Adami
Sabine Scholz
Michaela Thormaehlen

Text Lady Helen Taylor
Clic Sargent-Cancer Care for Children

Photography & Design Karsten Thormaehlen
www.karstenthormaehlen.com

Colour Separation Medien Team-Vreden, Germany

Translations SAW Communications,
Dr. Sabine A. Werner
Melanie Koster (German)
Silvia Gómez de Antonio (Spanish)
Céline Verschelde (French)
Elena Nobilini (Italian)

Published by teNeues Publishing Group

teNeues Publishing Company
16 West 22nd Street, New York, NY 10010, USA
Tel. 001-212-627-9090, Fax 001-212-627-9511

teNeues Book Division
Kaistraße 18
40221 Düsseldorf, Germany
Tel. 0049-(0)211-994597-0, Fax 0049-(0)211-994597-40

teNeues Publishing UK Ltd.
P.O. Box 402
West Byfleet
KT 14 7ZF, Great Britain
Tel. 0044-1932-403509, Fax 0044-1932-403514

teNeues France S.A.R.L.
4, rue de Valence
75005 Paris, France
Tel. 0033-1-55766205, Fax 0033-1-55766419

teNeues Iberica S.L.
Pso. Juan de la Encina 2-48, Urb. Club de Campo
28700 S.S.R.R., Madrid, Spain
Tel./Fax 0034-91-6595876

www.teneues.com

ISBN-10: 3-8327-9093-4
ISBN-13: 978-3-8327-9093-6

Printed in Italy

Bibliographic information published by Die Deutsche Bibliothek.
Die Deutsche Bibliothek lists this publication in the Deutsche Nationalbibliografie; detailed bibliographic data is available in the internet at http://dnb.ddb.de

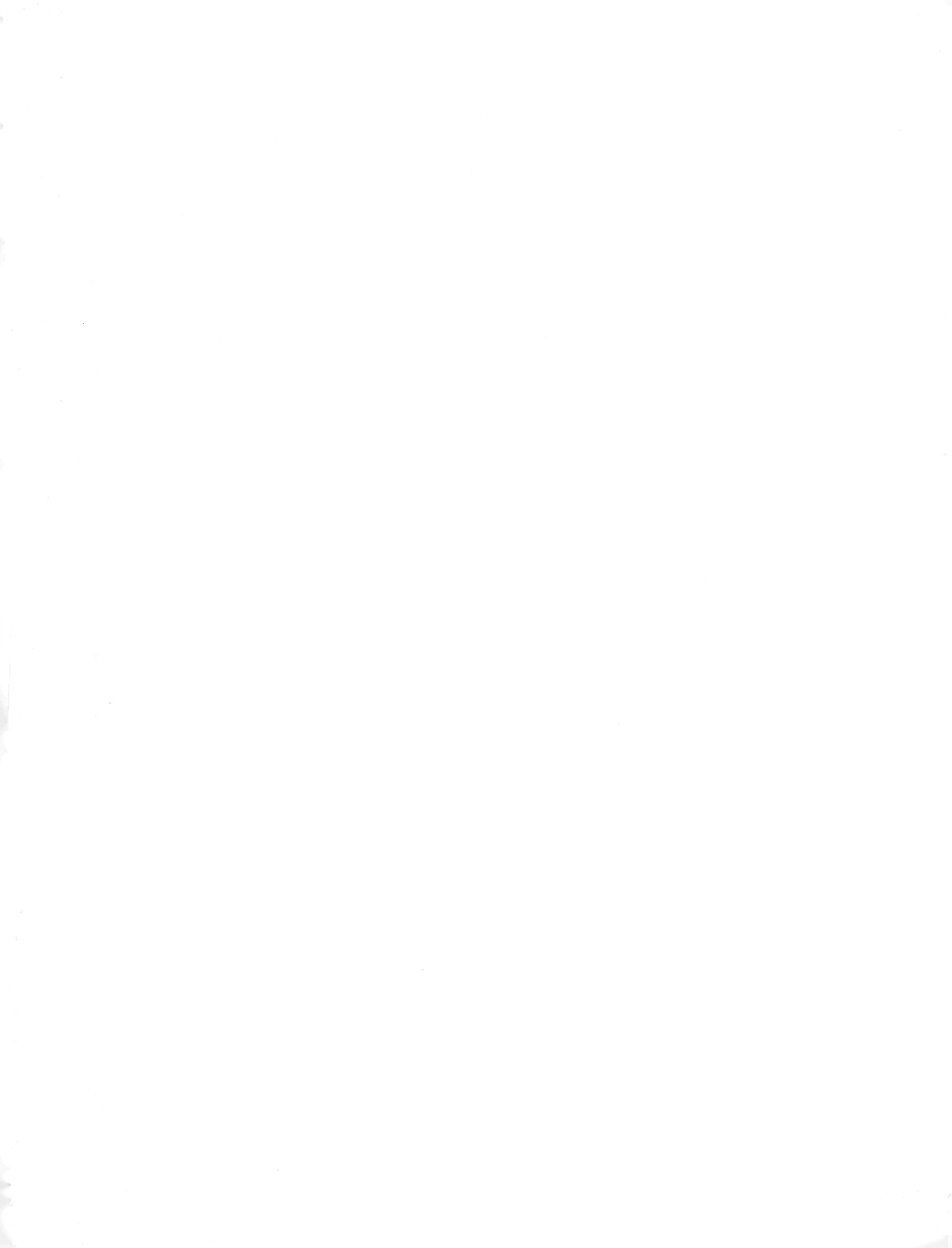